WOMEN'S FILM
AND
FEMALE EXPERIENCE

WOMEN'S FILM
AND
FEMALE EXPERIENCE

1940-1950

Andrea S. Walsh

PRAEGER SPECIAL STUDIES • PRAEGER SCIENTIFIC

New York • Philadelphia • Eastbourne, UK
Toronto • Hong Kong • Tokyo • Sydney

Library of Congress Cataloging in Publication Data
Walsh, Andrea S.
  Women's film and female experience, 1940-1950.

  Bibliography: p.
  Includes index.
  1. Women in moving-pictures.   2. Moving-pictures—
United States—History.   I.   Title.
PN1995.9.W6W3   1984   791.43'75'0909352042   83-24486
ISBN 0-03-061351-5 (alk. paper)

Stills courtesy of Jerry Ohlinger's Movie Materials Store, Movie Star News, and Cinemabilia.

The Production Code has been reprinted with permission of Ken Clark of the Motion Picture Association of America.

Published in 1984 by Praeger Publishers
CBS Educational and Professional Publishing
a Division of CBS Inc.
521 Fifth Avenue, New York, NY 10175   USA

© 1984 by Praeger Publishers

456789 052 987654321

Printed in the United States of America
on acid-free paper

Dedicated to the memory of my grandmother,
Anna Cotter Lally (1889-1981)

ACKNOWLEDGMENTS

This study had many phases — in classrooms, theaters, libraries, my study and late at night in front of the television. I have many people to thank for providing the intellectual, emotional, and practical support necessary for its completion.

This project began as my doctoral dissertation. I wish especially to thank my dissertation committee for their support, enthusiasm, patience, and insight. Terry Hopkins saw this project through from inception to completion. His guidance and probing insight helped me to sharpen and refine both theory and method. Joan Smith provided provocative criticism, and always encouraged me to disagree. Likewise, John Flint supported this study, encouraging me to ground it firmly within the larger field of sociology of culture. Mary Ryan helped me design the project initially and to link it to relevant scholarship in women's history. Sarah Elbert gave sisterly support and criticism, as well as guidelines for cultural and historical analysis.

I thank Joel Greifinger who provided boundless support — emotional and intellectual — and never acted bored or frustrated when asked to read and comment upon yet another draft.

Likewise, Sonya Michel, my collaborator in research on women's roles in the 1940s, provided sisterly support, perceptive (and always gentle!) criticism, and new and impossible-to-find sources.

Many friends, students, and colleagues accompanied me to movies, rekindled my enthusiasm, and read and commented upon all or parts of the manuscript. Marty Frum bought me my first movie stills, discussed an endless number of films with me, prepared the index, and guided me to a wide array of sources. Nina Shapiro and Anna Yeatman planted important ideas about women's culture in my head a decade ago. Linda Silver encouraged me to take my work as seriously as she did. My housemate and fellow media critic Ella Taylor contributed critical insight, humor, and many cups of tea. Myra Boime, Torry Dickinson, Lew Friedland, Robert Horwitz, Ruth Harriet Jacobs, Isaac Jackson, Bill Martin, Chinnah Mithrasekaran, Terry Kalb, Cheryl Klausner, Ellie Leiman, Lynne Layton, Linda Peterson, Barbara Richardson, Simon Rosenblum, Bob Ross, Karen Schachere, Ann Schofield, Mary Smith, Robbie Strongin, Steve Vogel, and Anna Yeatman read or discussed with me the ideas of my study, or sat with me in darkened theatres while I scribbled note after note, after note. Larry Meacham and Betsy Swart provided much-

appreciated research advice. I wish also to thank many of my
colleagues and students at SUNY-Binghamton, Cornell, and Clark
University, who shared their insights on women in film with me.
Lynda Sharp, my editor at Praeger, supported and encouraged this
study, while providing helpful criticism.

SUNY-Binghamton provided some of the financial support
necessary to complete this work. I would also like to thank the
People's Film Collective, Providence, Rhode Island and the Rhode
Island Committee For the Humanities for providing me an opportunity to show and discuss some of these films with large and
diverse audiences. Barbara Humphries and Emily Sieger, Motion
Picture Division, Library of Congress, assisted me in locating and
viewing many of these films. Elizabeth Bouché and Roxanne Rawson
typed several drafts and were more than willing to accommodate
crazy deadlines. Leslie Dowd and Patricia Hamilton assisted in
preparing the final draft.

Carmen Sirianni lived with this study through most of its short
but intense life, watching and listening to plots of more 1940s films
than he probably ever cares to remember. For his love, unfailing
support, and critical insight, I will always be grateful.

My parents Eileen and Michael Walsh and my aunt and uncle
Mary and Edward Fallon taught me long ago to love the "Bette
Davis" and "Katharine Hepburn" movies about which I would later
write.

And lastly, this book is dedicated to the memory of my grandmother, Anna Cotter Lally, who always believed that I would indeed
finish, but did not live to see the completion.

This study has been immeasurably enriched by everyone I have
mentioned; any errors, omissions, or inconsistencies are, of course,
mine.

CONTENTS

INTRODUCTION

Movies of the past are like samples — swatches of cloth — of the period in which they were made.

Pauline Kael, Reeling
(New York: Warner, 1972), p. 16

The year 1940 marks the onset of a crucial decade in the history of American womanhood. The draft and war emergency compelled Americans, temporarily at least, to question and re-evaluate Depression-era stereotypes of subordinate and subservient femininity. With over six million new female recruits joining the labor force by 1944, women comprised over 36 percent of employed persons in the United States. Rosie the Riveter, Norman Rockwell's super-competent blue-collar heroine, stepped off a 1943 Saturday Evening Post cover to become the all-American womanly ideal of World War II.

Wartime Rosies faced challenges unimagined by many of their sisters in the 1930s. They were as apt to find themselves wielding a shovel or welding torch as pounding away at a typewriter or carrying a bedpan. And, while they earned higher salaries than they had before the war, many women worked double shifts: at home as well as at the plant or office. Unlike her Depression-era counterpart, the typical female wartime worker was also a wife or mother whose dual role became more demanding with the enlistment of many husbands and fathers. Young single and married women alike experienced the war years in a much more female atmosphere than that of the Great Depression. At work and at play, women came to depend more on themselves and one another, cooperating with each other in child care, volunteering to aid the war effort, and relaxing together on all-female baseball teams.

1

Although wartime women discovered new opportunities in traditionally masculine fields, they encountered resistance as well — from government, industry, trade unions, husbands, and male coworkers. And significant obstacles to full equality persisted. Female wages remained unequal to those of males, opportunities for promotions and raises were restricted, and needs for child care and supportive community services were largely ignored by industry and government alike.

Despite the obviously unequal treatment accorded women in war era America, feminism failed to re-emerge as a social movement. However, historical evidence suggests that wartime challenges did affect female consciousness significantly. A 1944 Women's Bureau poll, for example, indicated that over 75 percent of women war workers in ten key production areas did not wish to surrender their jobs to returning GIs. However, their desires were largely ignored by male-dominated institutions such as federal and state governments, corporations, and trade unions. Peacetime spelled the rapid demise of Rosie the Riveter. From the halls of government, the pulpit, and the analyst's couch, women heard a similar message: discard your wartime overalls for the more "feminine" garb of a homemaker or service worker. The dominant culture of mid-to-late 1940s America encouraged women to sacrifice their own needs to ease the transition from a society of war to one of peace. The feminine mystique promised women fulfillment in husband, family, and carefully cultivated suburban home. Rosie, Americans were assured, had only been a temporary heroine. Now that peace had been achieved, women could return to their "natural" role as subordinate, helper, and comforter of men and children. The gains of wartime women appeared to have been eclipsed by the power of the mystique, and its seductive promise of security, happiness, and satisfaction.

Yet the feminine mystique failed to deliver total fulfillment. During the late 1950s, Betty Friedan interviewed countless suburban women suffering from "the problem that has no name." Approximately 20 years after Rosie received her pink slip, organized feminism was reborn. Among the feminists of the mid-to-late 1960s, we encounter Rosie, her literal and symbolic sisters, daughters, and granddaughters. Though we cannot immediately draw causal links between the 1940s and the 1960s, these observations compel us to re-examine the World War II era.

On both a popular and scholarly level, women are beginning to "rethink the 1940s," transcending that peculiar American amnesia surrounding war eras. The women interviewed in Connie Field's documentary, The Life and Times of Rosie the Riveter (1978), are living examples of that rethinking. Feminist scholars, especially historians, have also begun to grapple with the 1940s as a critical decade for American women.

Some historians such as William Chafe in The American Woman: Her Changing Social, Economic and Political Roles: 1920-1970 (1972) and Women and Equality (1977) have viewed World War II as a watershed in American women's history. Whereas organized feminism did not arise in the 1940s, the seeds of its development were sown in the increased labor-force participation of women. In contrast, Karen Anderson in Wartime Women: Sex Roles, Family Relations and the Status of Women during World War II (1981) and D'Ann Campbell in her unpublished Ph.D. dissertation, "Wives, Workers, and Womanhood: America during World War II" (1979) have asserted that wartime women experienced changes in family and work primarily as temporary and crisis-oriented rather than as signifying deeper and more long-lasting transformations in sexual ideologies and roles.(1) Susan M. Hartmann in The Home Front and Beyond: American Women in the 1940s (1982) has identified currents of traditionalism as well as change in the female wartime experience.(2) In her perspective, antifeminism and political con- servatism retarded the progress of wartime women, while the increase in female labor-force participation, the growth of higher education, and the rise of suburbia paved the way for a future resurgence of feminism.

The new feminist scholarship on the 1940s has addressed issues of continuity and change, rephrasing and refocusing the question initially posed by Chafe: Was World War II a historical watershed for women? Historians, sociologists, economists, and other scholars in the 1970s analyzed multiple dimensions of war era womanhood: labor-force participation; trade union representation; government policy; sexuality, family, and personal life; social welfare policy; and the demobilization of Rosie the Riveter.(3) Despite this renewal of interest in war era American womanhood, however, popular culture remains relatively unmined as the rich source it can provide for social historians.(4)

Through analyzing selected popular "women's films," this work explores the significance of the American female experience in the 1940s and addresses issues relevant to the recent historical debate: In what ways were American women affected by wartime trans- formations in work and family roles? How did they perceive themselves and each other as workers, homemakers, wives, lovers, mothers, sisters, daughters, and friends?

Underlying my research is the assumption that popular culture reflects, through the mediation of myth and symbol, significant themes within popular consciousness. Popular culture – in this case, the "women's film" – cannot simply be categorized as the "top-down" imposition of fantasy material on an all-receptive mass, the audience. Rather, its production and reception constitute an inter- active process, embodying the power relations and cultural conflicts of the larger society. Film production, for example, involves the collaboration of many individuals and teams. Sexual, class, gene- rational, racial, and cultural conflicts may play themselves out on the movie set. The final product is no auteur or studio mogul's fantasy, pure and simple. And media creations, e.g., films, books, records, and magazines, succeed and fail, in varying degrees, not simply due to the manipulations of industry executives and producers, but because of the extent to which they relate to the concerns of the audience.

Studying artifacts such as popular film yields insights that other historical methods cannot. Popular culture explores both the surface and underside of human experience and is particularly suited to discovering historical undercurrents since repressed or dissident fantasies can be expressed more easily through the mediation of myth and symbol. Our deepest fears, worst nightmares, and most rebellious fantasies do not have to stand naked. Rather, they are cloaked in more acceptable garb so that we may indulge them at the same moment that we try to deny, repress, or resolve them miraculously.

This work traces both maincurrents and undercurrents within American female consciousness by interpreting selected top-grossing women's films of the 1940s.(5) The first chapter traces the evolution and development of the Hollywood women's film; the second describes the social history of American women in the 1940 and further frames the historical debate. The last three chapter analyze dominant narrative patterns within popular women's films of the 1940s: the maternal drama, the career woman comedy and the films of suspicion and distrust. Taken together, these three film patterns can be analyzed as maincurrents and undercurrents in the fantasy world of female consciousness. The maternal drama (e.g. Mrs. Miniver), the most popular variety of women's film, portrays an appreciation of female power and bonding coupled with domesticit The career woman comedy (e.g., His Girl Friday) dramatizes both excitement and ambivalence centering on public achievement. Film of suspicion and distrust (e.g., Gaslight) depict a fear of and ang toward men, especially husbands.

The American female consciousness of the 1940s, as mediated through the women's film, embodied elements of resistance to male domination as well as acquiescence and submission. This interpretation takes issue with those who see the 1940s as a decade unmarked by significant changes in female consciousness. Its reality is far more complex. The films popular among female audiences in this period portray a view of womanhood as: strong, maternal, sisterly; desiring yet distrusting and angry toward men; excited about as well as ambivalent toward and frightened of independence and autonomy. We can view recurrent patterns within popular 1940s women's films as threads running through the lives of women American culture. In the 1940s, women in the United States did connect the feminist threads of their "common sense" to weave coherent feminist ideology. Yet, that fact alone neither obliterates the existence of these threads nor denies their historical importance. Analyzing popular women's films of the 1940s comp us to recognize the nascent feminism of wartime female consciousness.

POPULAR CULTURE AND POPULAR CONSCIOUSNESS: A THEORETICAL FRAMEWORK FOR INTERPRETING THE WOMEN'S FILM

Before entering the world of 1940s women's films, it is necessary to present a theoretical framework for interpreting artifacts of modern popular culture as potential mediators of popular consciousness.(6) It is beyond the scope of this discussion to provide a fully elaborated cultural theory. Rather, my aim is more modest: to introduce the reader briefly to the theoretical perspective by situating that perspective in the light of other influential currents in cultural criticism. The test of this theoretical model, however, is to be found in the chapters to follow that analyze the dynamics between the women's film and female experience in the 1940s.

The following basic assertions underlie my research: (a) popular culture — from production through reception — constitutes itself through social relations of conflict as well as consensus, of power and resistance, of subordinate versus dominant, of subculture and mainstream; (b) popular culture — because of its distinctive ability to cloak reality in symbol and metaphor — provides an indispensable source for discovering and tracing historical undercurrents as well as maincurrents within popular consciousness; (c) certain forms of mass culture — in this case, women's films — can be considered popular culture and hence, are invaluable in analyzing the dynamics of maincurrent and undercurrent in the construction of popular (and, in this case, female) consciousness.

POPULAR CULTURE AND SOCIAL HISTORY

Reconstructing social history requires several interrelated modes of interpretation. No one sociological or historical method, whether demography, survey research, participant observation or oral history, possesses a superior claim on "truth". Rather, each approach is distinctive, structuring questions in a particular way, illuminating certain areas of inquiry, while de-emphasizing others. Each method maps out its own dimension of society in its own specific way. Together, the various modes of historical interpretation challenge, enrich, and complement one another by posing new and different questions, uncovering new and sometimes contradictory data, and checking upon the others' validity. Taken together, they present a complex and multi-layered view of social reality.

The study of popular culture – and culture as a broader entity – plays an essential role in this interpretative process.(7) A culture is "popular" if it involves two-way communication and/or relates directly to the traditions and life situations of its audience-participants. In other words, popular culture cannot be simply created "for the people"; it must also be "of the people," that is, reflective of the realities of their everyday lives. The adjective popular describes cultural artifacts that embody widely held emotions, values, and aspirations of some (or many) of "the people."(8)

Women's films arose historically within a form of female-oriented popular culture created in response to the transition to industrial capitalism in the nineteenth century and popularized further through the media of mass communications in the twentieth. Modern popular culture – like the women's film – obviously differs in both form and content from a precapitalist folk culture, which was more likely to be directly and collectively produced by its partici-pants. Despite this significant historical transformation, however, as shall be discussed later, documents of modern media culture can in many instances be termed popular culture, expressing themes that are both historically specific and humanly universal.

The artifacts and rituals of popular culture – everyday language and customs, popular songs, and seasonal ceremonies – reveal a great deal about the ways in which societies (or social groups) with enormous historical and cultural variation, have interpreted birth, death, love, as well as sexual, economic, racial, and generational conflict. Yet popular culture reveals different dimensions of social reality than other historical methods. The analyst of popular culture must abandon the criteria of realism at the door of the theater, the cover of the novel, the dial of the television or radio. It is not sufficient to measure fiction against real life. Rather, to interpret popular culture, one must enter the world of cultural mediation, of symbol and metaphor, of collective dream and fantasy. The challenge of cultural analysis is to decode that symbolic structure, and analyze why audiences and readers in specific societies and subcultures prefer particular patterns of fantasy over others.

Popular culture offers insights that other historical sources cannot. Studying the artifacts of popular culture offers access to the dream world of popular consciousness as well as its surface manifestations. Popular culture is particularly suited to the discovery of historical undercurrent. Dissident or repressed fantasies can safely express themselves through the mediation of symbol and metaphor.

As Eugene Genovese (1972), E.P. Thompson (1963), and other scholars have shown, the analysis of popular culture unearths a rich body of insights for the social historian. Evidence uncovered in the study of popular culture is neither secondary nor derivative of other historical methods. Rather, it can compel one to ask new questions, rephrase old ones, or reinterpret an entire historical era. For example, the late-1970s American bestseller list featured numerous novels about demonic children threatening the adult community. Sociologists and historians of contemporary family life would do well to interpret a sample of these before drawing meaningful conclusions from the analysis of fertility trends, or interviews with parents, children, or childrearing experts. Taken together with other methods of social analysis, the study of popular culture is essential to understanding the multiple dimensions of historical reality.

The power of popular culture for its audience lies in its metaphoric or symbolic mode, which, like the unconscious, speaks for the forbidden. This metaphoric mode can express a variety of sentiments: those of support, acquiescence, submission, distrust, or defiance of mainstream mores and values. No dominant group is so powerful, nor is any society so seamless as to control its culture completely (or necessarily to want to). It is the task of the cultural analyst to interpret the range of social meanings within this symbolic mode.

Popular culture can be a volatile and potentially subversive sphere of society. Yet, the expression of forbidden or repressed material in popular culture serves at least a dual function: first, as an escape valve, simultaneously to release and defuse forbidden or painful emotions; secondly, as a safe space to express taboo or socially dissident sentiments without reprisal, and with the potential to develop into a future counterideology. As Eugene Genovese (1972) asserted, in his analysis of slave humor, the political potential of such sentiments is explosive, yet depends on social changes transcending the cultural realm:

> Oppressed peoples who can laugh at their oppressors contain within themselves a politically dangerous potential, but the weapons of popular culture also betray a conservative bias. They direct criticism, as Douglass feared, into channels acceptable to the regime — acceptable because in themselves they pose no direct threat and may even function as a safety valve for pent-up discontent. Their more dangerous content remains latent as long as the general conditions of life do not generate a crisis that heightens their critical thrust and points it to political terrain — a crisis that upsets the balance within the bittersweet laughter, and liberates the anger behind the laughter. At those moments the oppressor's legitimacy which the laughter ironically helps to authenticate by its very playfulness, suddenly faces challenge.(9)

Today's self-effacing joke may become tomorrow's political slogan. It is the task of the social historian to analyze the dynamic between text and context, between culture and society, and to identify the historical conditions that enable popular culture to effect political change.

MODERN POPULAR CULTURE AND ITS SOCIAL CONTEXT

Although modern popular culture — such as the women's film — occupies its own social space, it cannot be considered a completely autonomous sphere within advanced capitalist society. Rather, modern American popular culture is produced and received within a social fabric of both class and sexual domination. However, setting culture in context neither denies any autonomy nor reduces it to a mere reflex of dominant social relations. Like its preindustrial counterparts, mass-mediated popular culture often reflects a variety of social responses: from dominant to dissident, from maincurrent to undercurrent.

In conceptualizing the dynamic of popular culture in modern American society, one can draw upon the writings of Marx, the Frankfurt school, Antonio Gramsci, Raymond Williams, Stuart Hall, Annette Kuhn, and Tania Modleski, as well as mass communications scholars such as Paul Lazarsfeld and Herbert Gans.

However, if we utilize Marx's categories, it becomes necessary to recast orthodox notions of a determining economy (base) and a determined culture (superstructure), which accord a fixed, hierarchical, and spatially defined relationship between the two. Such rigid formulations contribute little to explaining, for example, why, in contemporary America, the films of Bernardo Bertolucci have become very popular or why feminist fiction like Marilyn French's The Women's Room became a best-seller. Clearly, the relationship of culture to society is far more complex than such one-dimensional models imply.(10)

A much more accurate conceptualization draws on the sense of multidimensionality present in some of Marx's writings, as well as the cultural theory and criticism of the Frankfurt school, Antonio Gramsci, and Raymond Williams. Writing in a society that afforded the laboring classes very little leisure, Marx never focused his attention on culture and vacillated in his conception of the relationship between economy and culture. However, seeds of a more open-ended and multi-dimensional model of culture appear in some of his writings:

The economic situation is the basis . . . but various elements of superstructural-political forms of the class struggle and its consequences form the course of the historical struggle and in many cases preponderate in determining their form.(11)

As an economistic Marxism found itself unable to explain the Russian Revolution, and the failure of revolutionary consciousness in

Depression America, and the rise of Fascism, culture and consciousness moved more clearly into the foreground of Marxist analysis. Frankfurt scholars, outsiders and refugees from Fascism, saw negation — the critique and transcendence of dominant values — as a hallmark of art and recognized the utopian moment in the artistic imagination. Later theorists, such as Jürgen Habermas, drawing on the work of Ernst Bloch and others, argued that symbolic representations, including those that are quite ideological, contain an irreducible core of critical truth that points to social relations free of domination. Whereas Frankfurt scholars focused primarily on "high" culture (and often conceptualized popular culture in one-dimensional terms), their insights can also be adapted to the study of popular culture.(12)

Most useful, however, in analyzing culture is the concept of hegemony developed by Antonio Gramsci and elaborated by Raymond Williams. Capitalist society, in the Gramscian view, is not held together primarily or automatically by economic force or political coercion. Rather, the "spontaneous consent"(13) of the masses must be won. Relations of domination must represent themselves as a privileged system of meanings. Whereas Gramsci stressed the ideological advantages that derive from the dominant group's function in production, he did place the cultural realm in the forefront of political analysis.(14)

It is Raymond Williams' elaboration of the dynamics of hegemony, however, that is most useful for this study. For Williams, hegemony constitutes a process in which dominant social values encounter, compete with, and often triumph over subordinate values. Cultural hegemony is not simply given, however. It must be won or maintained in continual struggle with less powerful groups in society. And rarely does hegemony maintain itself without serious challenge that at some point may sow the seeds of a counter-hegemony.

> A lived hegemony is always a process. It is not, except analytically, a system or a structure. It is a realized complex of experiences, relationships and activities, with specific and changing pressures and limits. In practice, that is, hegemony can never be singular. Its internal structures are highly complex, . . . it does not just passively exist as a form of dominance. It has continually to be renewed, recreated, defended and modified. It is also continually resisted, limited, altered, challenged by pressures not at all its own.(15)

In this light, the hegemonic is a more useful concept than the more static hegemony since it captures the dynamics of a dominant culture encountering subordinate power groups and interests.

Williams has also introduced three related categories helpful in conceptualizing the dynamics of cultural hegemony: dominant, residual, and emergent cultures. <u>Dominant</u> is synonymous with <u>hegemonic</u>; <u>residual</u> and <u>emergent</u> cultures challenge the dominant by their reference to alternative visions of the past and future. Residual culture is, in effect, the past living on in the present. However, for Williams, it is far from archaic or irrelevant:

> The "residual," by definition, has been effectively formed in the past, but it is still active in the cultural process, not only and often not at all as an element of the past, but as an effective element of the present. Thus certain experiences, meanings, and values which cannot be expressed or sub-stantially verified in terms of the dominant culture are nevertheless lived and practiced on the basis of the residue – cultural as well as social – of some previous social and cultural institutions and formations.(16)

Residual elements of contemporary culture, such as the longing for rural community, may form currents of opposition to the dominant culture. However, the resistant power of residual culture is often weakened by its basis in previous modes of production, symbolizing an impossible alternative, a <u>lost</u> or golden era.

The realm of "emergent" culture, however, represents the most serious challenge to the hegemonic culture:

> By "emergent" I mean, first, that new meanings and values, new practices, new relationships and kinds of relationships are continually being created. . . . It is true that in the structure of any actual society, and especially in its class structure, there is always a social basis for elements of the cultural process that are alternative or oppositional to the dominant elements.(17)

Emergent culture is always in struggle with the dominant culture, and as social historians have shown, is often most explosive when combined with residual elements. That struggle often results in the forced incorporation of oppositional elements within the dominant culture. Whereas more one-dimensional Marxists might term this process <u>cooptation</u>, i.e., the neutralization of alternative values through their absorption into the dominant ideology, a more critical view, deriving from Gramsci and Williams, is that of "forced incorporation." The latter describes a dynamic in which dissident elements both merge with and challenge the dominant culture in an uneasy coexistence. Incorporation does not necessarily signify the weakness of an emergent culture, but its strength and mass appeal as well. The dominant culture is <u>forced</u> to embody within itself oppositional elements, thus changing its character and compelling it to express (at the same time it tries to contain) the sentiments of its own transformation, a potential counterhegemony. Whereas the hegemonic culture may frame the limits of ideology, it does not always have the power to proscribe its content.

The sources of potential counterhegemony are numerous, reflecting the values and traditions of varied subordinate social groupings. Gramsci's concept of "common sense" is particularly useful here. For him, all people, even those with relatively little social power, are actively engaged in constructing meaning and in modifying their environment. "Common sense," or the world view of the common people, is invariably fragmented and disjointed, episodic and contradictory, and continually changing. It embodies elements of acquiescence and submission simultaneously with those of resistance and refusal. Yet it changes in dynamic and reciprocal interaction with those who perform more critical intellectual and artistic functions in society. Even popular theater, serials, and novels represent "the popular creative spirit in its diverse phases of development."(18) Common sense, therefore, is not in and of itself a counterhegemony. However, political struggle, education, and cultural production (through the influence of "organic intellectuals") can stimulate common sense to articulate itself more coherently as an oppositional culture. If we apply the categories of Williams, common sense can assume (simultaneously) both residual and emergent, as well as dominant forms.

The dynamic tension between common sense and the hegemonic forms the social context of popular culture. By investigating the ways in which popular culture is produced and received, this perspective becomes further concretized and enriched.

MASS-MEDIATED CULTURE AS POPULAR CULTURE

Any theory of modern mass culture as popular culture must recognize the fact that most contemporary popular culture differs radically from its preindustrial counterparts in its modes of production and transmission of meaning. Bestsellers emanating from large publishing houses are worlds away from folktales; television and the movies could not have been imagined by Americans two centuries ago.

Some contemporary Marxist critics consider modern mass culture as nothing but formulaic escape, designed to placate the masses and ensure the rule of the corporate elite.(19) Likewise, some recent feminist film theorists, influenced by Althusserian Marxism, semiotics, and Lacanian psychoanalysis, assert that "classic realist cinema" and its "seamless narratives" serve only to naturalize and render invisible the ideology of patriarchy. In this view, women in popular film are prisoners of a patriarchal discourse, fetishized as the spectacle for male viewers, without voice or power in the cinema.(20)

However, the history of mass media, and particularly film, seriously challenges such monolithic theories. The reality of filmic creation, content, and reception fails to support the model of a seamless corporate patriarchal hegemony, unambiguously representing the dominant interests in society. Whereas dominant values may struggle for ascendancy in Hollywood, they also encounter residual and emergent elements whose realities they must acknowledge and often incorporate into cinematic language, themes, and narrative structure. In fact, on occasion, the mass communications industry ironically supports the production of films challenging their own corporate interests. As Bertolucci (1978) said of his film 1900,

> This movie is a monument to the contradictions of the system in which we live . . . the same system in which every director works . . . It seems absurd — the contradictions between the capital which supports the movies and the idealistic themes of many talented directors but this contradiction had always existed. I tried to enter into it and make it explode, and judging from the reactions, I have succeeded.(21)

Given the political conservatism of Hollywood and the historical realities of the Red Scare, Bertoluccis are rare. However, every Hollywood film must meet the test of the box office. If the box office vote is positive, media moguls are sometimes compelled to produce socially critical films because they will net high profits.

On a more general level, there exists a tension between those who finance the movies and those who make them. Media moguls are not free simply to translate their ideas and values into popular movie fantasies. As will become clearer in the discussion of the women's film, they are dependent on the talents and skills of a vast army of film artists whose creativity cannot always be so easily controlled and channeled into avenues acceptable to studio heads. As David Talbot and Barbara Zheutlin (1978) asserted,

> Hollywood is controlled by large scale private interests and there is a tendency for its films and TV shows to reinforce conventional social values. Those who own and operate the major studios have an obvious stake in preserving the status quo. Yet it is not the media moguls themselves who perform the creative work in Hollywood. It is not they who manufacture the cultural products which bring Hollywood its profits. For this, the industry must rely upon a vast legion of creative employees. These employees, though they are generally anxious to please those who pay them, cannot always be trusted to follow the ideological line of their bosses. That is, they cannot always be counted on to sing the praises of rugged individualism, acquisitiveness, male dominance, and strong-willed authority.(22)

To reconstruct the history of American cinema is to describe the dynamic and often conflictual relationship between studio heads, directors, stars, other film artists, critics, audiences, and, especially in times of national mobilization or political repression, the state.(23)

Films reflect the dynamics of their production and reception, and thus constitute complex, contradictory, and multi-layered narrative structures. There is rarely, if ever, one "meaning" to a film; narratives usually open up several possibilities for audience and critical interpretation. As Stuart Hall noted in "Encoding/De-coding" (1980), there may be a "preferred" reading that usually supports the dominant or hegemonic culture. However, the point at which the dominant culture encounters its opposition may be at the moment of reception. The oppositional reading may stress under-lying sentiments within the narrative or may at times "read" a film almost entirely "against the grain." Annette Kuhn has remarked similarly, "This dynamic notion of reading as a relationship between reader and text then implies that no texts, 'mainstream' or other-wise, bear specific a priori meanings in and for themselves."(24) In this light, endings cannot be considered the clue to filmic meaning. Whereas some movie endings are integrated into the structure of the narrative, others are tacked on and, as such, are singularly uncon-vincing and are often easily forgotten. Filmmakers sometimes subvert the happiness of endings through the use of unsettling visual techniques (tilted camera angles, shadowy lighting) as in the 1940s' film noir. Cultural analysts who fail to recognize the complexity of film production, reception, and interpretation do a grave injustice to those who make and watch popular films.

The image of audiences as sponge-like masses or "well-positioned spectators" eagerly absorbing media messages and images is also not supported by communications research. In fact, during the heyday of the women's film, the 1940s, communications researchers consis-tently challenged the "audience as mass" image, as they discovered the media-audience relationship to be multidimensional and often unpredictable.

First of all, audience research such as that of George Gallup and associates and Hortense Powdermaker showed that movie viewers acted not as faceless, anonymous masses but as social groups – men, women, young, and older people – with specific and distinct media preferences. As Raymond Williams (1958) has noted, perhaps "there are no masses; there are only ways of seeing people as masses."(25)

An alternative formulation to that of mass audience is Herbert Gans' concept (1956) of the "taste public." This term refers to a sector of the media audience for whom a particular production is created. In the studio era, for example, westerns and war films were largely designed for males, whereas women's films were created primarily for female viewers. All taste publics are obviously not equal in social power. Their vulnerability to stereotyping, scapegoating, invisibility, and misrepresentation varies with their social visibility, level of political organization, and power within and outside the media industries. However, the power of the taste public does not begin at the box office, but rather in the studio. In the process of production, the taste public is represented (or mis-represented, in some cases) as an audience image in the minds of filmmakers. For Gans,

> Every creator is engaged to some extent in a process of communication between himself and an audience, that is, he is creating something for somebody. . . . it becomes an image of an audience which the creator develops as part of every creative process. . . .
> This image, though projected by the creator, functions as an external observer-judge against which he unconsciously tests his product even while he is creating it.(26)

As audiences vary, so do media effects. Communications researchers have shown — in studies done over the last 40 years — that the relationship between content and effect is neither self-evident nor easily predictable. For example, Paul Lazarsfeld and Elihu Katz (1957) found that media news affected listeners as part of a "two-step flow," filtered through the influence of significant opinion leaders.

> The image of the audience as a mass of disconnected individuals hooked up to the mass media but not to each other could not be reconciled with the idea of the two-step flow, i.e. networks of interconnected individuals through which mass communications were channeled.(27)

Lazarsfeld's research also seriously challenged the hypothesis of the totalitarian appeal of mass media. Instead, he found that voters rarely listened to opposing political opinions, making it very difficult to sway their beliefs. Similarly Hadley Cantril (1940) discovered that certain radio listeners were predisposed to believe or doubt particular kinds of information. In studying the infamous Orson Welles "Mars invasion" broadcast, Cantril found that, contrary to popular belief, only "predisposed" listeners really believed that an invasion from Mars had occurred. Predisposition could be traced to a variety of factors: family background, sex, class, religion, age, ethnicity, or idiosyncratic personality characteristics.

The media effects issue proved complicated in other ways as well. Some media creations seemed to exert a sleeper effect, audiences reacting months or even years later. Still other media productions boomeranged, audiences reacting in a manner completely opposite from that intended or predicted by the producers.

George Custen's research (1980) has shown the difficulty of applying one model of audience behavior. Custen analyzed audience response to a popular film (Jonathan Demme's Citizen's Band) through monitoring after-film conversations. Custen divided his sample into "heavy" and "light" viewers, and discovered that "heavy" viewers usually focus on the structure of the narrative as a whole, whereas "light" viewers concentrate their attention on specific events and characters that relate to their own lives. Many viewers, despite the realism of the film, continually refer to the artifice of the cinema, and comment as to how they would have made the film. Others spoke as if the film were a documentary. "Film talk", that is conversations about movies and movie themes, was very important to many of these viewers, serving as a "coin of social exchange"(28) and a mode of integration into their peer group.

For the purposes of this study, monolithic models of mass culture and mass audience must be replaced by a conception of mass-mediated popular culture and its audiences that is dynamic, historically specific, and constituted through the ongoing power relations and struggles of class, race, age, and sex. In this framework, mass culture, in specific time frames and situations, can be analyzed as a popular culture in which the hegemonic encounters the emergent and residual cultural currents drawn from the fragmentary world of common sense.

As the following chapters will show, this theoretical model can be applied to the study of women's films of the 1940s, which can be seen as constituted through the dynamics of sexual power and resistance — in the studios and in society. The common sense of American womanhood in the war era — in all its fragmentary and contradictory manifestations — finds a safe avenue of expression in Hollywood films created primarily for a female audience. And the residual and emergent dimensions of femininity can be uncovered through analyzing the interrelationship of plot, characterization, and narrative structure in women's films.

Women's films can be interpreted as a metaphorical avenue to the consciousness of American womanhood, particularly to the undercurrents of female history. It is to those maincurrents and undercurrents, as represented in the history of the women's film, that we now turn.

NOTES

(1)   See Karen Anderson, Wartime Women: Sex Roles, Family Relations and the Status of Women During World War II (Westport, Connecticut: Greenwood Press, 1981); D'Ann Campbell, "Wives, Workers and Womanhood: America during World War II" (unpublished Ph.D. dissertation, University of North Carolina, 1979). Anderson has stressed the ways in which women were influenced by

the dominant ideology of femininity, whereas Campbell has focused on the ways in which women themselves embraced traditional roles.

(2)   See Susan M. Hartmann, The Home Front and Beyond: American Women in the 1940s (Boston: G.K. Hall, 1982).

(3)   See Alan Clive, "Women Workers in World War II: Michigan As A Test Case," Labor History 20 (Winter 1979): 44-72; Nancy Gabin, "Women Workers and the UAW in the Post-World War II Period: 1945-1954," Labor History 21 (Winter 1979-80): 5-30; Sherna Gluck, "Rosie the Riveter Revisited," paper presented at the Fifth Berkshire Conference on the History of Women, June 1981; Sheila Lichtman, "Experiences of Women's Wartime Employment", paper presented at the Fifth Berkshire Conference on the History of Women, June 1981; "Women at Work 1941-1945: Wartime Employment in the San Francisco Bay Area" (unpublished Ph.D. dissertation, University of California-Davis, 1981); Sonya Michel, "The Reproduction of Privatization: Women, Families and Professionals during World War II," paper presented at the Fifth Berkshire Conference on the History of Women, June 1981; also "Contradictions of Privatization: American Families during World War II," paper presented at the Society for the Study of Social Problems, August, 1980; Ruth Milkman, "Women's Work and the Economic Crisis: Some Lessons From the Great Depression," Review of Radical Political Economics 8, 1 (Spring 1976): 73-97; "Organizing the Sexual Division of Labor: Historical Perspectives on 'Women's Work' and the American Labor Movement," Socialist Review 49, 10, 1 (January-February 1980): 95-150; "Redefining Women's Work: The Sexual Division of Labor in the Auto Industry during World War II," Feminist Studies 8, 2 (1982); Leila J. Rupp, Mobilizing Women For War: German and American Propaganda: 1939-45 (Princeton, N.J.: Princeton University Press, 1978); Karen Beck Skold, "The Job He Left Behind: American Women in the Shipyards During World War II," in Women, War and Revolution, ed. Carol R. Berkin and Clara M. Lovett (New York: Holmes and Meier, 1980): 55-75; also see Eleanor Straub, "United States Government Policy Toward Civilian Women During World War II," Prologue 5 (Winter 1973): 240-54; "Government Policy Toward Civilian Women During World War II," Ph.D. dissertation, Emory University, 1973; "The Impact of World War II on Sex Roles: Women in the Civilian Labor Force," National Archives Women's History Conference (1976); Sheila Tobias and Lisa Anderson, "What Really Happened to Rosie the Riveter: Demobilization and the Female Labor Force, 1944-47," (New York: MSS Modular Publications, 1974), Module 9; "New Views of Rosie the Riveter," unpublished, 1975; Joan Ellen Trey, "Women in the War Economy: World War II," Review Of Radical Political Economics 4 (July 1972).

(4)   Two studies on popular 40s films were done during that period: Barbara Deming, Running Away From Myself: A Dream Portrait of America Drawn From the Films of the Forties (New

York: Grossman, 1969) and Martha Wolfenstein and Nathan Leites, Movies: A Psychological Study (Glencoe, Ill.: Free Press, 1950). The few studies that have been done on wartime popular culture include: M. Joyce Baker, Images of Women in Film: The War Years: 1941-45 (Ann Arbor: UMI Research Press, 1980); Susan Hartmann, "Prescriptions for Penelope," Women's Studies 5 (1978): 223-39; Maureen Honey, "Temporary Equality: The Use of Magazine Fiction during World War II," paper presented at the Fifth Berkshire Conference on the History of Women, June 1981. These studies largely conclude that wartime popular culture reinforced the dominant ideology of femininity by presenting stronger, more resourceful models of womanhood during the war to encourage women to take their part in the defense effort. After the war, these authors conclude, more independent images of womanhood gave way to portrayals of women that stressed their weakness and vulnerability.

(5) The films analyzed in this study represent over forty top-grossing women's films of the 1940s, although in the process of this project I viewed hundreds of women's films and other cinema from this era. Though the films I have interpreted in detail represent a sample of some of the most popular women's films of the decade, they do not claim to represent all women's films of the 1940s. What distinguishes this body of films are both their common narrative patterns and their audience appeal, and hence, relevance for the study of female consciousness and social history.

I began this study without a clear sense of what narrative patterns would emerge among the films. After considerable viewing, I traced variations on three common patterns that repeated themselves in many popular women's films: namely, the maternal drama, the career woman comedy, and the film of suspicion and distrust. Other movies featured strong heroines and related somewhat to these themes, but did not clearly follow the patterns. Still other films (see Chapter 1, "The 'Women's Film' ") fell into smaller, less significant categories. Some movies combined aspects of two or more types, or fell between typologies. Still others stood alone. Since I believe that cycles and progressions among common filmic narratives derive from audience as well as studio preference, I chose a smaller sample of films from the three categories to analyze in more detail and compare to the larger body of films.

(6) I am using the term consciousness in a descriptive sense, i.e., "the totality of an individual's conscious thoughts and feelings" rather than the normative sense (e.g. to have "false consciousness," "feminist consciousness"). Consciousness, though it connotes feelings one is aware of, can trace its deeper roots to subconscious and unconscious phenomena.

(7) When studying culture, it is important to trace the historical roots of the concept. Raymond Williams, in Marxism and Literature (London: Oxford, 1977) and Culture and Society (London: Chatto and Windus, 1958), noted that the term culture only came

into its present usage in industrializing England. This is not to suggest that, prior to industrialization, social groupings did not impart meaning to their life patterns, but rather, that the meaning imparted was not viewed as a separate, compartmentalized realm, divorced from the world of production. Only for the elite, in their realm of high culture did there exist a demarcated cultural realm. Hence, folk culture is, in many ways, a retrospective term. For the majority of the population, culture occupied a sphere of its own when the vast economic, political, social, and psychological changes wrought by a developing capitalism fragmented and transformed the preindustrial world into a universe whose key distinction was that between work and leisure. An understanding of that material and conceptual dichotomy is central to the study of culture, and especially, popular culture. However, at the same time that we must recognize the historical separation of the concept culture from that of economy and society, we must acknowledge its humanly universal dimension as well. Whether a preliterate society called its funeral customs culture or not, human activity has been marked since its inception by a desire for self-understanding and the need to express symbolically the meanings of key human dramas such as birth, marriage, and death. Modern culture, both high and popular, thus has two wellsprings: the universal need of humans to come to terms with their existence and the historically specific compartmentalization of work and leisure created by the transition to industrial capitalism.

(8) See Oscar Handlin, "Comments on Mass and Popular Culture," in Norman Jacobs, ed. Culture for the Millions: Mass Media in Modern Society (Boston: Beacon, 1959): p. 63-70. Also see Daniel J. Czitrom, Media And the American Mind (Chapel Hill: University of North Carolina Press, 1982) for a discussion of the tensions and contradictions within the popular culture of advanced capitalist societies. See also Stuart Hall, Dorothy Hobson, Andrew Lowe, and Paul Willis (eds.), Culture, Media, Language (London: Hutchinson, 1980) for a discussion of the dynamics between the dominant ideology and oppositional elements within popular culture.

The conception of popular culture employed in this study is rooted in the notion of culture as a site of social conflict. This notion differs radically from the definition of popular culture as "the cultural world around us — our attitudes, habits and actions; how we act and why we act; what we eat, wear, our buildings, roads and means of travel, our entertainments, sports; our politics, religion, medical practices; our beliefs and what shapes and controls them . . . in other words to us what water is to fish; it is the world we live in." Ray Browne, "Popular Culture: The World Around Us," in Jack Nachbar, Deborah Weiser, and John L. Wright, (eds.) The Popular Culture Reader (Bowling Green, Ohio: Bowling Green University Popular Press, 1978), p. 12.

(9)   Eugene Genovese, Roll, Jordan, Roll: The World The Slaves Made (New York: Random House, 1972), p. 584.

(10)   See Raymond Williams, Marxism and Literature (Oxford: Oxford University Press, 1977), esp. pp. 75-82, for a discussion of (a) the ambiguity in Marx's conception of the relationship between culture and economy to society and (b) the rigid interpretation of the base-superstructure relationship by some Marxists.

Discussion of the work of Louis Althusser is beyond the scope of this study. However, a brief description of his contribution to cultural theory is in order, particularly since many recent feminist film theorists have been influenced by his conception of ideology and culture. Althusser appears to reconceptualize the economy to culture relationship in a manner quite different from the base-superstructure model. In an attempt to transcend economism, he has asserted that societal superstructures are "relatively autonomous" and "determined in the last instance." However, at the same time Althusser denies the reality of human subjectivity and defines ideology in the most deterministic sense. Ideology, for Althusser, always functions to naturalize and support relations of domination. Upon critical examination, notions of "relative autonomy" do not differ radically from the base-superstructure model. The Althusserian revision of economism does not change the unidirectional notion of the flow of power (economy determines culture); it merely renders the process more complex. See Simon Clarke, Terry Lovell, Kevin McDonnell, et al., One-Dimensional Marxism: Althusser and the Politics of Culture (London: Allison and Busby, 1980). For a feminist analysis of film based on Althusserian concepts, see Claire Johnston, "Women's Cinema as Counter Cinema," in Patricia Erens (ed.) Sexual Strategems: The World of Women in Film (New York: Horizon Press, 1979): pp. 133-43.

(11)   Karl Marx, Preface, A Contribution to the Critique of Political Economy (New York: International, 1970), p. 11ff.

(12)   See Theodor Adorno, Prisms, trans. by Samuel and Shierry Weber (London: New Left Books, 1973); Theodor Adorno and Max Horkheimer, Dialectic of Enlightenment, trans. by John Cumming (New York: Herder and Herder, 1972); Leo Lowenthal, Literature and the Image of Man (Boston: Beacon, 1957); for a discussion of popular culture from a rather one-dimensional perspective, see Adorno, "On Popular Music," Studies in Philosophy and Social Science, 9, 1 (1941); "A Social Critique of Radio Music," Kenyon Review 7, 2 (Spring 1945); "TV and the Patterns of Mass Culture," in Bernard Rosenberg and David Manning White (eds.), Mass Culture (New York: Free Press, 1957), pp. 474-88. For a more dialectical and multidimensional approach to popular culture, see Adorno, "The Stars Down to Earth: The Los Angeles Times Astrology Column," Jahrbuch für Amerikastudien, vol. 2 (Heidelberg, 1957); Walter Benjamin, Illuminations, ed. and intro. by Hannah Arendt, trans. by Harry Zohn (New York: Schocken, 1968). Also see Jürgen Habermas,

Theory and Practice, trans. John Viertel (Boston: Beacon Press, 1973), especially 239ff. See Diane Waldman, "Critical Theory and Film," New German Critique 12 (Fall 1977), pp. 39-60, for a discussion of the differences in Adorno's and Benjamin's writing on the progressive potential of popular film. Waldman argues that critical theory can be adapted toward a more open-ended theoretical perspective on popular film.

(13) Antonio Gramsci, Prison Notebooks (New York: International Publishers, 1970), p. 12.

(14) Gramsci's concept of hegemony contains many more elements than are relevant to my purposes here. For recent discussions, see especially Chantal Mouffe, ed. Gramsci and Marxist Theory (London: Routledge, 1979); and Perry Anderson, "The Antinomies of Antonio Gramsci," New Left Review, no. 100 (Nov. 1976-Jan. 1977): 5-78.

(15) Raymond Williams, Marxism and Literature, p. 112. Also see Stuart Hall, Bob Lumley, Gregor McLennan, "Politics and Ideology: Gramsci," Working Papers in Cultural Studies, 10 (1977): 77-106.

(16) Williams, Marxism and Literature, p. 122.

(17) Ibid., pp. 123-24.

(18) See Antonio Gramsci, Letters From Prison (New York: Harper and Row, 1973), p. 80; also Prison Notebooks, pp. 9, 10, 200, 265-66, 321-3, 333, 418, 423.

(19) See Stuart Ewen, Captains of Consciousness (New York: McGraw-Hill, 1976), for an example of a contemporary study that adopts this perspective.

(20) See Michael Renov, "From Fetish to Subject: The Containment of Sexual Difference in Hollywood's Wartime Cinema," Wide Angle, 5:1 (1982), pp. 16-27, for an example of this perspective. Renov's work has focused on some of the same women's films that are analyzed in this book.

It is beyond the scope of this study to present a full-blown discussion of recent developments in feminist film theory. But let me briefly indicate some of the major contours, and suggest the relevance of recent works in feminist film theory to this study.

Feminist film criticism began to gain ground in the early 1970s, reflecting the growing strength of the women's movement and the feminist critique of culture. Early feminist film criticism, however, was often impressionistic, atheoretical, and limited to the rather narrow cataloguing of static "images of women" (e.g., virgin, vamp). More popular film histories of women such as Marjorie Rosen's Popcorn Venus and Molly Haskell's From Reverence To Rape (both 1973) presented much more complex arguments about changes in female representation in cinema over time. However, neither employed a coherent feminist film theory, or attempted to conceptualize the dynamics of the viewer/film relationship.

Into this theoretical void stepped cine-feminists, drawing upon Althusser, cine-semiotics, and Lacanian psychoanalysis. Early theorists like Claire Johnston ("Women's Cinema As Counter-Cinema") drew upon Althusser and Roland Barthes to describe ideology as rendering invisible or "naturalizing" patriarchal social relations. Johnston's initial view was monolithic and totalizing: "Within a sexist ideology, woman is presented as what she represents for man." Laura Mulvey elaborated upon this theory by introducing the notion of "visual pleasure." In her classic article, "Visual Pleasure and Narrative Cinema" (in Kay and Peary (eds.), Women and the Cinema, pp. 412-28), Mulvey described "woman as image, man as bearer of the look." She contended that Hollywood cinema is created for the male spectator whose desire controls the narrative (and the female within it). Drawing upon Lacan, Mulvey saw film as replicating the nature of the human symbolic order, primordially and unequally divided between active male and passive female, and rooted in the Oedipal drama, with the phallus as key signifier. In this all-powerful system of male signification, woman equals "lack" and can only be expressed in a male-constructed and female-objectifying discourse.

Since the publication of Mulvey's classic piece, feminist film theory has become more open-ended and attuned to the contradictions within Hollywood cinema, the "ruptures" and "disjunctures" in the discourse, as well as the influence of women upon the popular film. In addition, the textual emphasis has become more integrated with the contextual, and the issue of "progressive" and "multiple readings" of texts more widely accepted. See Annette Kuhn, Women's Pictures: Feminism and Cinema (London: Routledge, 1982) for an excellent discussion of the recent developments and ongoing debates within feminist film theory. Also see Christine Gledhill, "Recent Developments in Feminist Criticism," Quarterly Review of Film Studies (Fall, 1978), pp. 457-93; E. Ann Kaplan, "Integrating Marxist and Psychoanalytical Approaches in Feminist Film Criticism," Milennium: Film Journal, 6 (Spring 1980), pp. 8-17. Also see Tania Modleski, "The Search for Tomorrow In Today's Soap Operas: Notes On A Feminine Narrative Form," Film Quarterly 33,1 (Fall 1979): 12-21, for a critique of the notion of masculine pleasure as the only pleasure for the viewer of modern media. Also see Noel Carroll, "Address to the Heathen," October 23 (Winter 1982), pp. 89-163.

The problems within structuralist cine-feminism are numerous: the one-dimensionality of Althusserianism, the totalizing character of its original formulations, its reliance on an unfalsifiable model of spectator-text relations. How can one ever truly prove or disprove Mulvey's model of male spectatorship and narrative pleasure? In addition, structuralists in general assume an audience of "positioned spectators" somehow mesmerized by the "realism" or "illusionism" of filmic texts, when, in fact, audience research tells us something quite different.

However, recent cine-feminism in its more open-ended and multiple readings of texts can be quite insightful in its analysis of filmic narrative. See Elizabeth Cowie, "The Popular Film as a Progressive Text: A Discussion of Coma, Part I," M/F, no. 3 (1979), pp. 59-82.

(21) Bernardo Bertolucci, quoted in David Talbot and Barbara Zheutlin, Creative Differences: Profiles of Hollywood Dissidents (Boston: South End Press, 1978), p. x.

(22) Ibid., p. viii.

(23) See Eric Rhode, A History of the Cinema: From Its Origins To 1970 (New York: Hill and Wang, 1976), particularly his discussion of the origins of the studio and star systems. See Part One, "Before 1920," pp. 3-45.

(24) Annette Kuhn, Women's Pictures, p. 12. Also see Stuart Hall, "Encoding/Decoding" in Stuart Hall, et al., Culture, Media, Language, pp. 128-38.

(25) Raymond Williams, Culture and Society, p. 299.

(26) Herbert J. Gans, "The Creator-Audience Relationship in the Mass Media," in Mass Culture, Bernard Rosenberg and David M. White, eds., pp. 316-17.

(27) Elihu Katz, "The Two-Step Flow of Communication" in Wilbur Schramm, ed., Mass Communications, p. 347.

(28) See George Custen, "Film Talk: Viewer Responses To a Film as a Socially Situated Event," Ph.D. dissertation, University of Pennsylvania, 1980.

Chapter 1

THE "WOMEN'S FILM"

What did I go to see during the '40s? Oh, mostly, you know, women's pictures, a Bette Davis or Joan Crawford movie. I loved them; the woman was always in the middle of every-thing. I used to go two times a week. I don't go to the movies much anymore, but I'd go if they brought those kind of movies back.

Margaret G., age 62

I liked Clark Gable and Errol Flynn, but mostly I liked women.

Barbara, one of Hannah's Daughters,
by Dorothy Gallagher (New York:
Thomas Crowell, 1976) p. 212.

"Women's film" or "Woman's picture" was a commonly understood term for American women who grew up watching Hollywood movies of the 1930s, 1940s, and early 1950s. For those of us coming of age in the last thirty years, the phrase had become a historical reference – to the world of our mothers and grandmothers. In the mid-1970s, with the impact of the women's movement, a new, more feminist type of women's film began to emerge in features like Julia (1977) and Girlfriends (1977).(1) The classic women's films, the movies of Joan Crawford, Bette Davis, and Katharine Hepburn, are still loved by audiences of all ages on television and in revival houses across the country.

What is the women's film and why has it proven so enduringly popular with female audiences? Women's film is an umbrella term referring to Hollywood films of the 1930s to early 1950s, created primarily for a female audience. No one is sure if the name

23

originated in the offices of studio moguls or on the pages of female-oriented fan magazines. Nonetheless, the term women's film became popularly identified with particular themes and narrative devices designed primarily for female viewers. The following discussion will delineate the woman's film by theme, narrative structure, visual style, film production, and critical and audience response.

The women's film cannot be considered a genre(2) by any definition of the term; it partakes of a variety of narrative moods (comedy, melodrama), visual styles (mainstream Hollywood and film noir), and plot structures (romantic triangles, female kin dramas, and murder mysteries). However, women's films do comprise a recognizable and analyzable mode of cinema because of common psychological motifs that distinguish films produced largely for female viewers from those created primarily for male or mixed audiences.

First of all, women's films revolve around women in a culture that clearly does not. The titles of many women's films are taken from the names of the heroines: Daisy Kenyon (1947); Jane Eyre (1944); Kitty Foyle (1940); Madame Curie (1943); Mrs. Miniver (1942); The Song of Bernadette (1943); Stella Dallas (1937). Other women's films make some reference to womankind in the title: Adam's Rib (1949); His Girl Friday (1940); Letter From An Unknown Woman (1948); A Woman's Face (1941); Woman of the Year (1942). Secondly, the themes of women's films differ radically from those of male-oriented cinema such as Westerns, crime dramas, and war movies. Male-oriented films often dramatize a fear of intimacy (especially with women) and an obsession for individuation ("a man's got to do what a man's got to do") and masculine bonding. In contrast, women's films convey the primacy of emotionality and human attachment, and often express a dread of separation from loved ones, whether they be female kin or friends, spouses, lovers, or offspring. It is easy to see why the women's film might be called a "child of the sound era." Usually shot indoors, women's films are quintessentially emotive and verbal, rarely violent, unlike masculine dramas that are often shot outdoors and whose hallmarks consist of sparse dialogue, repressed feelings, and plenty of action (often violent). Both types of films focus on dilemmas of moral choice, yet in very different ways. When male heroes of the classic Western, for example, fight for justice and honor, they usually do so in an abstract way, suppressing emotion, acting alone or with a male "buddy" and shielding themselves from the "weak" and "compromising" influence of women and children.(3) Heroines of the women's film, on the other hand, also often struggle for honor and justice, but do so in a less abstract, more complex moral context of choice often focusing on competing strong interpersonal bonds. The moral universe of choice presented in women's films shares much in common with that described by psychologist Carol Gilligan in analyzing differences in dominant masculine and feminine modes of moral reasoning:

> The moral problem (for women) arises from conflicting responsibilities rather than from competing rights and requires for its resolution a mode of thinking that is contextual and narrative rather than formal and abstract. This (feminine) conception of morality as concerned with the activity of care centers moral development around the under- standing of responsibility and relationships, just as the conception of morality as fairness (masculine) ties moral development to the understanding of rights and rules.(4)

The dilemmas of choice popular in women's films always involve ambivalence and usually entail loss. Molly Haskell (1973) has noted that "sacrifice" is the most common mode of choice in women's films.(5) In Haskell's schema, several popular variations on the sacrifice theme occur, in which the heroine must:

1. sacrifice her own welfare for that of her children — as in Madame X (1929, 1937, 1965) and Mildred Pierce (1945)
2. give up her (sometimes illegitimate) child for its own good — as in Stella Dallas (1937) and To Each His Own (1946)
3. abandon respectable marriage for her lover — as in Back Street (1932, 1941, 1961) and Now, Voyager (1942)
4. give up her lover (or possibility of one) because he is married — as in All This and Heaven, Too (1940) and Now, Voyager (1942)
5. relinquish her career for love — as in Lady In the Dark (1944)
6. give up love for her career — as in Morning Glory (1933) and Little Women (1933, 1949)

One might add to Haskell's list, other compelling themes:

7. choosing your happiness over your mother's — as in Now, Voyager (1942)
8. giving up wealth and status for true love — as in Kitty Foyle (1940)
9. sacrificing health, wealth, etc. to fight for a cause — as in Mrs. Miniver (1942) and Madame Curie (1943)

In these films, the everyday world of feminine role conflict is taken to melodramatic excess.(6) Tragedy becomes the handmaiden of joy in these classically bittersweet films.

Other women's films — usually more comic and less melodramatic in nature — focus on choice as well. In the 1940s career woman comedy (e.g., His Girl Friday and Adam's Rib), the conflict between femininity and achievement is dramatized through a hyperactive verbal duel between the heroine and her husband-lover-coworker. In general, feminist themes were most acceptable in Hollywood films if cloaked in historical garb or softened by a comic treatment.

These sacrifice films, though rarely feminist in ideology, are based on a feminist assumption: that women can make choices. Although these heroines are often "pushed" in conservative directions, they are not socially determined, mere objects and "others" in a system of male signification. They are, to an extent, authors of their own destiny. The fact that they are depicted as choosing subjects may be as important as the content of the life styles they choose.

Women's films fall into several major categories: maternal dramas, "working girl" movies, and films of suspicion and distrust. Maternal dramas like Meet Me In St. Louis (1944), the most popular type of women's film, especially in the 1940s, featured strong, sacrificial mothers embedded in close networks of female kin. Men were usually peripheral to the often melodramatic narratives that celebrated the resilience of traditional femininity. "Working girl" films such as His Girl Friday (1940) were classically lighter in tone, whether as dramas or comedies, and featured spunky professional heroines focused on the dilemma of career versus love. By the 1940s, these films would take a more feminist turn. The third major type, "films of suspicion and distrust" such as Gaslight (1944) featured noir cinematography and plots often centering on a murderous husband and a suspicious wife. These deliciously paranoid dramas flourished in the mid- to late 1940s.

A popular, but slightly less common fourth type might be termed a "woman in suffering" film. These movies portrayed women coming to terms with impending death (Dark Victory 1937; Sing No Sad Songs for Me 1950), madness (Snake Pit 1948), or other physical affliction. A fifth category, "good woman/bad woman" films, of which there are a small but significant number, featured good and evil cast stereotypically as sisters in conflict in films such as In This Our Life (1942) and A Stolen Life (1946).

These types constitute broad categories. Some women's films like Claudia (1943) or Tender Comrade (1943) fall outside or between these categories and others (like A Letter to Three Wives, 1949 and Mildred Pierce, 1945) combine aspects of two or more types. It is also important to recognize that audiences often viewed these films at the same time (sometimes literally in a double or triple bill) and that most major women's film stars appeared in several different types of movies. Taken together, the three types complement as well as contrast one another. For over 20 years, they constituted a cultural dialogue on the American female experience from the 1930s until the early 1950s, when the women's film would decline in popularity with the advent of television.

NARRATIVE FORM AND VISUAL STYLE

The heroines of women's films differ markedly from the female leading characters of more male-oriented movies (like Busby Berkeley's Fashions of 1934 or John Huston's The Maltese Falcon (1941) who serve primarily as objects of desire and/or fear for male protagonists. The women's film heroine is at the heart and center of the narrative. Men and children exist in the film in relation to her and are often seen through her eyes. Women's films typically employ either first person or omniscient narration. The first person narrator may be the major female character (Mildred Pierce), or her daughter (I Remember Mama). Memory plays a key role in women's films; cinematic narrative often unfolds through the recurrent use of flashbacks. Dialogue-based, women's films provide a very different sense of narrative pleasure, rooted in the complex unfolding of personal relationships. As Tania Modleski has asserted, in analyzing soap operas:

> "Narrative pleasure" can mean very different things to men and women. This is an important point. Too often feminist criticism implies that there is only one kind of pleasure to be derived from a narrative and that is a masculine one. . . . Feminist artists don't have to start from nothing: rather, they can look for ways to rechannel and make explicit the criticisms of masculine power and masculine pleasure implied in the narrative form of soap operas.(7)

And, one might add, women's films, as well.

VISUAL STYLE

No one visual style predominates in women's films. Rather the similarities and differences in camera and editing techniques mirror those within the major filmic types.

First of all, common to most women's films is the predominance of interior sets, whether homes or workplaces. And, often, even if a scene is located outside, it occurs within an enclosed space, such as a car. The reasons for this are numerous; economy certainly was a prime motive. Films could often be shot more cheaply on studio lots (it is not the audience's imagination that those houses look the same), saving the time, energy, and money of shooting on location. While economic and pragmatic considerations abound, however, there are deeper reasons why women's films are set in interior, and often domestic, spaces. Woman, unlike man, was not often associated in popular consciousness with the frontier, the conquering of open space, the separation of self from community. And although woman was often metaphorically linked to nature (Grapes of Wrath), she was usually portrayed in familial and community settings. Furthermore, intensive dialogue between individuals is often more suited to interior spaces.

Secondly, the ambience of most of these films is distinctly middle class. The world of the reporter, actress, lawyer, or homemaker was usually neat, ordered, and quite comfortable. Tenements were few and far between in these movies. Chintz curtains, sweeping staircases, glamorous offices, and well-manicured lawns were the visual hallmarks of the women's film.

Most of the stars such as Claudette Colbert, Joan Crawford, Bette Davis, Irene Dunne, Katharine Hepburn, and Myrna Loy were mature and accomplished actresses with experience and power in Hollywood. In the 1940s most were white women in mid-life, 30- to 45-years old; few were starlets. Many of these women had battled the studio brass to gain more autonomy. These leading ladies, although typecast in particular ways, share an aura of strength, perseverance, and verbal facility. Shots in women's films tend to linger on the heroines' faces, and the strong and conflicting emotions inscribed therein. "Pin-up" and "body spectacle" shots were employed less frequently. Nonetheless, these heroines were far from asexual. Although circumscribed by production code standards, many women's film stars express strong sensuality. Yet their projected sexuality is more controlled and self-directed than the more tawdry or sultry appeal of a Rita Hayworth or Betty Grable.

Black and other minority actresses did appear in women's films, but usually within the narrow confines of racial stereotypes – as a maid, or a mammy. Talented women like Hattie McDaniel, Louise Beavers, and Butterfly McQueen rarely rose above the station of the filmic mammy or domestic (e.g., McDaniel as Fidelia, a slightly less typecast role in Since You Went Away; McQueen as the high-pitched Lottie in Mildred Pierce.) As Donald Bogle notes in Toms, Coons, Mulattoes, Mammies and Bucks: An Interpretive History of Blacks in American Films, only the "tragic mulatto" plot (as in Pinky), popular in the late 1940s, gave some dignity to a black woman's role (e.g., Ethel Waters as Granny in Pinky). The racism of both the studios and the largely white audience suppressed the possibility of women's films that would sensitively portray the minority female experience.

Several distinct types emerged among the major female stars: the strong, sacrificial mother, the "wholesome girl," the assertive, witty career woman, the threatened (and sometimes mad) wife. With the significant exception of Katharine Hepburn, most major women's film actresses played strong, sacrificial mothers: Claudette Colbert (Since You Went Away), Joan Crawford (Mildred Pierce), Bette Davis (Watch on the Rhine), Olivia de Havilland (To Each His Own), Irene Dunne (I Remember Mama), Greer Garson (Mrs. Miniver). The assertive (and usually witty) career woman was played by Joan Crawford (Daisy Kenyon), Bette Davis (Old Acquaintance), Katharine Hepburn (Woman of the Year, Adam's Rib), and Rosalind

Russell (His Girl Friday, Roughly Speaking). With her slightly brittle, upper-class manner, Hepburn was the quintessential career woman of the silver screen. The frightened, suspicious woman (usually wife) was portrayed by Ingrid Bergman (Gaslight, Notorious), Claudette Colbert (Sleep, My Love), Joan Fontaine (Rebecca, Suspicion), Dorothy McGuire (The Spiral Staircase), and even brassy Barbara Stanwyck (Sorry, Wrong Number). Nonetheless, specific publicity images emerged for particular actresses: Bette Davis was typed as acid-tongued, witty, and independent. Until the public scandal of her affair with Roberto Rosselini in 1950, Ingrid Bergman was cast as the "Joan of Arc," a pure and wholesome wife and mother in a corrupt Hollywood. Joan Crawford played superwoman, juggling a demanding career and single motherhood. One needs only to consult star biographies to trace the disparity between the real actress and the publicity image. Nonetheless, publicity images were hardly the top-down creation of the Hollywood studios; fans also played a role in crystallizing the dream symbols they wished their favorite actresses to represent. Taken together, from Fontaine to Garson to Hepburn to Russell to Stanwyck, the studios and their audiences created a family of female stars situated firmly within a Hollywood woman's narrative.

Cinematography and editing in women's films draw upon two dominant Hollywood traditions: the classic realist narrative, and the film noir. Most women's films can be considered classic realist texts with a predictable and ordered narrative and a semblance of reality. On the other hand, films of suspicion and distrust draw upon the visual code of film noir, the twisted cinema of cynicism and despair.

Classic Hollywood films employed well-balanced lighting (sometimes called Hollywood or high-key lighting),(8) predictable punctuation devices (dissolves, wipe-offs, fade in/fade outs), balanced camera angles, and evenly composed shots. Visuals complement dialogue, rather than contradicting it with eerie light, unsettling camera angles, or out-of-balance frame composition. A sense of single, not double or triple message prevails. In I Remember Mama, for example, the matriarchal Hansen family sits in cameo around the kitchen table, Mama at the center. His Girl Friday creates visual comedy by deviating just slightly from the classic two-shot. As Rosalind Russell and ex-husband Cary Grant verbally duel, he (literally) is falling out of the frame. A comforting aura of predictability surrounds this camera and editing style. We are seeing what we think we are seeing.

In the movies of suspicion and distrust, strongly influenced by popular mid- to late 1940s film noir(9) style, the sense of visual order is turned on its head. Lighting becomes shadowy and low key, contrasting light to dark, security to fear, good to evil. Noir cinematography, by its eerie and unsettling contrasts, spells paranoia and menace. In addition, twisted camera angles and unbalanced frame composition combine to create an "antitraditional mise-en-scene".(10) In noir women's films (e.g., The Spiral Staircase, 1946), interior details such as winding staircases are often photographed in visually unsettling ways, symbolizing female terror and entrapment. Even when the dialogue connotes happiness and security, the noir camera style undercuts its promise. Are we seeing what we think we are seeing? Although women's films did not develop a distinct visual style, they elaborate on (as well as undercut) the classic and noir Hollywood traditions.

WOMEN'S FILMS: HISTORICAL AND CONTEMPORARY CONTEXT

The women's film does not stand alone as a type of female-oriented popular culture. It is part of a historical tradition stretching from the sentimental and Gothic novel in the nineteenth century to the radio soap opera in the twentieth. A female-oriented sphere of popular culture emerged in response to the sexual bifurcation of culture and consciousness in industrializing America. As home and workplace became physically separated, and parallel ideologies arose to support "true womanhood" and "real masculinity," men and women desired new and different forms of leisure and culture.(11) The women's film can only be fully understood within this cultural context. Before Mrs. Miniver and Adam's Rib, came Louisa May Alcott's nineteenth-century classic Little Women and the twentieth-century radio serials Stella Dallas and Backstage Wife.

FILM PRODUCTION

Women's films reflect a strong female influence, although they are not solely of female creation. Many of the screenplays (such as Stella Dallas, Back Street, Watch on the Rhine) were adapted (often by female scriptwriters) from already popular fiction written for and/or by women. Women like Vera Caspary, Lenore Coffee, Ruth Gordon, Anita Loos, Frances Marion, Tess Slesinger, and Catherine Turney, authored or co-authored women's films in the studio era. In addition, females often worked as scenarists; art, set, and costume directors (Bonnie Cashin, Edith Head, Natalie Kalmus); and sometimes as film editors (Alma Macrorie, Barbara McLean, Dorothy Spencer, Eda Warren). The dialogue and sets of women's films, thus, often have a distinctly feminine quality. Given the inferior and undervalued status of women in Hollywood, it is likely that screen credits do not always accurately reveal the role of women in the making of a film. Alma Reville, Alfred Hitchcock's wife, influenced his films more than her credits as sometime screenwriter suggest.(12) Vera Caspary lost her co-screenwriting credit for A Letter to Three Wives in a Screen Writers' Guild dispute with Joseph

L. Mankiewicz. And major stars, such as Davis or Hepburn, might work on dialogue but never receive screen credit.

The women who wrote, designed sets, and edited these films were, however, quite different in lifestyle from many of the women in the audience. Writers such as Ruth Gordon and Frances Marion, for example, were more educated, affluent, leisured, and "liberated" (by contemporary standards) than most female viewers. The dream world projected by female stars and film artists appealed to the fantasies of the female audience. Although females in this era wrote, designed, and edited women's films, by and large (with the important exceptions of Ida Lupino and Dorothy Arzner), they did not shoot or direct.

Imbued with machismo, cinematography and direction in the sound era were predominantly masculine domains.(13) There are few generalizations to be made about women's film directors. Some, like George Cukor, though not above high-camp misogyny (The Women-1939), were noted for their ability to nurture unknown talent (like Judy Holliday), and to work respectfully and cooperatively with female writers like Ruth Gordon and actresses like Rosalind Russell and Katharine Hepburn. Cukor's true love of the women's film becomes clear in his decision to remake Old Acquaintance as Rich and Famous in 1981. Others like Michael Curtiz were notorious for their arrogance and authoritarianism. Bette Davis claimed that Curtiz called her a "sexless son of a bitch."(14) Though some directors (e.g. Douglas Sirk, Max Ophuls) loved the women's film, others like William Wyler and George Stevens proceeded on to more mainstream subjects as soon as they were more popular. What is intriguing about this panoply of directors is that they created very similar films. The prudish Hitchcock, the congenial Cukor, and the egotistical Mankiewicz all directed similar 1940s' films of suspicion and distrust: Suspicion (1941), Gaslight (1944), and Dragonwyck (1946). Clearly these men were mediators of cultural currents transcending the individual auteur. Most importantly, they were dependent on women – as screenwriters, stars, and audience members – to give their filmic visions life.

Female stars often battled with studios and directors alike – for better parts, more flexible contracts, etc. Although they were not always successful, actresses knew they had that economic and cultural clout known as "box office draw" or "marquee value".(15) The tables of marquee value (Appendix) indicate the enduring popularity of women's film stars for female audiences in the 1940s. In fact, audiences were much more likely to know a film by its star (a Joan Crawford movie) than by its director (a Cukor film). Using her marketability as a bargaining tool, an actress like Katharine Hepburn might suggest (as she did) a screen coupling with Spencer Tracy. Or, as Olivia de Havilland in To Each His Own, propose a particular novel for adaptation to the screen. Bette Davis struggled against sexist ads for her films (The Corn Is Green) and advocated for the rights of other actresses.(16) Feminists have often (and quite correctly) criticized the manipulation of stars and female film workers by the male-dominated film industry, while downplaying the ways in which these women in Hollywood asserted themselves and sometimes won. To assert that a women's voice is absent from film is tantamount to asserting that women are absent from history.

THE WOMEN'S FILM, THE STUDIOS,
AND THE PRODUCTION CODE

The women's film represents an attempt – within the confines and constraints of Hollywood and a patriarchal society – to construct a feminine narrative. It is the nature of some of those confines and constraints that we now address.

All film artists – from directors on down – were constrained by the realities of a powerful studio system that, until the late 1940s, controlled production, distribution, and exhibition. Directors and screenwriters alike often complained of Hollywood's preference for formula over originality and the pressure to clone films quickly and cheaply. However, Hollywood artists and their employers remained in creative tension. In the last instance, movie moguls were dependent on often hard-to-control artistic talent. In general, the higher the box office potential of a director or star, the greater his/her clout in the studio. And, at least until the devastating cultural chill of the Red Scare came to Hollywood, stars and directors – particularly those with high popularity ratings – continued to assert their own visions.

Though female stars and screenwriters often battled for autonomy, however, all film artists were controlled by the Hollywood Production Code of 1934. Any interpretation of women's films must take into account the history and development of the code and the limits it placed on filmic narrative.

Although the code was adopted officially in 1934, its roots lie in the silent era. The boom in movie popularity had generated public concern with morality, particularly that of youth. In the early 1920s, demands for film censorship came from a variety of groups: Catholics, women's and parents' associations, and patriotic and community groups. Shocked by such Hollywood scandals as the Arbuckle affair, many adults claimed that "movies are ruining our youth".(17) To answer these protests, in 1922, leaders of the film industry formed the Motion Picture Producers and Distributors of America and drew up first the 13 Points of 1921 and later, the Formula of 1924 as moral guidelines for movie production.

Early censorship codes were broad guidelines rather than narrow restrictions. Thus, films of the late silent and early sound era often dealt with social and sexual issues that would be taboo or restricted again until the early 1960s. Women's films such as

Arzner's Christopher Strong and Lubitsch's Design for Living (both 1933) dealt with nonmarital sex, unwed pregnancy, and love triangles. The most popular female stars of the early sound era (1930-34) openly expressed their sexuality: Marlene Dietrich, Greta Garbo, Mae West.

This era was short-lived, however. Pressure groups (particularly the Catholic Legion of Decency) were not satisfied with broad guidelines; they demanded more rigid restrictions and they got them. Hollywood, eager to retain its audience(s), established the Production Code of 1934. After a decade of public pressure, Hollywood chose self-censorship over what it felt to be inevitable: censorship from without, threatening the very existence of the industry. The code (see Appendix) banned explicit and unconventional sexuality, unpunished crime, and racial and ethnic stereotypes.

The struggle for the code was, however, no simple movement of male or right-wing backlash. The moral crusaders ran the political gamut: from old Progressives, anti-Communists, religious fundamentalists, Catholic conservatives, to feminists and anti-racists. And the censorship movement chose several, sometimes contradictory, targets: ethnic and racial stereotyping, anti-Americanism, unconventional morality, and the sexual objectification of females. Women in this movement were counted all along the ideological spectrum, sharing a deep concern for the welfare of children:

> The interests of women's groups in the moral standards of the movies was a natural extension of their concern for the effects the medium was having upon their children. . . . Film censorship was almost an obsession with many social feminists in this period.(18)

The women's film developed along the parameters set by the code. And those parameters created contradictory effects. On the one hand, films could only portray heterosexuality and only within strictly defined limits ("Excessive and lustful kissing, lustful embraces, suggestive postures and gestures are not to be shown"). However, on the other hand, those limits generated new possibilities for the depiction of independent and working women. The sexual object was now much more difficult to portray; the career heroine and female buddies (but never lovers) were much more adaptable to code guidelines.

> Garbo, Dietrich, Mae West, and Harlow belong unmistakably to pre-code liberation; Katharine Hepburn, Jean Arthur, Rosalind Russell and most of the professional and working-class heroines come after. The paradox is unavoidable: while the Hays office, having assumed the mantle of our national superego, suppressed the salutary impulse of female

sexuality, it was also largely responsible for the emergence of the driving, hyperactive woman, a heroine more congenial to current tastes than her sultrier sisters. The "working woman" (fulfilling also a demand, created by the Depression, for a more down-to-earth heroine) was more at ease pursuing a career, whether for its own sake, or as a pretext for finding a husband, than languishing in a love nest.(19)

The screwball comedies, such as Bringing Up Baby (1938), Philadelphia Story (1940), and His Girl Friday (1940), directly emerged from the restrictions on sexuality legislated by the code. Heterosexual attraction became embodied in the fast-paced verbal "battle of the sexes," hallmark of the screwball comedy.

At the same time that certain doors opened, however, others shut. The code had established very rigid guidelines for the portrayal of female sexuality. Unconventional lifestyles (e.g., extramarital relationships), like crimes, could be shown, yet never condoned. This virtually outlawed all but the most moralistic treatments of many controversial issues. Homosexuality was virtually banned from the screen.(20) Heterosexuality, even in marriage, was allowed only to be suggested, never explicitly shown. Even pregnancy, childbirth, and naked children were defined as lewd! Twin beds for married couples with nighttables discreetly placed in between, and very pregnant women with 24-inch waists became the order of the day.

Yet the code proved to be no iron barrier. Rather, it acted more like a fence that Hollywood producers, directors, cinematographers, screenwriters, and stars slipped under, over, and around. The narrative structure and conventions of the women's film shaped themselves around the restrictions of the Production Code. The code did not prevent Hollywood from dealing with sex. It did, however, stop Hollywood from dealing openly with sex. The code forced film to speak a double language. Imaginative cinematic conventions evolved to express sexual themes tabooed by the code. Sensually lighted cigarettes, ambiguous language and gestures, and suggestive dances were some of the ways that film artists manipulated the code. In the code era (1930-1950s), it seems that nothing is sexual and everything is sexual at the same time. In addition, directors circumvented the code in other ways. Some, like Douglas Sirk, would treat a subject as they chose, and then attach a didactic ending (as in Imitation of Life) to please the censors. By his own assertion, Sirk intended audiences to find these endings (as he did) ridiculous.(21) Other directors would use their influence to convince censors to bend the rules. In women's films of the code era, double and triple meanings continually express themselves through the narrative. It is both within and against the strictures of the code that their filmic meanings unfold.

CRITICS AND THE WOMEN'S FILM

The critics – from newspaper and radio reviewers to media academics – stand between film and audience, marking certain productions as "artistic," "brilliant," "provocative," and others as "flawed," "poorly directed," or "unconvincing." The role of criticism in audience response to film varies. For more educated, affluent Americans, for example, the New York Times or Washington Post critics might provide a guide for film selection and interpretation. Less educated and less affluent audiences tend to rely more on peer advice, women's and fan magazines, radio (and later television) reviews, and the suggestions of religious groups such as the Legion of Decency. Across class and culture, however, negative critical reaction to women's films helped create the climate in which they were produced and received.

"Sudser," "tear-jerker," "weepie" – critics commonly applied these terms to women's films. Early on it became clear that females were the most avid viewers of these films. When, for example, a patriotic Hollywood sent women's films overseas for GI entertainment, they were met largely by rejection. Servicemen (and most males) preferred war pictures, westerns, and musical comedies.(22) The association of these films with women created the conditions for their sexist and patronizing treatment by (primarily) male critics.

> Among the Anglo-American critical brotherhood (and a few of their sisters as well), the term "woman's film" is used disparagingly to conjure up the image of the pinched-virgin or the little-old-lady writer, spilling out her secret longings in wish fulfillment or glorious martyrdom and transmitting these fantasies to the frustrated housewife . . .
> As a term of critical opprobrium, "woman's film" carries the implication that women, and therefore, women's emotional problems, are of minor significance.(23)

A general lack of respect for women – their experience, work, and art – is mirrored in critical attitudes toward women's films. Often a reviewer would characterize the female audience pejoratively, as in the following New York Times review of Mildred Pierce (September 29, 1945):

> If you can accept this rather demanding premise (Mildred's obsessive mother-love) – and there were not a few ladies in the Strand who were frequently blotting tears with evident enjoyment – then Mildred Pierce is just the tortured drama you've been waiting for.

Film surveys of the period often reflect patronizing attitudes as well.

> In the '40s, with the vast audience of lonely women left behind by their soldier husbands, lovers and sons, the need for escapist vehicles became clearly pressing.
> MGM decided to meet the need by mounting a succession of films that reflected the shrewdly sentimental mind of Louis B. Mayer, starring the radiantly genteel Greer Garson and Walter Pidgeon. Theirs were the "nice," safe films in which middle-aged women could find solace, a sense that, amid restrictions and . . . the long wait for letters from the fronts, Life, after all, could be Beautiful.(24)

Women's films that received critical acclaim were often treated as tokens, transcending their "inferior category," rather than reflecting its strengths. Westerns, crime dramas, and musical comedies range from high to low art in mainstream critical appraisal. The women's film however, has been relegated to a critical back room, ignored, devalued, and misunderstood.(25)

Critical disdain for women's films contributed to the general lack of seriousness with which they were treated in American culture. Women still flocked to the movies, but often found themselves apologizing for their "addiction to melodrama."(26) Only with the rebirth of feminism have these films and their audiences begun to receive the serious consideration they deserve.

THE WOMEN'S FILM AND ITS AUDIENCE:
THE OTHER SIDE OF THE SCREEN

> The average red-blooded American girl grew up at the movies.
>
> Jeanine Basinger, "Ten That Got Away," in Women and the Cinema, ed. by Karyn Kay and Gerald Peary (New York: Dutton, 1977) p. 61.

Though reams of paper have been written on film production and criticism, less attention has focused on audiences. Hollywood, in its financial heyday, saw little need to study moviegoers intensively. And mass communications scholars found more interest in media production and content than in reception. However, an incomplete and fragmented body of knowledge exists, suggesting that the relationship of women to cinema (and particularly, women's films) is particularly active and intense.

Most Americans were regular moviegoers in the 1930s and 1940s. During the Depression, 60-75 million Americans attended movies at least weekly; in the war years this figure rose to 90 million. By 1945, 73.6 percent of Hollywood's potential audience were moviegoers. (Potential audience was an industry term referring to all those who could possibly attend movies, excluding very young children, the homebound, institutionalized, and mentally deficient.)

Women comprised 51 percent of the population, and during the war at least the majority of the cinema audience.(27) Most female audience members attended the movies at least weekly. Younger women and teenage girls were represented in greater audience numbers than older women, and tended to attend movies approximately twice weekly. The most common pattern of attendance was to see one double-bill on a weekday afternoon or evening, and another on a weekend night. During the week the female viewer was likely to be accompanied by a woman friend or relative to a neighborhood movie house. Weekends were more likely to be reserved for dates and/or higher priced, first-run theaters. During wartime, with the exodus of millions of American men, the weekend viewing pattern for young women often shifted to one of shared female viewing.

Leo Handel (1950) noted that the film industry, influenced by less systematic studies such as those done by the Women's Institute of Audience Reaction, assumed that the majority of the cinema audience was always female. Handel concluded that this assumption resulted in more programming designed for women. Hollywood made special efforts to please its female audience. Ad campaigns for women's films like So Proudly We Hail (1943) were targeted specifically to women's clubs and associations.(28) Theaters also made special concessions: round-the-clock movie schedules, occasionally a "crying room" for infants and young children. The Rivoli theater in New Jersey presented war mothers with free passes, and other theaters organized salvage drives and car pools to aid female war workers and volunteers.(29)

Evidence suggests that the women's film fan was far from a passive spectator. Rather she was an active participant in the culture of viewing films, a participant whose response to media was conditioned by the "film talk" of relatives and friends.

Wartime studies done by the Women's Institute of Audience Reactions revealed that many women preferred movies to radio.(30) According to a 1942 survey of over 500 New York City moviegoers by the Motion Picture Research Bureau, women reported increasing their movie attendance in wartime because of: higher wages and more money for entertainment; afternoons off due to night shift work; extra free time due to the absence of boyfriends or husbands who were working late or in the service. Interestingly, some women reported a decline in moviegoing because their usual male escorts were working in defense or away at war. "Going to the movies" itself was perceived as an autonomous act by many women.(31)

Women, however, true to their audience image, preferred very different films than men. In general, women preferred movies with a romantic or interpersonal theme — in short women's films — and often actively disliked the war movies and Westerns loved by men. As one young waitress put it, "A big tank or bomber gets my boyfriend all excited but it leaves me completely cold."(32) Many women sought a real story rather than action-packed adventure. A 35-year-old wife of a bank clerk commented:

> I feel that there are only very few war pictures which have a real story to tell where the war scenes are only inci-dental. . . . In war pictures, fighting is made the most important thing, shutting out the real human values, conflicts and emotions.(33)

Women's preferences in cinema however, cannot be categorized as feminist. Though the more progressive sectors of the female audience were represented through some women's organizations and in wartime through the Bureau of Motion Pictures, Office of War Information,(34) other (often religious) women's groups influencing cinema were much more conservative. The commercial failure of a film with a feminist theme, A Woman Rebels (1936) is indicative of the traditionalism of the female audience.(35) In addition, many women supported the Production Code, either individually or through women's, parent's, or religious organizations. In response to a 1947 California survey that asked "Do you think movie censorship is about right, or is it too strict, or not strict enough?" only 9 percent of the women polled termed the censorship "too strict," whereas 46 percent stated that it was "about right" and 37 percent thought that it was "not strict enough."(36) The sexual conservatism of the female audience reflected itself in the public disdain that arose among many women when "pure and wholesome" Ingrid Bergman openly had an extramarital affair with Roberto Rosselini, bearing him an illegitimate child. Women's organizations flooded Hollywood with letters and resolutions; some wanted her film Stromboli banned, not because of its content, but because of the actress' lifestyle. Senator Edwin Johnson of Colorado, a leader of the Swedish community, even argued on the floor of the Senate for passage of a resolution that would ban Bergman from ever returning to the United States.(37)

The stars that most appealed to women were those who fit particular kinds of dream images: the tragic innocent (Joan Fontaine); the sacrificial mother (Irene Dunne); the wholesome girl (Ingrid Bergman); the witty aristocrat (Katharine Hepburn); the acid-tongued spunky careerist (Bette Davis); the superwoman (Joan Crawford). Some actresses were typecast, and public impressions were further intensified by complementary publicity images. Others, like Crawford and Davis, portrayed several of these images at different times. As Alistair Cooke noted in 1940:

> The majority of stars . . . combine good looks and certain typical whimsicalities or personal traits of humor, temper, sarcasm — some single quality that is entertaining because it is effective to dramatize. . . . Thus, Jean Arthur's husky downrightness and loyalty, Claudette Colbert's tongue-in-cheek, Carole Lombard's air of honest-to-goodness exasperation, Ginger Rogers' natural acceptance of hard facts: these are individual characteristics of current favorites who were all originally consigned to a career of solemn prettiness.(38)

And as a 1940s female college student enthusiastically remarked,

> Bergman is different and Crawford is wonderfully sophisticated and both have great dramatic ability. When looking at them, especially Bergman, there is a sort of idolization. I would like to be like her.(39)

As the tables in the Appendix indicate, women's film stars were much more popular among women than men. In 1944, for example, 58 percent of females polled by Gallup chose to see a film based simply on the fact that Greer Garson was starring, while only 37.3 percent of males surveyed responded similarly. In most cases these actresses increased in overall popularity among women during the 1940s. Many of these stars found their most avid fans to be over 30, urban, and somewhat affluent.

In contrast to actresses adored by women and loved less by men, were those despised by women and loved by men. Betty Grable, the GI's favorite pin-up, was disliked by many female viewers who favored emotionality to exhibitionism.(40)

Fan culture was largely female culture, representing a minority of intensely involved viewers, who on the average sent a quarter of a million fan letters a month to Hollywood stars.(41) In the women's film era, fan clubs were almost solely the creation of young women, students, homemakers, and workers, some of whom were would-be actresses themselves.(42) Whereas fan culture is not representative of audience culture as a whole, it is indicative of an intense involvement of women (mainly young) with their favorite stars. Leo Rosten analyzed a month's (January 1939) fan mail to two (unnamed) stars, male and female. As the following tables (Tables 1.1 and 1.2) illustrate, the overwhelming majority (85-90 percent) of letter writers, to either star, were females under 21.

Anecdotes told by stars reveal a strong identification of women with screen heroines. Bette Davis has recalled the overwhelming response to her portrayal of neurotic, mother-dominated Charlotte Vale in <u>Now, Voyager</u> (1942). Over two hundred letters from

Table 1.1:
Analysis of U.S. Fan Mail Received by Movie Actor: (Basic Breakdown of 1-Month's Fan Mail January, 1939)

	Number	Percent
Total number of postcards received	449	66.8
Total amount of letters received	223	33.2
Total amount of fan mail	672	100.0
Sex of fan writers:		
Female	598	89.0
Male	67	10.0
Unknown	7	1.0
	672	100.0
Approximate age of fan writers:[a]		
Under 13 years	356	53.0
13 to 21 years	287	43.0
Over 21	29	4.0
	672	100.0

Table 1.2:
Analysis of U.S. Fan Mail Received by Movie Actress: (Basic Breakdown of 1-Month's Fan Mail January, 1939)

	Number	Percent
Total number of postcards received	461	52.4
Total amount of letters received	419	47.6
	880	100.0
Sex of fan writers:		
Female	761	86.5
Male	119	13.5
	880	100.0
Approximate age of fan writers:[a]		
Under 13 years	194	22.1
13 to 21 years	574	65.2
Over 21	112	12.7
	880	100.0

[a]Note: Most writers state their age, or it can be inferred from references in the letters, internal evidence, handwriting, etc.

From: Leo Rosten, Hollywood: The Movie Colony, The Moviemakers. (New York: Arno Press, 1970, pp. 411-412).

daughters poured in, telling Davis how the film helped them resolve their own conflicts with an overbearing mother. Joan Crawford's My Way of Life was written in response to continual fan inquiries: how do you combine home and career successfully?

Women more than men tend to project themselves into the movie drama, to imagine themselves as their favorite actress. In Movies and Conduct (1933), a Payne Fund volume, twice as many females as males admitted fantasizing about playing opposite the romantic lead in a favorite film. A 16-year-old girl wrote:

> I've been thrilled and deeply stirred by love pictures and love scenes. Usually when I see them, it seems that I'm a looker-on and one of the lovers at the same time. I don't know how to describe it. I know love pictures have made me more receptive because I always thought it rather silly until these pictures.(43)

A wartime saleswoman commented, "These actresses I mentioned are great. They make me feel every emotion of their parts. I feel as if it were myself on the screen experiencing what they do."(44)

However, strong female identification with movies is hardly one of mesmerized viewer to all powerful media. Women carefully selected filmic fantasies on the basis of their own needs and life choices. Elizabeth Ewen (1980) has noted that immigrant daughters saw silent films as models for a new, more Americanized and less patriarchal way of life. The film "flapper's" lifestyle, for example, contrasted to that of traditional, family-centered immigrant women. An older Italian woman interviewed by Ewen remarks:

> The young Italian girls, my daughters, they're up to date, just as good, just as polite as the Americans. They were born here, they go to school together, they see the same movies, they know.(45)

In addition, whereas the impact of some stars, like Carole Lombard, boosted sales of peroxide, the effect of others, like Crawford, stimulated the confidence and self-assertion of female viewers. As the Lynds noted in Middletown in Transition (1937):

> Joan Crawford has her amateur counterpart in the high school girls who stroll with brittle confidence in and out of "Barney's soft-drink parlor," "clicking" with the "drugstore cowboys" at the tables, while the tongue-tied young male learns the art of the swift, confident comeback in the face of female confidence.(46)

Regular movie watching did not seem to weaken women's critical faculties. Rather, audiences became cine-literate, aware (often subconsciously) of filmic language and narrative devices. Numerous studies show that audiences become more sophisticated and discerning with experience. Movie life is compared and contrasted to real life. Usually only when audiences have little or no experience with what they see on the screen are they willing to believe it completely.(47) Otherwise, movie meanings take shape in the context of after-viewing dialogue or "film talk" between friends, lovers, and relatives, and within the viewer herself. Hortense Powdermaker noted a lack of female gullibility in her mid-1940s study of Hollywood:

> There are still the teenage girls infatuated with movie heroes who go to see any picture in which their favorite stars perform, and who squirm in their seats when the hero passionately kisses the heroine. But in a preliminary study of audience reactions of high school juniors and seniors a large number, in discussing a movie or one part of it, used the phrases and adjectives "weak," "corny," "no motivation," or "couldn't happen."(48)

The women's film thus developed in response not only to a majority of women in the audience, but to their intense involvement as well. Why women identify strongly with films (especially women's film) is an intriguing question; a full discussion of this issue lies beyond the bounds of this narrative. However, a few speculations are in order. Women's films are constructed around dilemmas of moral choice focusing on themes of interpersonal connection and the fear of separation from loved ones. Feminist scholars such as Nancy Chodorow, Lenore Weitzman, and others have suggested that separation-individuation is far more difficult for most women than most men.(49) Daughters are often socialized by their mothers into a model of femininity centered on nurturing — at home and at work. Raised to prioritize oneness over separateness, daughters are often unsure where their personality ends and their mothers' begins. This familial process is complemented by peers, media, religious, and educational institutions that encourage females, above all else to respond to the needs of others. In Weitzman's words, "the self that they (women) value is one that emanates from the appraisals of others."(50)

In addition, several studies indicate that women may be socialized to greater media sensitivity. Evelyn Pitcher's 1963 study of preschoolers revealed the interior world of the female child to differ sharply from that of the male:

> Analysis of some 360 stories collected from children from 2 to 5 years revealed that girls tend to present people more vividly and realistically and to identify themselves with the personality and experiences of others. Direct conversations

are often quoted in girls' stories, and people are more individually conceived and characterized by their names.(51)

From Pitcher's observations of preschool female memory and conversation patterns, one can conclude that most adult women, through socialization for motherhood, have more fully developed these characteristics, and would be quite able to adapt media fantasies to their individual and collective needs. Clearly in form and content, women's films dramatized themes that women could understand much more fully than men. And in a society characterized by confusing and contradictory images of womanhood, these films provided lessons in how to speak, dress, act, in short, "how to be a woman."

Yet perhaps the most significant aspect of women's films lies in their presentation of moral choice: as complex rather than abstract and as embedded in the network of interpersonal relations. This closely parallels Carol Gilligan's depiction of a common mode of female moral reasoning focusing on responsibility rather than right, and often prioritizing persons over abstractions.(52)

Why women identify more closely than men with movie themes and images is a matter for speculation. That they do, however, seems quite clear, and explains, at least in part, the popularity of a Hollywood woman's narrative, called the women's film.

THE WOMEN'S FILM IN THE 1940s

Women's films can provide rich source material for women's history. An analysis of their production, content, and reception reveals a multilayered reality. Monolithic theories of culture and society fail to illuminate their meaning. Neither the top-down mythology of Hollywood nor the bottom-up "collective unconscious" of American womanhood, women's films represent a dynamic, a power relationship and struggle between men and women within and outside the studio. Whereas they are not feminist films, they are important sources of feminist history. As fantasies, women's films present a historical dimension other sources do not and cannot. Taken together with other sources, they are essential in reconstructing the experience of women in a particular era.

The women's films analyzed in this study are of the 1940s, a crucial decade for American womanhood. In 1942, 11 million men left for war and women adopted new and challenging roles at home and at work. Several years later GIs would return to a different America, an America whose women had matured and expanded their sense of possibility. Yet a male-dominated society proved unwilling to grant female equality. Unrecognized and unorganized, American women lost their wartime gains. The feminine mystique — with repercussions at home and at work — soon dominated the culture.

The meaning of this period for American womanhood would be debated for decades to come.

The women's film however, enjoyed its heyday in the war era. With men away, more women moved into film production. And most of those sitting on the other side of the screen were female as well. Despite the persistence of male domination and resistance, a woman's narrative of both residual and emergent cultural currents bloomed in the Hollywood of the 1940s. As Karyn Kay and Gerald Peary have asserted,

> Yet while finding our culture impossibly weighted with patriarchal values and with sexism, women keep discovering hidden pockets in which vestiges of "female culture" have grown usually unnoticed, or condescendingly ignored, by this male media majority. One such place is the cinema.(53)

Such a "vestige of female culture" is the women's film.

NOTES

(1)   For a discussion of these films as transcending the Hollywood mainstream, see Annette Kuhn, Women's Pictures: Feminism And Cinema (London: Routledge and Kegan Paul, 1982) Chapter 7. For a discussion of some less well known contemporary "women's films", see Ellen Elizabeth Seiter, "The Promise of Melodrama: Recent Women's Films and Soap Operas," unpublished Ph.D. dissertation, Northwestern University, 1981.

(2)   "Genre" is a slippery term to identify for the critic of popular film. In Hollywood genre often had a commonsense and unarticulated meaning: a gangster film, a Western, a screwball comedy. In film as in literary criticism, there is a common understanding that genre is a term whose meaning spans that of several media. For example, as Stuart Kaminsky noted in American Film Genres: Approaches to a Critical Theory of Popular Film (New York: Dell, 1974), "Genre study in film is based on the realization that certain popular narrative forms have both cultural and universal roots, that the Western of today is related to both the archetypes of the past 200 years in the United States and to folk tale and the myth" (p. 12). However, beyond that level of understanding, conceptual confusion abounds. Is genre a common plot structure, a set of conventions, a visual style? Who defines genre, the film critic, Hollywood, the audience, or all of these? Also see "Cycles and Genres" by Richard Griffith and "Genre and Critical Methodology," by Andrew Tudor in Movies and Methods, ed. Bill Nichols (Berkeley: University of California Press, 1976), pp. 111-25. My definition of genre assumes a commonality of both visual and thematic motifs existing within and among a body of films. In the words of

Kaminsky, "a body, group or category of similar works; this similarity being defined as the sharing of a sufficient number of motifs so that we can identify works which properly fall within a particular kind of style of film" (p. 20).

(3)   See Will Wright, Sixguns and Society: A Structural Study of the Western (Berkeley: University of California Press, 1975); and Joan Mellen, Big Bad Wolves: Masculinity in the American Film (New York: Pantheon, 1977).

(4)   Carol Gilligan, In A Different Voice: Psychological Theory and Women's Development (Cambridge, Ma: Harvard University Press, 1982) p. 19.

(5)   See Molly Haskell, From Reverence to Rape: The Treatment of Women in the Movies (New York: Holt, Rinehart and Winston, 1973), especially chapter 4, "The Woman's Film," pp. 153-88.

(6)   For an excellent discussion of melodrama – its conventions and social contradictions, see Ellen Seiter, "The Promise of Melodrama," op. cit.

(7)   Tania Modleski, "The Search for Tomorrow in Today's Soap Operas: Notes on a Feminine Narrative Form," Film Quarterly 33, 1 (Fall 1979): 20; also Modleski, "The Disappearing Act: A Study of Harlequin Romances," Signs 5, 3 (1980): 435-48.

(8)   High-key lighting (achieved by the interaction of "key," "fill," and "backlights") sought to illuminate all areas of the frame, soften harsh shadows, and avoid unnatural darkness.

(9)   Film noir was a prominent visual and narrative style of the 1940s. See chapter 6 for further elaboration.

(10)   See J.A. Place and L.S. Peterson, "Some Visual Motifs of Film Noir," in Nichols (ed.), Movies and Methods (Berkeley: University of California Press, 1976) pp. 325-34.

(11)   See Mary P. Ryan, Womanhood in America (New York: New Viewpoints, 1979, 2nd ed.); Kathryn Weibel, Mirror, Mirror: Images of Women Reflected in Popular Culture (Garden City: Doubleday, 1977); Barbara Welter, "The Cult of True Womanhood," American Quarterly 18 (1966): 151-74. Also see Sandra M. Gilbert and Susan Gubar, The Madwoman In the Attic: The Woman Writer and the Nineteenth Century Literary Imagination (New Haven: Yale University Press, 1979) who argue that women's writing in this period conveys images of entrapment and oppression. This nineteenth-century popular literary subculture, though not explicitly or consistently feminist, was created primarily by or for women. Its female origin must always be kept in mind when discussing its popularization and mass production through the media industries. For a contrasting point of view, see Serafina Kent Bathrick, "The True Woman and the Family-Film: the Industrial Production of Memory," unpublished Ph.D. dissertation, University of Wisconsin-Madison, 1981, who has argued that modern mass culture, especially cinema, neutralized any true woman's culture. Ann Douglas in The

Feminization of American Culture (New York: Avon, 1977) has asserted that Victorian ladies together with clergymen produced a sentimental, oppressive mass culture.

(12) See John Russell Taylor, Hitch (New York: Pantheon, 1978).

(13) Ironically, sound films, though providing a better medium for female representation, were much more costly to make. Thus, independent production with sound became further closed to women and minorities.

(14) Bette Davis, quoted in Sidney Rosenzweig, Casablanca and other Major Films of Michael Curtiz (Ann Arbor, Mich: UMI Press, 1982), p. 7.

(15) For comparison between younger and older female stars of the 1940s, see Hortense Powdermaker, Hollywood: The Dream Factory (Boston: Little, Brown, 1950).

(16) See Whitney Stine, with Bette Davis, Mother Goddam (New York: Hawthorn, 1974).

(17) "Fatty" (Roscoe) Arbuckle was accused of the manslaughter of Virginia Rappe, a Hollywood starlet, at a party. Allegedly Ms. Rappe died as a result of Mr. Arbuckle's cruel and unusual sexual practices. Other Hollywood scandals, such as Mary Pickford's divorce, the murder of director William D. Taylor, and the overdose death of Wallace Reid sparked national concern. See Eric Rhode, A History of the Cinema: From Its Origins to 1970 (New York: Hill and Wang, 1976).

(18) Garth Jowett, Film: The Democratic Art (Boston: Little, Brown, 1976), pp. 179-80. The issue of feminist support for censorship is a very complicated one with repercussions in the present. The line between "sexual objectification" and unrepressed sexuality is a thin one. Though I would not deny that feminist support of censorship can have repressive and undemocratic consequences, the issue can never be reduced to the question of puritanism versus libertarianism.

(19) Haskell, From Reverence to Rape, p. 92.

(20) For a discussion of the effect of code censorship on the portrayals of lesbians and gay men, see Vito Russo, The Celluloid Closet: Homosexuality In the Movies (New York: Harper and Row, 1981).

(21) See Jon Halliday, Sirk on Sirk (New York: Viking, 1972).

(22) See Leo Handel, Hollywood Looks at Its Audience (Urbana: University of Illinois Press, 1950).

(23) Haskell, From Reverence to Rape, p. 154.

(24) Charles Higham and Joel Greenberg, Hollywood in the Forties (New York: Coronet, 1968), p. 157.

(25) For further discussion of the critical double standard, see David Thomson, America in the Dark, particularly chapter 7, "Woman's Realm and Man's Castle," pp. 192-223.

(26) In interviewing many women who enjoy (or have enjoyed) women's films, I have consistently noted a tone of apology for their attraction to a disdained variety of film. "These films are junk, but I love them" is a common sentiment.

(27) See Leo Handel, Hollywood Looks at Its Audience.

(28) See Pressbook, So Proudly We Hail, 1943, Library of Congress, Division of Motion Pictures, Television and Recorded Sound.

(29) Variety, November 11, 1942, pp. 6 and 13.

(30) Variety, November 25, 1943, p. 7.

(31) Leo Handel, Hollywood Looks at Its Audience, pp. 116-117.

(32) Ibid., p. 125.

(33) Ibid., p. 123.

(34) See M. Joyce Baker, Images of Women In Film: The War Years, 1941-45. (Ann Arbor: UMI Research Press, 1980). The Bureau of Motion Pictures (domestic branch), an agency of the office of War Information, developed guidelines for film production, previewed Hollywood features, and reviewed scripts. Liberals and feminists within the BMP advocated for the production of more films with feminist themes. They were successful in the case of So Proudly We Hail.

(35) Speculations of the failure of A Woman Rebels in 1937 and the success of Adam's Rib in 1949 are numerous. Possible explanations include: (a) growth of feminist consciousness among audiences; (b) the appeal of comedy over drama; (c) the superior scripting and acting of Adam's Rib; (d) the popularity of Tracy/Hepburn as a team; (e) all of these.

(36) Leo Handel, Hollywood Looks at Its Audience, p. 128.

(37) See James Damico, "Ingrid From Lorraine to Stromboli: Analyzing the Public's Perception of A Film Star," Journal of Popular Film IV, no. 1 (1975): 3-20.

(38) See Richard Griffith and Arthur Mayer, The Movies (New York: Simon and Schuster, 1970), p. 47.

(39) Leo Handel, Hollywood Looks at Its Audience, p. 150.

(40) Ibid.

(41) Ibid., p. 10.

(42) Leo Rosten, The Movie Colony, The Movie Makers (New York: Harcourt, Brace, 1941).

(43) Quoted from Blumer, in Robert Sklar, Movie Made America, p. 128.

(44) Leo Handel, Hollywood Looks at Its Audience, p. 147.

(45) Elizabeth Ewen, "City Lights: Immigrant Women and the Movies," Signs: A Journal of Women in Culture and Society 56, no. 3 (Spring 1980): 63. Ewen concluded that movies connect to the American female experience only until the birth of the Hollywood studio system. After that point, Ewen conceptualized movies as "agencies of mass impression" (p. 47) that liquidated traditional cultures and laid the basis for a homogeneous mass consumer

culture. Though I disagree with Ewen's conception of the sound era, I find her treatment of immigrant women and silent film useful for this study.

(46) Helen Merrell Lynd and Robert S. Lynd, Middletown in Transition: A Study in Cultural Conflicts (New York: Harcourt, Brace, 1937), p. 262.

(47) Hence, the concern with the misrepresentation of history and stereotyping of minorities (ethnic, racial, sexual preference) is well taken.

(48) Hortense Powdermaker, Hollywood: The Dream Factory (Boston: Little, Brown, 1950), p. 297.

(49) See Nancy Chodorow, The Reproduction of Mothering; Lenore Weitzman, Sex Role Socialization.

(50) Weitzman, "Sex Role Socialization," pp. 117-18.

(51) Evelyn Goodenough Pitcher, "Male and Female," in And Jill Came Tumbling After, ed. Judith Stacey, Susan Bereaud, and Joan Daniels (New York: Dell, 1974), p. 83.

(52) See Carol Gilligan, In A Different Voice.

(53) Karyn Kay and Gerald Peary (eds.), Women and the Cinema: A Critical Anthology (New York: Dutton, 1977), p. xiii.

Chapter 2

DIVIDED AND UNITED:
American Womanhood on
the Homefront

A war is an opportunity to start again, to see new things, to
escape from old chains.

> E.F.M. Durbin & John Bowlby,
> "Personal Aggressiveness and War,"
> in War, Studies from Psychology,
> Sociology and Anthropology, ed.
> by Leon Bramson and G.W. Goethals,
> rev. ed. (New York: Basic, 1968), p. 102.

I loaf here leafing ancient copies of LIFE from World War II.
We look so poor and honest there: girls with long hair badly
combed and unbecoming dresses – where are you now?

> Adrienne Rich, "Readings of History,"
> in Snapshots of a Daughter-In-Law (New
> York: W.W. Norton, 1960), p. 39.

And, perhaps most importantly, who were you then? Over 50
million American women encountered the war era as: blacks, whites,
Hispanics, Japanese, and Native Americans; Christians, Jews,
agnostics, and atheists; poor, working, middle, and upper class;
single, married, separated, widowed, and divorced; heterosexual,
lesbian, and bisexual; mothers, mothers-to-be, grandmothers, and
mothers-in-law; disabled and able-bodied; homemakers, welders,
servicewomen, nuns, doctors, secretaries, retirees, and volunteers;
northerners, easterners, westerners, and southerners; "city women,"
suburbanites, and "country girls."(1) The fabric of female experience
in the 1940s was woven of sameness and difference.

49

THE LEGACY OF THE GREAT DEPRESSION

"Today there is no time for feminism: the problems are not feministic, but economic."
(Chase Woodhouse, Director, Institute for Women's Professional Relations, quoted in Peter G. Filene, Him/Her Self (New York: Harcourt, Brace, Jovanovich, 1974), p. 158.)

The war erupted in a culture shaped by the hand of the Great Depression. Feminism, as a social movement, had lain dormant for nearly 2 decades. For many Americans, feminism evoked images of humorless, aging spinsters battling militantly for rights won and forgotten about long ago. Flapper working-girl chic had been replaced by frilly and demure fashions.

Even many women's organizations, though arguing for women's rights in employment, prioritized male unemployment as the primary social problem of the 1930s. Working wives were often seen as stealing jobs from needy male breadwinners; some states even legislated against hiring married women. Clearly, blaming working wives or feminists diverted public attention from the recurrent and allegedly natural business cycles of capitalism in crisis. Female unemployment rose as male unemployment declined during the 1930s; the percentage of women workers in 1940 equalled that of 1910.

The culture heroine of Depression America was strong, yet safely maternal. Ma Joad, populist heroine of Steinbeck's The Grapes of Wrath symbolized the image, mother as savior of family and society:

Ma was heavy, but not fat; thick with childbearing and work. Her hazel eyes seemed to have experienced all possible tragedy and to have mounted pain and suffering like steps into a high calm and a superhuman understanding. . .

She seemed to know that if she swayed . . . the family will to function would be gone.(2)

Her man's plight may have combined with her resilience to empower Ma Joad within the home. Yet her matriarchy was temporary and reluctant, at least in the popular mind.

Yet sexual egalitarianism still survived. Public opinion polls of Depression-era women, for example, revealed a tension between feminism and traditionalism. In one Ladies' Home Journal survey, 75 percent of the women polled believed that both husbands and wives should make important family decisions, and 60 percent objected to the word "obey" in the marriage vows. However, 90 percent felt that a wife should quit her job if her husband wished her to stay at home.(3)

As American women encountered the economic and social changes wrought by war, these contradictions in "common sense" would multiply and intensify.

WAR BREAKS OUT

America's declaration of war however, did not immediately challenge dominant ideologies of femininity. At first leaders in government and industry merely urged women to "attend nutrition classes, hang blackout curtains, and 'build morale by being beautiful'."(4) Throughout the war, millions of American women contributed countless hours in unpaid defense work: selling war bonds, planting victory gardens, and assisting the Red Cross.

A minority of women answered their nation's crisis by joining the armed services. In all, 140,000 enrolled in the Women's Army Corps (WACS), 100,000 became WAVES, 74,000 nurses joined the army and navy medical corps, 13,000 became Coast Guard SPARS, and 1,000 aviators flew planes as WASPS. Although most women in the military performed traditionally female jobs, they achieved more equal status than they had in previous wars, largely due to both the military crisis and the efforts of women's organizations and sympathetic legislators.(5)

Another minority was deprived of civil rights, unable to live as full citizens during the war. These were the over 50,000 female Japanese Americans whose story lies outside the major narrative of women's lives in World War II. Concentrated on the West Coast, these women and their families lost home, work, and possessions as they were held in relocation camps as aliens throughout the war.

THE HOME FRONT

The Women's Bureau, among other organizations, lobbied for increased employment opportunities for women, asserting that females were willing and able to do defense work. Furthermore, GI wives and children could not live adequately on low Dependents' Allowances. And, most importantly, the war necessitated the mobilization of women.

However, it was mid-1942 before America confronted the womanpower issue. Fearing that even the draft and a revitalized economy would fail to employ jobless men, employers rationalized underutilizing female labor by asserting that women, especially homemakers, were physically, emotionally, and/or intellectually incapable of performing "male" jobs. Management also argued that plants would need costly revamping to accommodate female workers: smaller tools and machinery and more rest facilities. Furthermore, they feared women might disrupt plant morale by seductively distracting men!(6) As of early 1942, only one-third of defense jobs in 12,000 factories were open to women, and females comprised only 1 percent of the 1,775,000 war workers who had received special training.(7)

The United States, major supplier of allied food and arms, could not meet her production quotas, however, simply by hiring jobless men. America had no accessible alternative labor source, such as easily mobilized migrants or war prisoners. The solution proved to be womanpower. Historically a labor reserve, women were needed to fill the positions of servicepeople, as well as newly created defense jobs.(8) Management also may have welcomed women with interrupted work lives, dual roles, and low rates of unionization, as a cushion against possible labor strife.

RECRUITING WOMEN WORKERS:
THE PROMOTIONAL CAMPAIGNS

By mid-1942, government and management turned quickly about-face, hastily reversing previous arguments against the hiring of women. During the war, many states suspended protective legislation, barring females from "heavy" and night work. Clearly, the dual labor market proved an impediment in wartime.(9)

Aided by opinion leaders such as Eleanor Roosevelt, industry and government initiated a massive joint campaign to promote war work among women, especially homemakers, as well as reluctant unions, employers, husbands, and male co-workers. The message to women to "Get a War Job" boomed out across radios, movie screens, and pulpits,(10) as the mass media cooperated generously with the government to aid the war effort (and, of course, to raise their own profits).(11)

Although the promotional campaigns shared a common goal, their appeal to women proved contradictory. Two trends emerged, mirroring tensions within American society: (a) a dominant ideology advocating temporary war work for women with a peacetime demobilization (b) a feminist undercurrent supporting the increased integration of women into the labor force, aided by supportive community services.(12)

The dominant approach appeared in film shorts such as Glamour Girls of '43, which assured women they needn't sacrifice beauty while doing "dirty" war work. Other ads portrayed woman as wife, girlfriend, or mother first, worker second.(13) The promotional campaigns also aimed to limit women's career aspirations. Fearing a female exodus from dead-end jobs and anticipating a demand in the service sector, a 1943 federal campaign was begun, "America at War Needs Women At Work":

Many women are urgently needed today in thousands of apparently humdrum, unglamourous and frequently ill-paid jobs in stores, restaurants, offices, laundries . . . Any job that brings victory sooner is a war job.(14)

Literature aimed at anxious or resentful husbands or male co-workers portrayed women workers as "pinch-hitters," and advocated patriotic appreciation and tolerance. Little attention focused on the 12 million females already employed; immigrant and minority women were noticeably absent from campaign imagery.

Simultaneously, however, the campaigns advocated an increased sense of female possibility. The following is from a billboard, which depicted homemaking skills as assets in employment: "What job is mine on the Victory line? If you've sewed on buttons . . . you can learn to do spot welding."(15)

While the woman of leisure may have been the culture heroine of Victorian America, she was seen as a potential parasite in wartime. Countess Josephine von Miklos' I Took a War Job (1943) urged "club women" to overcome their aversion to manual labor and work to "save democracy." Management, in addition, may have viewed affluent women as the ideal labor reserve, able to survive postwar layoffs without hardship.

The most feminist theme of the campaigns contrasted the freedom of American women with the shackles of their German sisters.(16) A War Production Board radio script reads:

Goebbels: The Nazi movement is a masculine movement. When we eliminate women from public life, it is not because we want to dispense with them, but rather because we want to give them back to their essential function.

Narrator: Yes, the Nazis cheered. Women are to be broodmares.(17)

The campaigns' ideology proved contradictory, however, urging women to express power and autonomy, yet within traditional bounds. A shaky and confusing ideology, it helped sow the seeds of its own demise.

AMERICAN WOMEN RESPOND TO THE WAR CRISIS

In 1941 only 12 million women were employed, comprising 25 percent of the labor force. Two-thirds of these workers were unmarried, many were working class, immigrant and minority. And most could be found in the "pink collar ghetto"(18) of dead-end, low-paid service jobs.

The war transformed the nature of the female labor force and redefined "women's work." Most of the 6 1/2 million new recruits had left the kitchen or nursery to take defense jobs previously designated as "male." Mary Anderson of the Women's Bureau commented, "Almost overnight women were reclassified from a marginal to a basic labor supply."(19) The power of the promotional propaganada, however, is difficult to assess. Depending on class and lifestyle, women sought work for a variety of interconnected motives: financial need; social interaction; self-fulfillment; economic and psychological autonomy; and patriotism.

Three and one-half million new workers were homemakers in 1941; another one-half million had been students.(20) Of America's 5 million service wives, about 50 percent were employed during the war.(21) In contrast, wives with husbands at home comprised only a little over 19 percent of the wartime labor force.(22) Nonetheless, the number of working wives doubled: Rosie the Riveter was more likely "Mrs." than "Miss," and was also likely to be a mother or grandmother.(23) The woman worker could no longer be typed as young, unmarried, or minority. She became Everywoman in wartime America.

With the majority of new female workers concentrated in defense, the percentage of women in manufacturing rose 140 percent from 1940 to 1944. In metals, chemicals, and rubber, the increase was astronomical: 460 percent.(24) As National Geographic columnist Verne Bradley noted in 1943,

> The balance of power rests in women's hands. Literally.
>
> Behind the whine of sawmills and roar of blast furnaces, the hammer of arsenals and thunder of machine shops — in shipyards, factories, slaughter-houses, and laboratories — women are manipulating the machinery of war.
>
> About one third of America's manpower today is womanpower.(25)

Female union membership more than tripled, skyrocketing to over 3 million by 1945, with heaviest concentrations in CIO, electrical, auto, and steel unions.(26)

Norman Rockwell's Rosie the Riveter stepped off the cover of the May 29, 1943, Saturday Evening Post, becoming the nation's sweetheart and a household word. Strong and maternally sensual, the "longlashed, snub-nosed, rosy-mouthed buxom lass wearing coveralls with a blue bandanna on her head"(27) quickly symbolized millions of American working women. Together with other popular symbols of wartime womanhood such as Eleanor Roosevelt, Rosie challenged the domestic ideal of the 1930s. In fashion, "welder chic" favored durability and safety over fragile glamor. Padded shoulders, straight skirts and comfortable shoes became wartime vogue.

Rosie was the most talked about worker in the land. Yet her unsung sisters on farms and in offices also contributed enormously. A severe agricultural crisis occurred in 1942-43, as many farm workers left for active duty and machinery shortages delayed further mechanization.

Despite resistance and ridicule by farmers, hands, and agricultural leaders, women mastered the challenges of agriculture. In the absence of husbands and hired hands, wives and children successfully managed family farms. In addition, many business women, professionals, homemakers, and students pitched in for a month, a summer or longer, harvesting, planting, and raising livestock. The number of women in wartime agriculture (laborers and volunteers) soared to 1.9 million, a 900 percent increase from 1940.(28)

"No job is ever finished 'til the paperwork's done," a popular contemporary office poster proclaims. The proliferating paperwork of defense bureaucracies demanded over 2 million new workers. The popular image of clerical work was, however, neither heroic nor glamorous; women's work connoted low status and pay. Not surprisingly, wartime women migrated en masse to factories, earning almost twice the pay of clericals, with less clothing expense and few extra educational requirements.

Some women, however, preferred clerical work which seemed more feminine, and respectable. Furthermore, the offices usually ran on a 9 to 5 basis; working mothers could more easily juggle their dual roles. Traveling home for women was often quicker and safer at 5 P.M. than at 5 A.M. Perhaps most importantly, most white-collar women did not fear that a veteran would claim their place at the typewriter or file cabinet.

Despite its appeal, however, serious white-collar wartime shortages prevailed. Jessica Mitford (1956) recalled:

> that the shortage of clerical(s) . . . was so severe that the applicant . . . was taken into a room with a typewriter and a washing machine; if she could identify the typewriter, she was hired.(29)

The lower echelons of the professional world (or "semiprofessions") also suffered shortages. Teachers and nurses abandoned classrooms and hospital wards to earn much more in factories and in the armed services. Despite propaganda claiming "any job is a war job," in June 1943, American schools were in need of 15,100 teachers, and the Army was short over 2,000 nurses.(30)

Although American women hardly welcomed war, their homefront experience created exciting, and often unimagined, possibilities. The gains they experienced range from tangible to intangible, from realities easy to perceive to complex realities more difficult to interpret. Documenting increases in income and status proves simpler, however, than interpreting changes in self-perception and familial power. Yet the two dimensions intertwine. The meaning of changes in income, status, and power varied for women by race, class, age, sexual orientation, and lifestyle. Two welders might have earned equal pay and encountered identical work conditions. Yet if one were a 55-year-old white, middle-class homemaker with adult children, and her co-worker, a 32-year-old black single mother of five young children and former domestic, the meanings of that common experience for their everyday lives may have been worlds apart.

Economic gains were apparent for many female war workers who enjoyed increased spending power and greater economic independence. The worth of their labor was quantified in rates per hour, per day, per week. The paycheck empowered many women — with respect to husbands, fathers, and children.(31)

Material gains were paralleled by less easily measured but consistently documented increases in self-esteem. Wartime ship-fitter Virginia Wilkinson recalled (1943):

> In the early morning I made my way to the shipyards. . . . For me, a housewife who had not held a job since that year's schoolteaching before marriage this was adventure indeed.(32)

For ex-college student Mary Danvouris (1977) the excitement of self-discovery was heightened in a predominantly female world as well.

> It was interesting how fast these plants converted to an almost all-female crew. . . . The first summer that I worked at the plant it was almost like a picnic. . . . People knew each other; there was lots of camaraderie. Most people had relatives and boyfriends in the service, and the discussion was where and what they'd heard and trying to dope out what was going on.(33)

Homemaker turned riveter Mabel Gerken has described female workplace solidarity (1949):

> You'd think we were a couple of heroes this morning, the way the girls crowded around us, kidding us about the mistake we'd made . . .

> "No use feeling bad," they chattered and giggled, "we all do it, sooner or later." Each had her own private boner to relate. Yesterday we were all strangers: today we are friends. . . .(34)

Whereas the wage liberated some women from economic dependence on men, it freed others from reliance on the state. For many women in poverty, war work signified an end to the Depression and the stigma of welfare. How many women on relief joined the labor force we do not know. Yet wartime observers, like journalist Agnes Meyer (1944) suggested that the number was significant. Meyer noted that defense opportunities challenged the fatalism of the poor women she interviewed; expectations soared along with income. Yet uneasiness paralleled economic boom: What if the bubble bursts?(35)

Handicapped women also found new employment opportunities, challenging popular stereotypes, and forcing physically able workers to deal with their handicapped counterparts. An industrialist commented:

> In our plant we have several paralysis victims who cannot walk far or well but whose finger dexterity . . . is excellent. We also have a blind girl who is doing a splendid job of gauging automatic screw machine parts.(36)

THE "OTHER ROSIES": UNEXPECTED MOBILITY

Whereas the new "Rosies" monopolized America's attention, however, the majority (60 percent) of women war workers were already employed in 1941. Yet, for these 12 million, defense work also spelled significant social mobility.(37)

First of all, war work provided an escape from the "pink-collar ghetto." Despite government propaganda, over 700,000 women left service jobs for the higher status and pay of "men's work."(38) Receptionists and file clerks saw their salaries double and triple when they entered defense plants.(39)

Yet psychological as well as material incentives attracted "pink-collar" women to blue-collar work. Working-class and minority women already employed were less likely to experience the headiness of middle-class homemakers asserting simultaneously their power and patriotism. Working class women probably considered employment both alienating and necessary. Yet developing new skills and utilizing talents and muscles they may not have known they possessed, led women like Celia Sapersteen Yanish (1982) to perceive themselves with pride:

> I loved that job, because I produced something. I knew it was precision work, and it required skill. It gave me a self-respect I didn't have before.(40)

Ruth Wolf (1982) found war work easier and more challenging than her pre-war job in an all female pottery factory:

> In the steel mill, . . . it was easy work, more intelligent work. You weren't just standing up all day and working like a robot.(41)

Defense opportunities also allowed some service workers to escape troublesome clientele.

> Joanne, who had previously been a waitress . . . preferred welding because "you don't have to take so much from the public."(42)

Even the "world's oldest profession" lost members; Mary Damon, an aging prostitute, left the street corner for a Midwest war plant.(43)

Black women experienced rapid wartime occupational mobility. Although black females in the prewar labor force (40 percent) outnumbered whites two to one, they were heavily concentrated in domestic service (70 percent) and farming (16 percent). Although discrimination persisted, the war crisis and the political mobilization of blacks challenged racial as well as sexual barriers in employment. As the ranks of black female domestics and farm laborers dwindled rapidly, the number of black women working in defense more than doubled.(44)

As black women entered the mainstream of American labor in wartime, many received their first Social Security coverage. Living environments also changed, as black women and their families migrated en masse to the war boom towns such as Detroit, San Francisco, Mobile. The Second World War did not simply provide more and better jobs for blacks; it altered the course of Afro-American history.(45)

STILL UNEQUAL: RESISTANCE TO SEXUAL EQUALITY AT WORK

Sexual inequality endured, however, despite the gains women experienced in income and status. Although wartime profits soared, women in manufacturing averaged about $.65 to every dollar earned by men.(46) Some female defense workers received training that was inadequate and crisis-centered, leaving them unprepared for employment in the postwar era.(47) Although the government tacitly supported the equal pay principle, the National War Labor Board rarely enforced it. In fact, some sectors of government advocated lower wages for women as a weapon against inflation!

The persistence of sexual imbalance at work is due, in large part, however, to the failure of trade unions to struggle significantly for female equality. Although women comprised 25 percent of union membership by 1944, their influence on policy failed to match the strength of their numbers. Rank-and-file women, many newly arrived in the workplace, found themselves divided by class and race, burdened by dual roles, and unprepared to battle militantly. Many male co-workers saw them as auxiliaries, not equals. Although female union leadership increased during the war, the United Electrical Workers, with a one-third female organizing staff, was an exception to the rule. Furthermore, female leaders supporting demands such as childcare often encountered a hostile male membership.

Some unions advocated sexual equality and most at least supported the equal pay principle. However, they often advocated equal pay in fear that lowered female wages would also diminish male salaries.

More blatantly sexist unions advanced spurious and conflicting arguments against female hiring and promotion: that women only work for extras; that women only work for money, not craft; women are too slow, forcing males to work harder; women are too fast, resulting in speedup; women are prone to accidents, emotional upset, and illness; the demand for day care would only give employers more control over personal life.(48)

CIO unions, particularly those with a sizable Communist Party membership, were most likely to support sexual equality. Yet, the Communist Party's influence on the struggle for women's rights was weakened because of its wartime political strategy and its ambivalence on the "woman question." Under Earl Browder, the Communists adopted the strategy of the Popular Front, i.e., a progressive coalition prioritizing the fight against Fascism. The Popular Front policy supported a wartime "no-strike pledge"; labor unrest would have to wait until the demise of world-wide Fascism. Feminist issues were viewed contradictorily. Whereas sexual equality remained a Communist ideal, it might not have been the historically appropriate moment to address the "woman question." The lack of female Party leadership did little to further debate and strengthen the cause of women. The Communist Party remained a vocal, but weakened and divided, force for sexual equality. The failure of feminism in the wartime labor movement is partly due to the ambivalence of the Communist Party.

It is hardly surprising that wartime women often responded with hostility or indifference toward unionism. A 1943 Roper poll asked women if they would prefer working in a shop that was (a) nonunionized, (b) unionized by the company, (c) unionized and open, or (d) unionized and closed. Close to half surveyed chose the nonunionized shop; working-class, black, Jewish, and Catholic women expressed stronger pro-union sympathies.(49)

Management and unions responded similarly to womanpower, yet with different motives. Management aimed to maintain high profits, a docile work force, and flexible labor reserve, whereas unionists sought to retain their jobs and maintain wage and benefit levels. Managers and co-workers often rationalized these practices arguing that women, by nature, enjoyed monotony. As a Connecticut Valley industrialist remarked, "they do the monotonous work that drives a man nuts."(50) The effects on women were mutually reinforcing; females were often relegated to the more repetitive and poorly paid jobs.

Wartime management literature expressed a fear of male power and prerogative lost. Donald Laird's The Psychology of Supervising the Working Woman (1942) depicted women as flighty, irrational, and unsuited for leadership. He warned supervisors that women working too closely together develop powerful "crushes" on one another that threaten to disrupt the workplace.

> Those wonderful "friendships" which spring up quickly are usually crushes between the girls. They walk around together during the lunches, . . . buy birthday presents for each other, temporarily lose interest in boys.

> When a crush is just starting, the alert executive will transfer one of the girls.(51)

How many wartime women workers turned to one another for sexual and emotional comfort we do not know. What Laird's advice reveals, however, is a deeply rooted male fear that men were becoming increasingly irrelevant to women.

As women entered the masculine enclaves of the blue-collar and professional world, men experienced a loss of territory, and a challenge to an often misogynist work culture. The resulting backlash took several forms: fear of lesbianism, sexual harassment, and the simultaneous depiction of women as prudish and hypersexual. Some men taunted their new workmates by whistling, ogling, or complaining that the mere sight of an attractive woman might provoke an accident. Sexual harassment was strongest in plants in which women were few and isolated, and did not retaliate by counter-whistling, ogling, or ridicule.(52)

The days of the "boys' club" were numbered, at least for the duration of the war. A masculine culture that once dominated the workplace threatened to be relegated to the washroom, bar, or men's club. As men retaliated (and management sometimes complied), women workers often confronted behavior they found repulsive. Von Miklos (1943) has related an encounter with tobacco chewing:

> "Spitting?" Penny asked. "What about spitting?"

> "Well, you see, it isn't very pleasant to sit at your machine and work hard and then a guy comes by and spits practically at your feet. They don't do it on purpose. They chew tobacco and they've got to spit."

> "How awful," Miss Perry exclaimed.(53)

Some male workers transcended the bounds of an informal culture of resistance and enlisted a sympathetic management to demote women. Virginia Wilkinson (1943) recalled,

One woman burner reported that they were "seething with resentment" that women should be given a unit to construct. . . . I could not believe it. The men had always been so decent, so respectful. . . . But this was the first time that we were seen in the light of competitors.

The next day, with no explanation, the XAK, our baby, was taken from us and given to the men. . . . Cora, whose boy friend was in one of the groups, said the men were afraid the assemblies would be . . . overrun with women.(54)

While some plants utilized group incentives to encourage male-female cooperation, others did little to curb the backlash. Winifred Raushenbush, in How to Dress in Wartime (1942), compared the fear of male war workers to that of male students encountering collegiate coeducation at the turn of the century. Raushenbush surmised that men most easily accepted women at work if males could serve as teachers or trainers. When women refused to subordinate themselves, masculine resistance grew.(55)

Male resistance expressed itself perhaps most strongly in persistent discrimination against professional women. Although space opened for wartime women to train for, enter, and advance in the professions, sexism prevailed. For example, despite the urgent need for doctors, the Army refused to commission female physicians until legally compelled by a 1943 Act of Congress, passed due to an aggressive campaign by various women's organizations.(56)

Wartime management literature depicted women supervisors as unstable, jealous, petty, authoritarian, and over-sensitive, better suited to serve than to lead. Male managers also often failed to encourage female leadership and isolated women from decision-making networks. In addition, management sometimes placated males who balked at working "under a woman." Some women workers also internalized their own inferiority and preferred male supervisors.(57) It seemed a no-win situation for the wartime female foreperson or manager.

In defense planning, inequality also prevailed. The National War Labor Board, Board of Economic Warfare, and War Production Board were exclusively male; on the War Manpower Commission one woman sat among nine members.(58) The presidentially appointed Women's Advisory Commission (WAC) to the War Manpower Commission had no formal power. For Alice Baker, economist for the Lend-Lease Program:

It was quite a handicap to me to be a woman. . . . I did have this dread of the telephone because . . . I was treated rudely. The assumption was that I was the secretary. . . . Finally, I had to leave the job because I married Ed Baker and they didn't want both of us working in the same office.(59)

Promoting female leadership would clearly have strengthened women's networks advocating sexual equality in the postwar era. The "old boys' network" jealously guarded its terrain, denying women a system of role models and contacts through which to achieve occupational mobility.(60) Yet perhaps the most important obstacle to female equality lay in the inadequacy of childcare and community services.

THE CHILDCARE AND COMMUNITY SERVICES CONTROVERSY

Although "working mother" became a household word in wartime,(61) childcare was still considered an individual and maternal responsibility by most federal agencies as well as by many women themselves. For Paul McNutt, head of the War Manpower Commission, "The first responsibility of women with young children in war and peace is to give suitable care in their own homes to their own children."(62) A 1943 Gallup Poll asked women if they would take defense jobs if free childcare were provided. Only 29 percent would, whereas 56 percent replied with a resounding "no."

Childcare in America historically has borne a dual stigma of welfare and maternal neglect. U.S. day-care policy has been oriented toward the children of the poor (i.e., the offspring of women who could not fulfill the ideal of continuous mothering in a nuclear family). Childcare, in the Depression Era, for example, was seen by its architects as a necessary evil. If America could conquer poverty, day care would become obsolete. Mothers then could "afford" to stay home and provide children with an ideal environment. Thus, day care spelled welfare, not education; charity, not public right.

Whereas public day care spelled familial failure and maternal neglect, the nursery school, its middle-class counterpart, promised social and cognitive enrichment. The nursery school movement, however, strongly upheld the ideal of full-time mothering; its role was only to supplement maternal care.(63)

Childcare in America has rarely been associated with women's right to employment. It is easy to see why the word "childcare" connoted fear and shame for women. If given the option, most working mothers probably would have chosen higher pay and privately arranged childcare. But, given unequal pay and inadequate day care, working mothers would have neither public nor private childcare on a mass scale.

As mothers flooded the labor market, some federal agencies, such as the Women's Bureau, saw the need for childcare. Yet other opinion leaders asserted that the state should not assume women's "natural roles."

Industry and government began to respond when war production suffered the effects of the "double day." Female workers had double the male rates of turnover and absenteeism. In a 1943 survey, 40 percent of women interviewed who had quit jobs had done so because of family responsibilities.(64) In addition, many working mothers were recent migrants without familiar female support networks. Some women stayed home, as they discovered that outside employment left them no richer on payday. As one wartime nurse commented, "It costs me from $.20 to $2.20 plus nine hours of my time to help relieve the nursing shortage."(65)

The West Coast Air Production Council estimated the need for day care quite dramatically: "Lack of twenty-five childcare centers can cost 10 bombers a month."(66) Conflict ensued between those supporting public childcare as an emergency measure and those advocating childcare as a desirable long-range precondition for expanding the female labor force. Though financial considerations dominated, perhaps equally important was the challenge that a viable childcare system posed to traditional female roles.

A token, compromise solution finally came in August, 1942. Roosevelt appropriated $400,000 to help communities assess the need for daycare and a 1943 ruling allowed childcare centers to be built under the pre-existing Lanham Act.

Roosevelt's allocation however, generated a proliferation of studies stating the obvious: a desperate need for childcare. The Lanham decision was also more hopeful in appearance than reality. The average Lanham grant provided only a fraction of the cost of constructing or maintaining a center.(67) Funding was often held up in bureaucratic disputes between the administering agencies, the FWA (Federal Works Administration) and the FSA (Federal Security Agency), whose conflicts mirrored those in society at large.(68)

The Lanham centers, at their peak, (spring, 1945) served only about 100,000 youngsters,(69) although the government estimated that over 2 million children needed some surrogate care.(70) A few companies such as Kaiser in Portland, Oregon, and some areas of heavy war industry set up adequate and, in some cases, quality programs. However, on the whole, childcare appropriations were grossly inadequate. The Thomas Bill, providing for increased child-care funding, was introduced in Congress in 1943. However, opponents of day care like the Roman Catholic Church triumphed. The bill passed the Senate after a day of hearings, but died in committee in the House.(71)

Throughout the war, day care was available for less than 10 percent of the children in need.(72) In addition, many of the hastily constructed centers were inadequate. It is no wonder that half of wartime working mothers made private arrangements.(73) However, for an estimated 40 percent of working parents, no regularized surrogate care existed. For Betty Covello, that meant leaving her baby in the alleyway of her shop.(74) Lyn Childs did not see her child for several years as her daughter was cared for by her grandmother in another area of the country.(75) Some women became more desperate. The New York Times reported, on February 16, 1944, the case of a Mrs. Stanfanski who abandoned a baby she claimed could not be cared for while she worked.

Homemakers in wartime found their job more difficult: rationing and shortages rendered housework more tiring and time-consuming. Working wives often encountered an added barrier as most stores, banks, and laundries closed early, leaving only Saturdays for errands. Transportation often also posed a problem, with gas rationed and defense plants located "in the middle of nowhere." Furthermore, a severe housing shortage forced many to accept substandard and inconveniently located quarters.

The Women's Bureau urged the United States to emulate Great Britain by establishing community services to aid working wives and improve production. Such support systems, however, did not materialize in the United States. Although government propaganda supported voluntary community services, business and government provided working wives only minimal assistance. Edsel Ford even suggested that women neighbors alternate work shifts so they could do each other's housework! Some banks and groceries established late hours, and prepared foods became commercially more available. Some plants set up shopping services: A store representative took orders from employees on break and delivered goods at the end of the day. Yet, comprehensive community services never materialized. Perhaps the idea of viable public alternatives to private familial functions too seriously threatened traditional conceptions of femininity as well as rising corporate profits.

WOMEN, HOME, AND FAMILY: THE DOMESTIC WORLD IN WARTIME

"They're either too young or too old, they're either too gray or too grassy green, the pickings are poor and the crop is lean"

(They're Either Too Young or Too Old by Frank Loesser and Arthur Schwartz. Copyright 1943, M. Witmark and Sons, Warner Bros. music.)

Transformations in personal life paralleled those in the public sphere. As 11 million men left for war, the homefront quickly became a much more female universe. This simple yet dramatic change "rippled" throughout personal life, altering patterns of sexuality, marriage, motherhood, leisure, and friendship.

However, the GI exodus did not affect all women equally. Whereas most women of all ages had at least one close male relative in uniform, women, 15-35, most of whom were current or future wives and lovers of servicemen, experienced the greatest life changes. The war stamped itself uniquely as a generational experience on their individual and collective consciousness. And as they grew older, worked, married, raised children, they would transmit the meanings of their war experience to daughters and grand-daughters, literal and symbolic. Thus, this section focuses heavily on the lives of young women.

Taken together, two factors set the stage for significant changes in lifestyles: the exodus of servicemen and female migration. For young women, the departure of GIs created a comparatively manless world. The 1944 ratio of females to males, aged 20-24, averaged a little over two to one nationally; in key defense centers like Detroit it soared to three to one.(76)

Over 7 million women (mostly young) migrated across the United States to war-boom areas following GI husbands, fathers, and boyfriends or seeking defense work. Migration created added strain for women performing dual roles in new surroundings without familiar female networks. However, migration proved double-edged, as women found new employment opportunities. In addition, loosened family ties and increased economic power opened oppor-tunities for personal freedom. Although marriage still remained a primary goal, young wartime women became more sexually active and assertive, and sometimes shared the costs of dating.(77) Reflecting changing mores, the number of wartime illegal abortions was estimated at over eight thousand yearly.(78)

Although the dominant culture remained homophobic, lesbians, estimated by Kinsey to average between 3-12 percent of the female population, experienced greater freedom in wartime. The woman-centered atmosphere of the war-boom towns allowed for the growth of an urban gay culture, underground yet vibrant.

> The need for women to take the places of absent men increased the incidence and acceptability of women in public places. Women had more money to spend and enjoyed greater freedom of movement, congregation and opportunity to meet other women-identified women. As it became more cus-tomary for women to be out alone and to socialize with other women, the social lives of lesbians became less overtly deviant and consequently less vulnerable to public hostility or ridicule.(79)

A public symbol of female sexual freedom was the "Victory Girl" (V-girl). These young women were usually not career-oriented, and often travelled from city to city seeking sexual adventure with GIs. The popular stereotype was that of a patriotic "prostitute without pay." Victory Girls however, may have seen themselves as sexual pioneers rather than "volunteer prostitutes."

However, for most Americans, the V-girl was a social pariah, symbolizing uncontrolled female sexuality and threatening the family. Federal and state campaigns focused on the rehabilitation of the V-Girl. Venereal disease and prostitution were the official targets of the campaigns. Prostitution, however, was defined as "promiscuous intercourse." Young women engaging in frequent, casual heterosexual activity were labelled "sex delinquent" and diagnosed as love-starved, maladjusted, and a threat to the American family.(80) Whereas federal propaganda described male sexuality as a drive which women must both restrain and tolerate, female sexuality became an arena of control. A similar set of negative rumors surrounded the WACS: "That WACS were frequently drunk, that they were sexually promiscuous, that the army provided them contraceptives, and — contradictorally that hundreds of them were pregnant."(81) Morals charges for women rose 95 percent from 1940 to 1944. A backlash against female sexual power paralleled and intertwined with a backlash against female workplace power.

Yet V-girls were the minority. Most young American women were still oriented toward heterosexual monogamy and marriage. However, wartime America — with mass migration, female employment, scarcity of men, and family separation — challenged traditionalism and facilitated a wider range of sexual expression. Secondly, war inspired panic. As youth feared it was the "last generation," the time table of courtship often accelerated rapidly. Women in defense areas had unforeseen chances for casual encounters with GIs. The old morality did not work in an era when the world could end, your partner die, or disappear forever.

Yet, the sexual freedom of the 1940s, like the sexual revolution of the 1960s, was not as radical as its name. For most young women, marriage still retained primacy. And the economic prosperity and psychological insecurity of the war years generated a marriage boom. Between 1940-1943 there were 1,118,000 more marriages than would have been predicted to occur given prewar conditions.(82) Some marriages represented the sealing of long Depression engagements made possible by wartime economic recovery and the employment of wives.

However, other marriages were much more hastily contracted. As Americans feared personal and global annihilation, love affairs were initiated, speeded up, and sealed quickly. Some women may have feared that the opportunity may not arise again; perhaps they would be too old by the end of the war. For both sexes, a spouse became a very concrete "something to fight for." The wedding band sanctioned sex, legitimized possible offspring, and promised hope for the future postwar family and world.

The "hasty marriage," characterized by a whirlwind (sometimes weekend) courtship and wedding, was the focus of much national attention. As Grace Reeves (1945) described,

> Marceline, a senior in high school, met Harry in a USO. They "fell" for each other immediately. They danced and played together for the next week which was all that was left of Harry's furlough. Marceline . . . gave freely of herself to

Harry who was hungry for the love and affection of a girl. . . . they talked of marriage . . . though the only thing they had in common was dancing. . . . The future was fogged with the passions of the moment. And so they were married.(83)

How many Marcelines and Harrys there were we do not know, but the postwar U.S. divorce rate, highest among vets, testifies to the prevalence of wartime marital instability.

Historians such as Anderson and Campbell have viewed the "rush to the altar" as evidence of an enduring conservatism.(84) Doubtless, this interpretation is partially correct. For many women, raised in traditional families and living in insecure times, becoming a wife probably crystallized their sense of identity. Marriage also legitimized sex and symbolized adulthood.

However, marriage "cost" war brides very little in terms of sacrifice or compromise. A young woman could marry, and, after her GI mate left, continue her premarriage lifestyle. Over 50 percent of service wives worked outside the home; they did not feel forced to choose between marriage and career. They also did not usually experience a decline in personal power upon marriage, and their loneliness was perhaps not so very different from a GI's girlfriend. For poor, working-class, and minority women, particularly, marriage also possessed a financial incentive. Service wives received a monthly government allowance of at least $50.

In addition, although long separation created its own strains, distance often allowed a couple to idealize each other from afar. The "end of the honeymoon" and its classic disillusionment, characteristic of early marriage, were postponed for many newlyweds. The war bride often felt simultaneously married and single; Kinsey statistics indicate that some women allowed themselves sexual freedom as well.(85)

In interpreting the wartime marriage boom, it is imperative to consider also the parallel rise in divorces. The war intensified already progressing twentieth-century trends toward companionate marriage and serial monogamy. As traditional patriarchy declined, the ideal of companionate marriage arose, embodying rising expectations of love, communication, and friendship. If these needs were not met, after a period of mutual effort, the marriage (in this model) should terminate. And the spouses would again search for a partner of the companionate mode. This ideal became more popular and affordable during the war.

In the relentless wartime search for happiness, all family processes were accelerated. The "now or never" ethic supported as well as challenged traditionalism, pushing some women toward marriage, others toward divorce. The wartime divorce rate for women over 15 rose — from 8.8 per 1,000 in 1940 to 14.4 per 1,000 by 1945.(86) Economic independence and the common condition of female singlehood gave unhappy wives the incentive to divorce. Whereas the war era marriage and divorce booms reveal an enduring ideal of heterosexual monogamy, they also express a growing power and freedom of women vis-à-vis men.

Paralleling these trends, the national birth rate (both legitimate and illegitimate) climbed from 17.9 percent to 22 percent from 1940 to 1943. Did the wartime baby boom also signify an embracing of traditionalism? While it clearly expresses a strong desire for motherhood, motherhood in and of itself does not equal subordination.

And most American women favored contraception, at least for married couples. Among white urban women, surveyed in the late 1930s and early 1940s, over 80 percent used contraception. Although statistics are lower for black women, family planning was accepted in mainstream American culture. Abortion, although illegal (except for rare therapeutic abortions) and less accepted, was fairly common. Close to a quarter of the urban affluent women interviewed by Kinsey had had illegal abortions. Over 75 percent of these women reported few long-term negative emotional consequences.(87) Thus, except for very young or religiously conservative women, we can assume that most wartime pregnancies were wanted.

With expanding wartime job opportunities and changing social roles, a woman could parent child(ren) and also be independent and employed. For GI wives, single parenting created numerous strains, but also entailed a de facto temporary matriarchy. And, as Max Lerner (1944) suggested, children represent hope and affirmation in wartime.

To bring children into the world, especially now, is an act of faith in life, and an affirmation that — in the face of all the powers and principalities of reaction — life is worth living.(88)

SEPARATION OF THE SEXES AND FAMILIES IN WARTIME

Whereas war unites some people, it divides others. In patriarchal societies, the most significant division war creates is that between men and women. Wartime sexual segregation significantly alters love, work, and family relationships. Ironically, as war undermines narrow sexual stereotypes, it glorifies the most "masculine" identity: that of warrior.

Although wartime America was hardly manless, it was a society largely without young men. Thus for young women (15-35), wartime had a manless quality, with the contradictory effect of increasing job opportunities while decreasing possibilities for stable heterosexual relationships. For young wives, except for spouses of COs, Japanese-Americans, deferred defense workers or 4Fs, wartime separation was the rule. In Seattle in 1944, over half of teenage wives and over a third of those aged 20-24 had GI mates away from home. By 1945, about one-half of the married GIs had children. The average tour of duty was 33 months, with additional months of long, slow demobilization. America's 5 million service wives endured long marital separations. For GI girlfriends, whose ranks at least equalled that of wives, separation was the rule as well.

How did these women experience wartime separation? In the absence of extensive oral histories, information can be gleaned from demographic data, diaries, memoirs, biographies, social commentary, and social work literature. These sources indicate that the realities of separation challenged as well as supported traditionalism. The space created by male absence was a source of opportunity as well as strain. As men went to war, women went to work. However, the loneliness, anxiety, and uncertainty of waiting were psychically interwoven with the new freedoms. As Margaret Mead noted, wartime women kept asking and re-asking "will he return to love the woman I am now?"

Social work literature noted mixed reactions of women to wartime separation. In a 1944 study of 77 service wives and sweethearts, loneliness was the most frequently mentioned problem. Twenty-eight percent of respondents, like the wife in the following quote, reported extreme loneliness:

> I can't sleep when I'm alone in the house. I just lie awake all night listening to the water faucet drip, and the window panes creak. . . . I guess I'm never really happy without my husband. I'm always lonesome.(89)

Those reporting extreme loneliness were usually wives, not sweethearts, and often suffered clinical symptoms of depression such as early morning awakening, insomnia, weight gain or loss. The degree of isolation rather than length of marriage or number of children determined their degree of loneliness.

Moderate to considerable loneliness was described by 45 percent. However, for these women the companionship of other women and their families eased the waiting period. For other women, like this mother of two, work provided the key to alleviating loneliness:

> At first I was very blue at times . . . With the children it is so confining and my vocabulary has to be so limited . . . At last, I decided to be a Nurse's Aid and I like it very much. I see so many people and it is a change from the house.(90)

Parenthood relieved loneliness for some, but only if the mother was not completely isolated. Wives in extended households reported that children provided affection, companionship, and a tie to the absent father, whereas grandparent(s) provided much appreciated childcare while the mother worked and/or socialized. For several women, leisure activities such as movie going and card playing alleviated loneliness. However, a little over one-fourth reported little loneliness. For Mrs. M,

> I'm really busy and don't have much time to feel terribly lonesome. It seems as though things were happening so often and fast for L_____ and me, that I just can't realize he's gone yet.(91)

A small minority described separation as positive. One wife claimed she was "coming along fine": "I am at an advantage. . . . I can read in bed now. He used to turn off the light."(92) This study, though by no means exhaustive, suggested that women coped creatively, alone and together, with wartime separation. Loneliness, though creating pain and anxiety, also gave wives freedom to pursue activities they might not have been able to if husbands were home. In peacetime, that same autonomy might require sustained struggle. Ironically, for many women in wartime, increased personal freedom was something that just "happened."

Loneliness, however, was only one emotion evoked by separation. Many service wives, as Mary described below, experienced "role confusion": Were they married, single, both, or neither?

> Mary didn't follow her husband. She kept her job in her home city and . . . her husband had been away for two months. Her first sentence states her problem. "I'm a married woman, yet I'm not."
>
> How was she to act? . . . If she went out, even with the girls, she would have to be with other fellows. . . . She loved her husband and missed him dreadfully and wanted to be loyal now. What could she fill her life with and still remain a faithful wife?(93)

MOTHERS IN WARTIME

> I was at the terrible, growing years. War Years. I do not remember them well. I was working, there were four smaller ones now, there was not time for her. She had to help be a mother, and housekeeper . . .
>
> There was so little time left at night after the kids were bedded down. She would struggle over books . . . and I would be ironing, or preparing food for the next day, or writing V-mail to Bill, or tending the baby.
>
> Tillie Olsen, "I Stand Here Ironing," in Tell Me A Riddle, (New York: Dell, 1981), p. 18.

Role confusion also prevailed for service wives with children, after having become temporarily single parents who simultaneously experienced increased power and responsibility. The time and energy quotient of many wartime mothers was taxed to the maximum, and fear of juvenile delinquency ran high, particularly in war-boom areas. Though historical evidence indicates that most mothers did not seriously neglect their young, older children were pushed more quickly into adulthood, as workers, babysitters, and companions for parents.

For younger children, mothers became stronger, but less available, role models who often combined and juggled "masculine" and "feminine" traits. GI fathers were shadowy figures kept alive through memory, occasional visits, phone calls and letters, and through the mother's initiative. Wartime social work literature has noted contradictory reactions by mothers to father absence. Some women clearly enjoyed their new-found matriarchy. As Reuben Hill (1944) noted,

> The well adjusted wife and mother . . . has frequently grown as a result of the separation. She has been treated to a liberal and technical education in the ways of a "man's world." Indeed, men have become dispensable as wives mastered the traditional duties . . . great and small for which men claimed a special talent.(94)

Yet wartime culture also glorified masculinity: "Separation also causes the wife to idealize her soldier-husband. She sees him as a dashing hero in shining uniform, capable of great deeds."(95) Idealization probably had a multiple effect. Returning fathers inevitably disappointed families as they could never live up to the image. However, during the war, this worship of masculinity may have encouraged sons of GIs, especially older sons, to play "little daddy" ("Take care of Mom while Dad's away") and became more dominantly masculine than their counterparts in other family types. There is considerable evidence that "war play" was encouraged and increased among boys. For mothers, military play was most likely a double-edged sword, as they feared its possible consequences in crime and violence. As one mother anxiously asked a wartime counselor: "What shall I do with Jim? I am afraid he will become a delinquent, . . . He always talks about killing Japs and the Germans."(96)

The impact on daughters of wartime father absence has not been extensively studied. However, some evidence does suggest that strong female role models affected the occupational aspirations of young girls. For example, a 1945 Senior Scholastic poll of high school girls found that 88 percent wished to combine career and homemaking. Only 4 percent aspired solely to become home-makers.(97)

Some young women may have welcomed father absence. For Doris F., patriarchy was at its weakest when men were away:

> You have no idea how much I dread my dad coming home. . . . It's been heavenly at home without him around. My mother and I are pals. . . . He's just going to blow up when he finds I'm engaged.(98)

Some fathers proved unable to accept their daughters' autonomy.

> The father discharged after four years . . . in the Navy returned to find his 19-year-old daughter a grown-up young woman. When he left home she was an adolescent . . . On his return he found her an independent woman, a war worker earning $40 a week . . . The father was horrified to find that his "little girl" sometimes stayed out as late as 2 in the morning, and he felt that her mother had allowed her to go to the dogs.(99)

As wartime family separation promoted stronger female bonding and power, it simultaneously encouraged the glorification of the absent male, the heroic father, and the primacy of the eldest son.

THE DARK SIDE OF WAITING:
FEAR, SUSPICION, AND DISTRUST

Wartime separation evoked not only loneliness and anticipation but fear as well. The most easily expressed fear of waiting women was that their GI loved ones would die. In all, over 400,000 American men died during World War II.(100) In fact, the homefront proved more dangerous; more workers died in industrial accidents during the war than soldiers succumbed in combat. However, risk in the factory was publicly downplayed, or ignored, whereas danger in battle was emphasized. Nonetheless, although the actual risk of death for servicemen was low, fear ran high. War casualties could affect any woman at any time, without respect for age, class, race, or ability to deal with crisis. Most women experienced a death close to home; a relative, friend, neighbor, or co-worker who had lost a son, brother, father, friend, husband, or sweetheart.

Fear of death was paralleled by another gnawing dread: that loved ones would return physically maimed. Over 500,000 GIs did return with serious levels of disability. As the mass media attempted to generate optimism about the rehabilitative potential of handicapped veterans,(101) wives and girlfriends may have wondered: What will he look like? Will I still find him attractive? How independent can he be? Can he support the family? How will the child(ren) react? Will we still be able to have a satisfactory sex life? Will he be sterile? Will he be bitter? Will I? Will I want to be with the man he is now? Will he want to be with the woman I am now?

Fear of psychological disability among vets also manifested itself among wartime women. How widespread this fear was we cannot tell, but various sources have confirmed its haunting presence. Coleman R. Griffiths of the National Conference on Family Relations warned (1944):

> But others will be maimed . . . in spirit . . . And the homes to which they return, and even whole communities will likewise be maimed, almost beyond the power of word to tell. . . . The strand of continuity between the boy . . . who left home and the warrior who returns will be broken. As warriors they will have practiced deceit, treachery and killing — evil means to the good that ought to be at the end of the road.(102)

The press featured sensational tales of blood-crazed vets. As Joseph C. Goulden (1977) has noted,

> Any former serviceman who got into trouble was seized upon in support of the War-Crazed Veteran theory. Daily news-papers exploited the fears, and the following were not atypical:
>
> "Vet Beheads Wife"
> "Ex-Marine Held in Rape Murder"
> "Sailor Son Shoots Father"(103)

One psychologist warned of a postwar crime wave by bloodthirsty GIs.(104) Did women share this fear of the familiar loved-one-turned-brutal stranger? Were visions of domestic violence and rape lurking in female minds?

Separation provoked another gnawing fear for both sexes: that of infidelity. In the cynicism of the late war years, the seeds of mutual distrust found fertile soil. Historical research indicates that men as well as women feared betrayal and infidelity by their loved ones.

There is evidence that women feared male infidelity at the same time that advice columns, women's magazines, and popular psychology books encouraged them to "forgive and forget." One mother wrote an advice columnist that she viewed her husband's enlistment as abandonment.(105) And army psychiatrists reported a sizable number of husbands who saw military service as a last bachelor fling:

> To some it represented a socially acceptable excuse for deserting their families . . . Others, . . . anticipated the army experience as a sort of return to bachelor freedom and

displayed only face-saving reluctance in accepting Uncle Sam's invitation.(106)

The press covered stories about prostitutes, V-girls, and servicemen. Dr. Howard Kitching, in the popular book, <u>Sex Problems of the Returned Veteran</u> (1946), linked the need for casual sex with the experience of violence:

> It is impossible to tell men to go and kill an enemy and risk their lives and expect them at the same time to be honest, chaste, kind and unselfish all the time.(107)

Women's fear of male infidelity and desertion did not stand alone. Most likely, it intertwined itself with other anxieties generated by war: Will he find someone more "feminine" than I (some GIs praised submissive Japanese and French women)? Will he miss his service buddies?(108) And perhaps most importantly, will he return a different man? As war further segregated the already divided worlds of the sexes, suspicion and distrust grew.

The American female experience during World War II was rich and varied. At work, women encountered new and unexpected opportunities and exerted greater power. Yet their movement forward occurred suddenly, threatened to be temporary, and met resistance. At the same time, the exodus of GIs changed the constellation of family power, rendering women more powerful, yet lonely and overburdened. Between the young of both sexes, the war erected a wall of alienation and mistrust. As women moved into the postwar era, their emotions were very likely to have been complicated and contradictory.

DEMOBILIZATION: THE DEMISE OF ROSIE THE RIVETER

Despite the dominant ideology of temporary, patriotic war work, historical evidence suggests that women were, nonetheless, significantly affected by their war experience, particularly their success in previously male sectors of labor. Whereas polls taken in 1941 indicate that 95 percent of new female workers expected to leave in peacetime(109), surveys taken near the war's end tell quite a different story. The Women's Bureau interviewed over 13,000 female workers in ten major defense centers about their postwar plans. This 1944 study included all types of workers, except domestics, and examined women's motivations for working, as well as employment histories. Close to 75 percent of the women surveyed indicated that they hoped to continue their employment in peacetime.(110) The highest proportion of those wishing to remain employed were minority (94 percent) and older women (81 percent), as well as those already working in 1941.(111) Approximately 75 percent of ex-students and 50 percent of prewar homemakers planned continued postwar employment; 70-75 percent of women aged 21-44 wished to remain on the job. These statistics reflected the fact that the role of working woman was most easily adopted either, when it was of financial necessity, or least conflicted with the maternal role. Yet, the fact that 50 percent of the prewar homemakers (most of whom were probably mothers) wanted to keep working (despite the lack of strong social support) testified to the fact that the experience of waged labor did heighten female aspirations. In addition, approximately 90 percent of those wishing to keep working, wanted not simply a job, but their wartime jobs. They had encroached on male territory and wanted to stay.

Meanwhile, popular attitudes had shifted, but not radically. Most Americans still saw outside employment as secondary to woman's primary duty: her family. In a Fortune survey (1946), for example, most Americans accepted female labor force participation if it did not conflict significantly with wifely or maternal duties.(112)

An enduring traditionalism reflected itself as America demobilized. Despite the clear preference of many female defense workers to remain on the job, their wishes went largely unheeded.

Leaders of government and industry reacted in conflicting and ambivalent ways to the future of Rosie and her sisters. Eleven million veterans were returning; factories and bureaucracies were slowing production. The economy had not been "normal" since 1929 and many feared a postwar depression.

In American society at large, the view that all veterans should return to full-time jobs was never questioned. Where individuals, as well as government and industry, differed was in the implication of reconversion for women. Some government agencies, such as WAC, supported economic planning for full employment, continued growth in the female labor force, and the maintenance and development of community services. However, the dominant ideology was that women, although to be commended, should "step down" for returning soldiers. "Stepping down" implied a return to one of two "female spheres": the home or the expanding clerical and service sector. The Brookings Institute argued that female demobilization would create few problems since few women would wish a long-term identification as workers anyway! Many labor leaders supported seniority practices automatically favoring the returning vet over his wartime (usually female) replacement. Cultural pressures, particularly from the popular media, encouraged women to "step aside." Their maternal role, they were told, was in jeopardy; rising delinquency rates were held up as a warning to working mothers. Mothering was stressed as central for postwar women, and central not only for children. The returning veteran, with physical and emotional scars, sorely needed attention. Social stability, in this framework, was not to be sacrificed to the readjustment crises of veterans; women would ease America back to normalcy. Ma Joad had helped pull us through in the Depression – why not again?

In the first 6 months after the war, as 11 million vets came home, production was cut in half and the ranks of the jobless rose to 2.7 million.(113) It comes as no surprise that women comprised the majority of the unemployed. The number of women who quit jobs or were fired during demobilization rose to 4 million. The female labor force declined rapidly in the immediate postwar period, from 19.5 to about 15.5 million, approximately the prewar figure.(114) The Selective Service Act of 1940, as well as prevailing stereotypes, provided the legal and cultural mechanisms for female demobilization. As Hattaway (1976) has noted,

> Women found that their jobs were in jeopardy if they had replaced a man or woman who had entered the armed forces; had been employed to meet emergency conditions produced by the war; if they had changed jobs since the war began; if they had seniority status less than or equal to a male fellow employee; if they had reached the age set by their employer as an employment deadline in their field; or if they had an employed husband.(115)

What skeletal community services existed were abolished, making the double day in the context of a stressful postwar adjustment particularly difficult. Lanham aid ended March, 1946, and all state assistance to day care was cut by November 1, 1948. By 1947, the New York World Telegram red-baited public childcare as a plot against the family concocted by Communist social workers. McCarthyism stood waiting in the wings. National admiration for patriotic wartime Rosies quickly turned to scorn for postwar working women who were depicted as "neglecting families" and/or "emasculating husbands." For homefront female "soldiers," there was no GI Bill.

Some demobilized women, however, viewed their unemployment as temporary; many unions promised female workers their jobs back with reconversion. Protests tended to occur when ex-Rosie the Riveters perceived these promises as false; some even filed individual union grievances.(116) Collective protests, however, like the picketing of the Ford Detroit Highland Motor Plant in December 1945, were rare. Although women's organizations had gained momentum during the war, they found themselves divided by class and race and unable to build a mass base. In the absence of a strong, vocal, unified, and coordinated women's movement, the voices of angry female ex-war workers went largely unheard.

The dominant culture supported female demobilization by stressing the importance of traditional femininity. Freudian psychology (particularly its popularized variety) provided a more sophisticated and scientific rationale for sexual inequality.(117)

According to Ferdinand Lundberg and Marynia Farnham in their classic work, <u>Modern Woman: The Lost Sex</u> (1947), for example, the "career woman" was far from a culture heroine. Rather, through "penis envy" and "masculine overcompensation," she violated the biological dictates of her nature: to nurture children and to be dependent on men.

In 1947 Christian Dior introduced the "New Look" in fashion, with padded brassieres, tiny waists, and long flowing skirts. Dior was fed up with "Amazons," as he put it, and eager to see feminine attributes. Many women objected to the new styles from Paris; women picketed Dior on his visit to Chicago. Yet the majority of women conformed to the new look.

Even those who subscribed to the feminine mystique, however, were not immune to criticism. "Momism," as popularly articulated in Philip Wylie's <u>Generation of Vipers</u> (1942), castigated "parasitic mothers," who, with little outside stimulation, fell prey to "smother-love," emotionally crippling children. And particularly, emasculating their sons. For many American women, the postwar years were riddled with strain and contradiction: "Damned if you do, and damned if you don't."

Even for those women who failed to embrace domesticity eagerly, the postwar transition was marked by increased anxiety and attention to personal life. Waiting was over; "life" again could resume. Sweethearts, husbands, brothers, and fathers returned to re-encounter fiancees, wives, sisters, and mothers whose reality had changed greatly during the war. Anxiety surrounded reunion; would American family life ever be the same? As Margaret Mead noted,

> In wartime, men and women get out of step and begin to wonder about each other. What will he be like after all those years in the Army? What will she be like after all those years alone at home? Will he be harder on the children and want them to toe the line too hard? After all that's all he's seen for years. Will she have learned to be so independent that she won't want to give up her job to make a home for me . . . what's happened to his morals? What's happened to her morals? I do hope he won't have changed too much. I hope she will look the same.(118)

The 1946 national divorce rate, highest in the world, reflected postwar confusion and disruption.

Despite its anxieties, however, postwar family life took on a new meaning for both sexes, symbolizing the calm following the storm. A child-centeredness reflected not only a new domesticity but a faith in the future. As Betty Friedan (1963) has noted,

> After the loneliness of the war and the unspeakableness of the bomb, against the frightening uncertainty, the cold

immensity of the changing world, women as well as men sought the comforting reality of home and children. In the foxholes, GIs had pinned up pictures of Betty Grable, but the songs they asked for were lullabies. And when they got out of the army, they were too old to go home to their mothers.

We are all vulnerable, homesick, lonely, frightened. A pent up hunger for marriage, home and children was felt simultaneously by several different generations, a hunger, which in the prosperity of postwar America, everyone could satisfy. The young GI made older than his years by the war, could meet his lonely need for love and mother by recreating his childhood home.(119)

The new cult of domesticity, however, did not drive all wives out of the labor force. The feminine mystique colored the female role at work as well, affecting women differently according to age, race, and class. Postwar women were encouraged to return to their "place" as "nurturers." However, that place now also included the expanding service (and especially clerical) sector of the labor force. The postwar re-employment of women occurred primarily in this "pink-collar ghetto." By late 1946, 80 percent of wartime women workers were still employed but only 40 percent occupied their wartime positions. In addition, despite skyrocketing postwar inflation, the average weekly wage for women plummeted – from $50 to $37. By 1950, half of all female workers and 66 percent of white women workers were employed as clericals.(120) As the percentage of women in skilled blue-collar jobs, business, and the professions declined, the proportion of women in the "white-collar mass" expanded.

The period of reconversion and postwar expansion necessitated an expanding service sector. And the work-place experience of American women in World War II provided ideological justification for female employment in that sector. Femininity and employment need no longer conflict, if employment occurred within the parameters of the dominant ideology of womanhood.

In the cultural climate of postwar America, antifeminism was bolstered by a growing conservatism and anti-Communism. However, the legacy of the war remained in the minds of women. As Susan M. Hartmann has noted (1982),

Historians who emphasize continuity should not ignore what it meant for a married woman to learn welding and earn unprecedented wages, for a black woman to exchange domestic service or field work for a factory job; for younger women to nurse soldiers under enemy fire or to train combat pilots; for a musician to have a chance at playing with a major symphony.(121)

Women experienced complex and contradictory changes in the spheres of work, family, and personal life from 1940 to 1950. Though the dominant ideology of the era contrasted images of overalled welders in wartime to those of aproned consumers in peacetime, the reality of American culture, its maincurrents and undercurrents, has proven far more complex. In the next three chapters, as we analyze top-grossing women's films we will explore these themes in more detail.

NOTES

(1)   The demographics of the female population during the war are cited at length in D'Ann Campbell, "Wives, Workers and Womanhood: America during World War II" (unpublished Ph.D. dissertation, University of North Carolina, 1979), Chapter 1. Also see Susan M. Hartmann, The Home Front and Beyond: American Women In the 1940s (Boston: G.K. Hall, 1982).

(2)   John Steinbeck, The Grapes of Wrath (New York: Viking, 1964), p. 64.

(3)   See Filene, Him/Her Self, p. 167.

(4)   Kymberly Hattaway, "Did Rosie the Riveter Give Up Her Job?" Work, Family and Social Change: University of Michigan Papers in Women's Studies (1976): 92.

(5)   See Hartmann, The Home Front and Beyond, especially Chapter 3.

(6)   Ibid.

(7)   William Chafe, The American Woman: Her Changing Social, Economic and Political Roles 1920-1970 (New York: Oxford, 1972), p. 136.

(8)   The history of women workers in the U.S. during World War II raises a significant question beyond the scope of this narrative: Are women a reserve army of labor, in the classical Marxian sense? Clearly women war workers performed an important function for capitalists as a malleable labor force hired in time of need, demobilized in peacetime. Whether or not, in other senses, they functioned as a "reserve army" is questionable. Did they discipline other workers because they often worked for less? Was their economic marginality a grim spectre of possible poverty for the rest of the working class? (Since most women lived in families of more than one earner, the latter is dubious.) Was World War II, as Chafe asserted, a watershed, integrating women as a permanent rather than temporary sector of labor, thus ending their reserve army status? Or do women now, despite the fact that they are currently over 43 percent of the labor force, still embody aspects of the reserve army? See articles in The Political Economy of Women, Review of Radical Political Economics 4, 3 (July 1972), for further discussion.

(9)   During periods not characterized by a labor power crisis such as World War II, the "dual" or segregated labor market (by race, sex) had been advantageous to capitalists as it limited applicants for more highly paid and skilled positions, while creating a massive pool of unskilled or semiskilled labor for lower paid and less socially desirable jobs. Taken together, sexual and racial stereotyping, educational tracking, and overt discrimination have maintained a system in which white males have competed for more highly paid and skilled white- and blue-collar jobs, whereas women applied for clerical, domestic, and other service work, and minorities found easiest acceptance in the world of unskilled blue-collar labor. During the war the segregated labor market threatened successful defense production, since minorities and women would have to move out of their "assigned" slots to replace GIs.

See Sonya Michel, "Contradictions of Privatization: American Families During World War II," paper presented at the Society for Study of Social Problems, August 1980, for a more detailed discussion of the tensions between patriarchy and capitalism in this period. Also see Ruth Milkman, "Organizing the Sexual Division of Labor: Historical Perspectives on 'Women's Work' and the American Labor Movement," Socialist Review, No. 49, 10 (January-February 1980): 95-150, for a further discussion of the historical development of 'women's work' in the labor force, the influence of trade unions, and labor segmentation theory. Milkman asserts that labor market segmentation is a process whose historical development has been conditioned by the strategies of both capital and labor.

(10)   "Get A War Job" is the name of a specific 1942-1943 government campaign. See Eleanor Straub, "The Impact of World War II on Sex Roles: Women in the Civilian Labor Force," paper presented at the National Archives' 1976 Conference on Women's History (1976): p. 8.

(11)   This is not to suggest that ideology and economy marched in lock-step in this or any other historical period. However, it is important to assert that the climate of wartime exerted considerable pressure on the mass media to respond to the cry for patriotism as well as stifle the overt criticism of the government. Criticism of the war effort, hence, was often channeled into less obvious and more oblique cultural manifestations (e.g., film noir, popular in the latter part of the war).

(12)   See Sonya Michel, "The Reproduction of Privatization: American Women, the Family and Professionals During World War II," paper presented at the Berkshire Conference on the History of Women, June 1981, for a more detailed discussion of the relationship between these factions in the childcare debate.

(13)   Straub, "The Impact of World War II on Sex Roles," p. 15. Also see Leila J. Rupp, Mobilizing Women for War: German and American Propaganda, 1939-1945 (Princeton: Princeton University Press, 1978).

(14)   Ibid., p. 10.
(15)   Eve Lapin, "Mothers in Overalls," in America's Working Women, ed. by Rosalyn Baxandall, Linda Gordon, and Susan Reverby (New York: Random House, 1976), p. 284.
(16)   Leila J. Rupp, Mobilizing Women for War, has contradicted the popular view that the U.S. government ideology regarding women was radically more egalitarian than that of Germany.
(17)   Straub, pp. 17-18.
(18)   "Pink collar workers" is a term coined by Louise Kapp Howe in Pink Collar Workers (New York: Avon, 1977). The term describes the occupational world of service work (domestic and clerical) a primarily female universe or ghetto in which job duties mirror those of the homemaker. Low pay, low rates of unionization, and slim chances for advancement entrap "pink-collar" workers.
(19)   Mary Anderson, quoted in Chafe, The American Woman, p. 137.
(20)   Campbell, "Wives, Workers and Womanhood," op. cit. p. 10. This figure must be analyzed carefully as a significant proportion of the 14 percent who were students were probably prospective home-makers as well. For these young women, who potentially experienced the greatest life disruptions when male partners were drafted, war work may have provided an unexpected step in the life cycle. Interrupting a school-marriage transition, war work may have created an intermediate stage of independence for some young women with long-ranging effects.
(21)   Ibid., p. 17.
(22)   Ibid., p. 18.
(23)   Data revealing the exact proportion of wartime mothers working outside the home are not currently available. A Women's Bureau survey of major defense centers showed that 20 percent of all employed women had children under 14. Another 1943 estimate reported that 20 percent of all working women were mothers of children under 18, and 12 percent of children under 6. Mothers of preschoolers increased their labor-force participation from 9 percent in 1940 to 12 percent in 1944 and 1946, an increase of one third. For further discussion of the difficulty in estimating the total number and proportion of working mothers, see Campbell, op. cit., Chapter 1, "Women Numbered and Armed: The Demographics of the Bloodless War."
(24)   Ruth Milkman, "Women's Work and Economic Crisis: Some Lessons of the Great Depression," Review of Radical Political Economics, 8, 1 (Spring 1976): 86; also see Milkman, "Organizing the Sexual Division of Labor," Socialist Review 49, 10 (January-February 1980): 128.
(25)   Verne Bradley, "Women at Work," National Geographic 86, no. 2 (1943): 101.
(26)   Barbara Deckard, The Women's Movement: Political, Socioeconomic and Psychological Issues (New York: Harper and Row, 1975), p. 302.

(27)   Donald I. Rogers, Since You Went Away (New Rochelle, N.Y.: Arlington House, 1973), p. 39.

(28)   Campbell, "Wives, Workers and Womanhood," pp. 53-54.

(29)   Jessica Mitford, A Fine Old Conflict (New York: Random House, 1956), p. 28.

(30)   Campbell, "Wives, Workers and Womanhood," pp. 62, 66.

(31)   Numerous research studies have asserted that labor-force participation translates into increased familial power for working women. Rooted in the "resource theory" of familial power, this research has asserted that the more socially valued resources (like money) one brings into the family, the more power one attains. Economic resources translate more easily into power than noneconomic assets (like housework skills). See Lois W. Hoffman and F. Ivan Nye (eds.), Working Mothers (San Francisco: Jossey-Bass, 1974), esp. Stephen J. Bahr, "Effects on Family Power and Division of Labor in the Family"; also see Stephen J. Bahr, "Comment on the Study of Family Power Structures: A Review, 1960-69," Journal of Marriage and the Family 34 (1972): 239-43. Lillian Breslow Rubin, Worlds of Pain (New York: Basic, 1976) has aptly commented that resource theory is often based on the assumption that housework is less important than wage labor. Rubin's point is well taken. However, one may assert that paid employment "counts for more" in our society than homemaking without asserting that it should. During World War II, the issue of power in the family is further conditioned by: (a) the assumption of work by some women for primarily patriotic reasons; (b) the absence of many men from the homefront. The second point will be elaborated further as we discuss home and family.

(32)   Virginia S. Wilkinson, "From Housewife to Shipfitter," Harper's, 187: 331.

(33)   Mary Danvouris, quoted in Roy Hoopes, Americans Remember: The Home Front (New York: Hawthorn, 1977).

(34)   Mabel Gerken, Ladies in Pants: A Homefront Diary (New York: Exposition Press, 1949), pp. 17-18.

(35)   See Agnes E. Meyer, Journey through Chaos: America's Home Front (New York: Harcourt Brace, 1944), especially pp. 53-54. Meyer visited over 25 American defense centers to gain a broad picture of homefront life. This book is a revised collection of articles originally published in serial form in the Washington Post. Meyer feared that moral and familial disintegration loomed on the horizon. Wartime migration, working mothers, rapid social mobility and family separation all contributed to the chaos she ascribed to wartime life in the U.S. Meyer advocated a strong childcare policy and urged Americans to repair the unraveling moral and social fabric. Although her perspective is somewhat conservative, her descriptions of wartime cities are compelling and useful to social historians.

(36)   Campbell, "Wives, Workers and Womanhood," p. 85.

(37)   See Sheila Tobias and Lisa Anderson, "What Really Happened to Rosie the Riveter: Demobilization and the Female Labor Force, 1944-47" (N.Y.: MSS Modular Publications, 1974) and "New Views of Rosie the Riveter," unpublished manuscript, 1975. These authors have challenged the bias of feminists who focus on upper and middle-class women, while ignoring their working-class, immigrant, and minority sisters.

(38)   Chafe, The American Woman, p. 142.

(39)   Campbell, "Wives, Workers and Womanhood," pp. 73-74.

(40)   Celia Sapersteen Yanish, quoted in Miriam Frank, Marilyn Ziebarth, and Connie Field, The Life and Times of Rosie the Riveter: The Story of Three Million Working Women During World War II (Emeryville, Ca: Clarity Educational Productions, 1982), p. 24. Also see Augusta Clawson, "Shipyard Diary of a Woman Welder," quoted in Baxandall, et al., op. cit., p. 289. Clawson's 1944 book Shipyard Diary of a Woman Welder (New York: Penguin, 1944) is one of a handful of personal accounts written by female war workers. Among the others are Nell Giles' Punch In Susie: A Woman's War Factory Diary (New York: Harper, 1943); Josephine von Miklos' I Took a War Job (1943); Ann Pendleton's Hit the Rivet, Sister; Mabel Gerken's Ladies in Pants: A Homefront Diary (New York: Exposition Press, 1949).

These works share a common perspective, and present similar problems for the social historian. They are not written by average women. Rather, each was undertaken with a patriotic purpose: to help persuade more women to work in defense. And each author stepped down from a middle or upper-middle-class status to help "save democracy" and write about war work. Augusta Clawson was a white-collar federal employee who became a welder specifically to write a book to inspire other women to do the same; von Miklos gave up the whirling social life of a countess; Giles, a Boston Globe reporter, spent only 8 weeks as a machinist to "tell the true story" of women's war work. Giles' book is the most useful yet it, too, exudes a romantic gloss. These works are revealing in two ways. They give a picture of what defense work was like for middle-class women who may have otherwise scorned factory work in peacetime. And they portray the largely female world of the defense plant, albeit somewhat sentimentally. Taken together with other primary and secondary sources, however, these accounts shed light on the female experience in wartime.

(41)   Ruth Wolf, quoted in Frank, et al., p. 27.

(42)   Clawson, op. cit., p. 290.

(43)   Jeane Westin, Making Do: How Woman Survived the Thirties (Chicago: Follett, 1976), p. 147. Leaving aside psychological motive, Damon's decision was probably conditioned by several factors. Firstly, her age probably lessened her value on the sexual market. And V-girls, young women who considered it their patriotic duty to satisfy GIs sexually, economically undercut prostitutes.

Furthermore, the V-girl scandal fueled a massive campaign against prostitution as a carrier of both moral decay and venereal disease. The May Act of 1941 enabled localities to close brothels; by 1944 over 700 cities had closed "red-light districts." See Richard Polenberg, War and Society (New York: Lippincott, 1972). Also see Meyer, Journey through Chaos.

(44)   See Chafe, The American Woman, p. 143.

(45)   The wartime migration of blacks and their increased incorporation into the industrial workforce set the stage for the historical events of the next 25 years. One might interpret this experience as both heightening contradictions and raising expectations. The Civil Rights and Black Power movements may be seen as the logical outcome. See Richard Polenberg, War and Society, especially Chapter 4, "The Struggle for Equal Rights"; see Chafe, Women and Equality (New York: Oxford, 1978), for a discussion of the possible links between World War II and black and women's liberation.

(46)   Baxandall, et al., America's Working Women, p. 281. This wage comparison represents the multiple influence of overt discrimination, educational tracking, interrupted female work histories, unequal experience, unequal representation in unions, and occupational segregation.

(47)   See Sheila Tropp Lichtman, "Women At Work, 1941-45, Wartime Employment in the San Francisco Bay Area" (Ph.D. dissertation, University of California-Davis, 1980).

(48)   These arguments are elaborated in Campbell, op. cit., especially pp. 136-144. I have reproduced them here in abbreviated fashion to demonstrate the "grasping at straws" characteristic of threatened male unionists.

(49)   Campbell, op. cit., pp. 150-151.

(50)   Chafe, The American Woman, p. 152.

(51)   Donald A. Laird, with the assistance of Eleanor C. Laird, The Psychology of Supervising the Working Woman (New York: McGraw-Hill, 1942), p. 140.

(52)   Campbell, op. cit., has documented several instances of women fighting back against workplace sexual harassment. One woman asserted, "Oh, when a fellow whistles at me, I whistle right back at him. He doesn't know what to do next." (p. 101) At other worksites, women held "indignation meetings" and whistled and ogled as a group when male workers walked by. Obviously, these creative strategies were only possible if a sizable group of women worked together.

(53)   Josephine von Miklos, I Took a War Job (New York: Simon and Schuster, 1943), p. 131.

(54)   Wilkinson, "From Housewife to Shipfitter," p. 336. Male defense workers may have been particularly susceptible to feeling "demasculinized" since they were often the recipients of military exemptions and deferments. Masculine overcompensation may have

been a defense mechanism for feelings that women (and other men) viewed them as "slackers," "cowards" or "weaklings."

(55)   See Winifred Raushenbush, How to Dress in Wartime (New York: Coward-McCann, 1942).

(56)   See Mary Roth Walsh, "Doctors Wanted: No Women Need Apply:" Sexual Barriers in the Medical Profession, 1835-1975 (New Haven: Yale University Press, 1977).

(57)   Campbell, "Wives, Workers and Womanhood," p. 99.

(58)   Myra Moss, "The Use of Women as a Surplus Labor Force in World War II," paper presented at the North Central Sociological Association, May 1975, p. 26.

(59)   Alice Newcomer Baker, quoted in Hoopes, Americans Remember, p. 57.

(60)   See Rosabeth Moss Kanter, Men and Women of the Corporation (New York: Harper & Row, 1977) for an analysis of the impact of the lack of supportive networks for contemporary women workers.

(61)   The term working mother is problematic. It subtly implies that mothers who labor at home do not work, only wage labor counts. Hence, the slogan, "Every mother is a working mother" is quite on target, asserting the social value of housework. I use the term, however, because it is used colloquially to mean "a mother who also works outside her home."

(62)   Paul McNutt, quoted in Rosalyn Baxandall, "Who Shall Care for Our Children? The History and Development of Day Care in the United States," in Women: A Feminist Perspective, 2nd ed., ed. by Jo Freeman (Palo Alto: Mayfield, 1979), p. 291.

(63)   See Michel, "Contradictions of Privatization," p. 1.

(64)   Chafe, The American Woman, p. 159.

(65)   Campbell, "Wives, Workers and Womanhood," p. 68.

(66)   Ibid., p. 162.

(67)   Chafe, The American Woman, p. 166.

(68)   The Federal Security Agency, a grouping of federal social welfare agencies, included the Office of Education and the Children's Bureau. The FWA saw public nurseries as temporary, while the FSA viewed day care centers as a permanent feature of the American social welfare system. See Chafe, The American Woman, p. 168.

(69)   Ibid., p. 170.

(70)   Ibid., p. 162.

(71)   Michel, "Contradictions of Privatization," p. 3.

(72)   Chafe, The American Woman, pp. 170-171.

(73)   Baxandall, et al., America's Working Women, p. 291.

(74)   Personal interview with author.

(75)   Frank, et al., The Life and Times of Rosie the Riveter.

(76)   Karen Anderson, Wartime Women: Sex Roles, Family Relations and the Status of Women During World War II (Westport, Conn.: Greenwood Press, 1981), p. 94.

(77)   See Linda Gordon, Woman's Body, Woman's Right (New York: Grossman, 1976), p. 356. Also see Norman S. Hayner, "Women in a Changing World," Marriage and Family Living (Summer 1943) for a discussion of a study of wartime college-dating patterns. Dating was less formal and involved a wider circle (though smaller number) of potential male partners, including servicemen.

(78)   Nadina Kavinocky, M.D., "Medical Aspects of War Time Marriage," Marriage and Family Living (Spring 1944), p. 26.

(79)   Hartmann, The Home Front and Beyond, p. 180. Also see John D'Emilio, Sexual Politics/Sexual Communities (Chicago: University of Chicago Press, 1983).

(80)   See Anderson, Wartime Women, 137 ff.

(81)   See Hartmann, The Home Front and Beyond, p. 39.

(82)   U.S. Bureau of the Census, 1943, quoted in Marriage and Family Living, "News and Notes" (Winter, 1943), p. 21.

(83)   Grace Reeves, "The New Family in the Postwar World," Marriage and Family Living (Autumn 1945), p. 75.

(84)   Anderson, Wartime Women, and Campbell, "Wives, Workers, and Womanhood." Anderson's perspective emphasized the effects of social control on women, while Campbell's stressed the conservatism of women themselves.

(85)   See Anderson, p. 136.

(86)   Ibid., p. 102. Also see Hornell Hart and Henrietta Bowne, "Marriage and the Family," Social Forces 22 (December 1943), pp. 191-94.

(87)   Hartmann, The Home Front and Beyond, Chapter 9: "The Unshaken Claim of Family."

(88)   Max Lerner, in Marriage and Family Living (Spring 1944), p. 34.

(89)   This study included 67 service wives and 10 fiancees. The men have been away for periods ranging from two months to several years, serving in several branches of armed services and ranking from privates to captains. The length of marriage varied from eight months to several unions of over 15 years. About 50 percent of the wives worked outside the home, and about 50 percent were mothers. Duvall does not differentiate her sample by age, social class, race, religion, or regionality. See Evelyn Millis Duvall, "Loneliness and the Serviceman's Wife," Marriage and Family Living (Autumn 1945), p. 77.

(90)   Ibid.

(91)   Ibid., p. 78.

(92)   Ibid., p. 77. Duvall did not ask these women to rate their marriages as "happy" or "unhappy," so there is no way of knowing if the wives who weren't lonely were unhappily married. In their responses, however, there is no clear reference to unhappiness.

(93)   Evelyn Millis Duvall, "Marriage in War Time," Marriage and Family Living (Autumn 1942), p. 76.

(94)   Reuben Hill, "The Returning Father and His Family," Marriage and Family Living (Spring 1944), p. 32.

(95)   Ibid.

(96)   Maria Piers, "The Role of the Family in Preventing Delinquency," Marriage and Family Living 6 (Spring 1942), p. 26.

(97)   Chafe, the American Woman, p. 179.

(98)   Hill, "The Returning Father and His Family," p. 34.

(99)   Ibid., p. 33.

(100)   Hartmann, The Home Front and Beyond, p. 22.

(101)   See Joseph C. Goulden, The Best Years, 1945-50 (New York: Atheneum, 1976), especially Chapter 2, "Preparing for Ulysses."

(102)   Coleman R. Griffiths, "The Psychological Adjustments of Returned Servicemen and Their Families," Marriage and Family Living (Autumn 1944), p. 65-66.

(103)   Goulden, p. 38. See also Mead, "The Women and the War," in While You Were Gone, ed. Jack Goodman (New York: Simon and Schuster, 1946): pp. 274-289.

(104)   Ibid., p. 37.

(105)   Anderson, Wartime Women, p. 97.

(106)   Hill, "The Returning Father and His Family," pp. 31-32.

(107)   Dr. Howard Kitching, cited in Goulden, p. 43.

(108)   I have found no direct evidence for female fear of male homosexuality during the war. See John F. Cuber, "The College Youth Goes to War," Marriage and Family Living (Winter 1943), for a discussion of the alleged increase in male homosexuality in the military during World War II.

(109)   Joan Ellen Trey, "Women in the War Economy — World War II," Review of Radical Political Economics 4 (July 1972): 47.

(110)   "Postwar Plans of Women Workers," in Baxandall et al., America's Working Women, p. 310.

(111)   Obviously, as from previous discussion, these three categories (particularly those of "minority women" and "women employed before the war") overlap.

(112)   Chafe, The American Woman, p. 189. Also see Campbell, "Wives, Workers and Womanhood," for a discussion of wartime polls (Roper 35 and Roper 54) that revealed a persistence of traditional attitudes toward the roles of men and women.

(113)   Jane Humphries, "Women: Scapegoats and Safety Valves in the Great Depression," Review of Radical Political Economics 8, no. 1 (Spring 1972), p. 114.

(114)   Hattaway, "Did Rosie . . .?" p. 99.

(115)   Hattaway, "Did Rosie . . .?" p. 97.

(116)   Ibid., p. 180. See Tobias and Anderson, "New Views of Rosie the Riveter"; also see Julie Boddy, Separated and Unequal; interviews with Margaret Wright, Lola Weixel, et al., in The Life and Times of Rosie the Riveter, documentary film by Connie Field.

(117) While the relationship between Freudianism and feminism is a very complicated one, the effect of Freud (and particularly Freudian popularization) seems quite clear as an ideological buttress of the feminine mystique. However, this assertion does not imply that Freudian thought is, of its essence, antifeminist.

(118)   Mead, "The Women and the War," p. 274.
(119)   Friedan, The Feminine Mystique, p. 174.
(120)   Chafe, The American Woman, p. 183.
(121)   Hartmann, The Homefront and Beyond, p. 214.

Chapter 3

WOMAN FLOWS LIKE THE RIVER:
The Evolution of
the Maternal Drama
in the 1940s

Time was I had a tender heart,
But time hath proved its foe;
That tenderness did all depart,
And it is better so;
For if it tender did remain
How could I play my part,
That must so many young sustain?
Farewell the tender heart!

> "Maternal Love Triumphant," or "Song of the
> Virtuous Female Spider" (1932) by Ruth Pitter,
> in The World Split Open: Four Centuries of
> Women Poets in England and America, 1552-1950,
> edited by Louise Bernikow (New York:
> Random House, 1974) p. 172

"Boston liquor licensing board asks cafe proprietors to stop
serving liquor to women with babies in arms and discourage
baby carriage parking outside saloons."

> New York Times, March 30, 1944, 24:6

"She'll be so nice to come home to"

> caption under Arthur Sasse's 1944 photograph
> of a GI mother (cited in Culture and Commitment,
> 1929-1945, ed. by Warren Susman New York:
> Braziller, 1973 Figure 24b, Appendix)

89

Mother, Mama, Mom, Mommy — no other words sound so sacred and intimate. Spanning history and culture, no role has proved more central in defining womanhood than that of mother; the female sex has assumed (and been forced to assume) primary responsibility in rearing the young. From that persistent sociocultural fact stems the uniqueness of woman's experience — her joy, pain, anger, power, and possibility.(1) Mothering took on a different face as women flocked to offices and defense plants. And as wartime mothers found their roles to be more complex, exhausting, and autonomous, American society responded with confusion and backlash. Maternal dramas, loved by wartime women, reflected the dynamic of traditionalism and change — on screen and in society.

The maternal drama, with its cultural roots in women's fiction and radio soaps, emerged in the silent and early sound era in films like The Mothering Heart (1913), Sunrise (1927), and Stella Dallas (1937). Melodramatic in tone, featuring noble, sacrificial wives and mothers valiantly encountering crisis upon crisis, the maternal drama captured an audience of women by portraying conflicts at the heart of the feminine role. Christiane Viviani comments on the narrative excess of the maternal melodrama:

> Elements are juxtaposed, telescoped, multiplied, in order to maintain the pathos at an intense level, simultaneously creating both an outer layer, which seems unreal by virtue of its excessiveness, and an inner core, which calls upon a collective experience of real life.(2)

Stella Dallas, the tragi-comic maternal heroine of the 1937 film of the same name, became a household word. The maternal drama entered the world of women's language and culture.

As war rearranged the sexual landscape, Hollywood's performers and audience became increasingly female. The 1940s could be termed the decade of the maternal drama. Mary Astor, Claudette Colbert, Jane Darwell, Bette Davis, Irene Dunne, Greer Garson, Myrna Loy, Dorothy McGuire, and other stars portrayed women of valor who expressed power in a motherly fashion. The most popular type of women's film, the maternal drama celebrated the exercise of female power in the service of others — family, community, and nation. However, as American womanhood evolved, so too did the maternal drama.

MA JOAD: A DEPRESSION IDEAL FOR WARTIME WOMEN

Images of sacrificial, resourceful motherhood were not new to wartime America. The Great Depression had inspired the ideal of Ma Joad, head of the impoverished migrant clan in Steinbeck's classic of social protest, The Grapes of Wrath. On January 24, 1940,

John Ford's critically acclaimed 20th Century Fox screen adaptation opened at Manhattan's Rivoli Theatre.(3) Jane Darwell, in a masterful performance as Ma Joad, portrays the life force of the Okies, providing a quintessentially maternal model for American women on the brink of war.

Ma Joad is neither young nor traditionally attractive — in the codes of femininity popular in society or on screen. A plump, earthy, older woman, Ma wears plainly styled iron gray hair, drawn off her ample, moon-like peasant face. Rotund, graying, paying no homage to fashion, Ma is hardly an image to step off the pages of a women's magazine. Yet cinematographer Toland evokes her beauty, in ways that cannot fail to challenge dominant aesthetic ideals. In the third sequence, as the family is leaving dusty Oklahoma for the promise of California, Ma fondly reminisces, leafing through postcards, trying on old jewelry, saying goodbye to her past. One of Toland's finest shots is of Ma in close-up, gazing in a mirror, holding to her ears the jewels of her youth. Ma's face fills the frame, gently painted in soft focus. Her forehead is obscured, as light shines on the optimism of her upturned mouth. Ma Joad's life, symbolized by her shadowed face, may be more than half over, yet her beauty and courage endure. Ma is awesomely beautiful, yet not in the naive or adorned manner of youth. Ma possesses a beauty of epic, almost religious quality, born of experience and simplicity, interconnected to the flow and richness of the earth and seasons.(4)

Ma Joad

As Ma Joad's determined face fills the frame, so is her character central to the Okie epic. On the Joads' journey, they encounter repeated misfortune: the deaths of the grandparents, the desertion of son-in-law Connie (Eddie Quillan), exploitation at Hooverville, and the stillbirth of Rosasharn's (Dorris Bowdon's) child. Despite this exhausting round of crises, Ma perseveres; she is the lifeblood of the family. And, like her counterpart Mother York in the top-grossing Sergeant York (1941), Ma Joad has earned the respect of her community as well. As Ma Joad, the eternal populist, says in her final monologue, "We're the people and we go on forever."(5)

Ma Joad however, is no feminist. She did not fight to displace Pa (Russell Simpson) and become a matriarch. Nor does she consider women equal to men in the family or society; Ma's rule is born of necessity. Pa, unemployed and broken, can no longer lead; Ma sees no other choice than to assume the reins of power. Ma is contradictory, however. Her final monologue is one of female moral and emotional superiority:

> Man – he lives in jerks – baby born and a man dies, and that's a jerk – gets a farm and loses a farm and that's a jerk – Woman, it's all one flow, like a stream, little eddies, little waterfalls, but the river, it goes right on. Woman looks at it like that – we ain't gonna die out. People is going on – changing a little, maybe, but going right on.

For Ma, women are the backbone of society. Like a rolling river, they can ride out misfortune, illness, and hard times, only to rise again. The source of woman's resilience lies in her reproductive capacity and its closeness to nature, its ebbs and tides, its eternal persistence. In contrast, men are prone to emotional upset from the "jerks" of life; they lack the fortitude of femininity. Broken, jobless husbands, the Pa Joads of the world, must rely on their wives in crisis. And their impetuous young sons, the Tom Joads (Henry Fonda), who struggle for freedom and dignity, draw their lifeblood from the serene strength of their mothers.

As a farm woman at the heart and center of her family, Ma dramatizes that woman's work is neither easier nor less important than that of men. Motherhood and maturity enhance rather than diminish her power. Ma's beauty flows from age, experience, and strength, a clear digression from the ideal of womanly beauty as youth, innocence, and powerlessness. Furthermore, Ma possesses an ethnic aura that an immigrant woman might easily identify with.(6)

Ma's power, however, proved acceptable in 1940 because it grew of necessity, not struggle, and confined itself to the family. Furthermore, motherhood totally eclipses Ma Joad's individuality and sexuality. The audience never even learns Mrs. Joad's first name. Ma's character also smacks of political as well as sexual conservatism. As a populist symbol, Ma Joad, underscored by the

"Red River Valley" theme, is an "enduring peasant," a mythic survivor. As Roffman and Purdy (1981) have noted, Ma portrays the populism of a bygone rural era. Tom, although he is inspired by his mother, symbolizes a radicalism and class consciousness that conflicts with her enduring stoicism.

> Ma . . . is Ford's populist heroine, fighting against the onslaught of progress. . . . Every time, anger and frustration are filtered through Tom, Ma is always on hand to placate his rage and thus subtly undermine the social criticism. To his rebellious "there comes a time when a man gets mad . . . ," she answers with "You got to keep clear, Tom. The Fambly's breaking up. You got to keep clear."(7)

Teenage Rosasharn mirrors her mother. Through the power of maternity (although her baby is stillborn), she is able to nurture and guide her people. (In the novel's last scene, for example, she nurses a starving vagrant.)

The sense of woman's nature in The Grapes of Wrath is strong and supportive, yet static and conservative. Inklings appear throughout the film to suggest that Ma is unhappy as matriarch. She and Pa seem to have enjoyed better times, and there are clues to imply that she might prefer him to lead. Yet Pa simply cannot. Like the dusty taste of the roads and the hunger gnawing in their bellies, the Joads' sex-role reversal is a hardship born of poverty and despair. Perhaps, if she could, Ma would rather move backstage, leaving the reins of leadership of the family to Pa.(8)

Ma Joad is a complex character, expressing simultaneously power and reluctance, epitomizing the contradictions within popular ideologies of femininity and the female experience itself. As men left for war and women and children migrated across America, Ma Joad endured as a powerful symbol etched in the minds of women. And, as the war progressed and female power — at home and work — increased, Hollywood continued to produce films evoking Ma's imagery as well as challenging the reluctance and tenuousness of her power.

MRS. MINIVER: COMING OF AGE IN WARTIME

Greer Garson, in William Wyler's MGM production of Mrs. Miniver (1942), was perfectly cast as a fortyish British suburban homemaker whose comfortable complacency is shattered by the reality of war. Garson's Oscar-winning performance conveys beautifully a middle-class orderliness and polite composure; Mrs. Miniver is attractive, sensual, yet distinctly ordinary. An architect's wife and mother of three, she is a British Junior Leaguer, content in a world of tea parties and charity bazaars.

Our first visual introduction to the heroine occurs as the camera cranes down to capture her frantically running, loaded with shopping bags, down a busy city street. She barely makes her bus, and alights at a hat shop to make a rather expensive purchase: "I know it's foolish and extravagant and I don't know what my husband will have to say but I've got to have it." Attractively coiffed and suited, she is pretty, but frivolous.

Yet her comfortable homefront soon turns to battlefront, as husband Clem (Walter Pidgeon) becomes an air warden, oldest son Vin (Richard Ney) joins the air force, and bombs explode near her well-manicured lawn. Unlike Ma Joad, however, Mrs. Miniver is not static or superhuman. Rather, she must rise to the challenge. As England goes to war, Mrs. Miniver comes of age.

The pacing of Mrs. Miniver is central to the production of filmic meaning. The first sequences dramatize trivial incidents within the relaxed pace of an English village — Kay purchases a hat and Clem buys a car that neither can quite afford, Lady Beldon (Dame May Whitty) sponsors a rose-growing contest, Vin returns from Oxford with a "social conscience." Early on, the film compares Kay Miniver to the common people. The trainman, Mr. Ballard (Henry Travers), has grown a rose to enter the Beldon competition (a rather rebellious act for a commoner to compete with an aristocrat). As Kay Miniver returns home, Ballard shows her his rose; he's named it "The Mrs. Miniver." The film cuts between close-ups of Kay's delighted face and the lovely rose. The intended identification is clear: between the hardy beauty of the flower and that of its namesake, symbol of the common people.

In the later sequences, the mood and pace of the film change. The war, literally, comes home, as a wounded Nazi pilot (Helmut Dantine) enters Kay Miniver's kitchen, ordering her to feed him. He is about as old as Vin; her maternality encourages her to nurture him. Yet she cannot. His very presence threatens the existence of herself, her family, and her country. As he collapses, Mrs. Miniver disarms him and calls the police.

A series of incidents occur to test Kay Miniver: an over-zealous Vin joins the RAF, bombs hit her home and Vin's bride, Carol (Teresa Wright) is killed. Throughout these crises, Mrs. Miniver manages to sustain herself and her family. The film visually portrays Kay Miniver, like Ma Joad, as the center of the family, and the family in turn as the foundation of society:

In the course of a brutal air raid Wyler remains in the shelter with the Minivers; we hear but don't see the falling bombs and the destruction they cause . . . the tight framing, short pans and tilts, and low shooting angles Wyler employs . . . force us to share both the togetherness and the claustrophobia of shelter existence. Here and throughout Mrs. Miniver the emotional world, the rituals of family and societal life receive primary emphasis.(9)

In the sequence depicting the evacuation of Dunkirk, family ties form the basis of community bonds in the Allied war effort. Wyler employs models, lap dissolves, glass shots, and matte photography to create a series of images depicting small boats (like Clem's) progressing through larger and larger fleets and culminating in a massive flotilla. The familial and community world expands to form the nation.

By the last scene, Mrs. Miniver has become a symbol of the homefront, mother of the Allied cause. Yet she is not just "worth fighting for"; she, too, is a soldier in the fight against Fascism. Mrs. Miniver has come a long way from the silly woman in the hat shop. And for that reason, this film, narrative of her transformation, bears her name.

As Bosley Crowther contended, "Greer Garson . . . as Mrs. Miniver glows with compassion and womanly strength."(10) Yet, Mrs. Miniver, like Ma Joad, is no feminist. Her strength is mobilized out of necessity and always for others. Furthermore, she seems content to return to the status quo in peacetime. Indeed, the status quo — her mundanely comfortable life — is what she has fought for. Yet, in the process, she has changed, in ways she may never have imagined. As a woman in mid-life "coming of age," Mrs. Miniver challenges static and ahistorical notions of woman as the "weaker sex" or "junior partner."

For female audiences, Mrs. Miniver, like Ma Joad, linked an enduring traditionalism with an assurance that women were as courageous as men, and as severely affected by the ravages of war. World War II is cast in feminine terms, validating the homefront role of American women, particularly homemakers.

> Kay Miniver's portrait . . . struck a nice balance between the rural and urban heroines who vied for domination in American popular thought before the outbreak of World War II. She was a middle class, suburban woman, happily and competently playing a traditional role, but at the same time . . . enormously resourceful.(11)

Mrs. Miniver, drawing in overflow matinee crowds, grossing over six million dollars and winning six Academy Awards (Best Picture, Best Director, Best Actress and Supporting Actress, Best Screenplay, Best Black and White Cinematography) in 1942, might be considered the first major "women's war film."

WATCH ON THE RHINE: A NOT SO "TENDER COMRADE"

Sara Muller (Bette Davis) in Herman Shumlin's Warners production of Lillian Hellman's play, Watch on the Rhine (1943), is also a woman in mid-life who meets the challenge of Fascism.(12) The 41-

year-old daughter of a late Supreme Court Justice, Sara left her wealthy American family 17 years ago to marry a leading German anti-Fascist, Kurt Muller (Paul Lukas, in an Oscar-winning performance). Because of the underground nature of her husband's activities, Sara has evaded telling her family of his work, referring to Kurt simply as an "engineer." Since the Mullers were an ocean away, the truth was never necessary. However, Kurt falls ill and Europe grows dangerous. As the film opens, in the late 1930s, the Mullers and their children (two sons and a daughter) seek temporary refuge with Fanny (Lucile Watson) and David Farrelly (Donald Woods), Sara's widowed mother and brother in suburban Washington, D.C.

The worlds of Fanny Farrelly and Sara Muller are separated by more than the Atlantic. Our first image of Fanny is one of plump elegance. Sixtyish Fanny, rotund and ruffled, buzzes excitedly about her palatial home, summoning servants, and preparing for Sara's return. At the same time, the impoverished Mullers enter the United States through Mexico and approach Washington by train. Sara is almost the opposite of her mother. Slim, serious looking, dressed in a shabby dress and coat, Sara Muller is far from a socialite. As mother and daughter meet for the first time in many years, the film juxtaposes their images in close up. Each must acknowledge the other, their current differences, their common past.

Watch on the Rhine, like Mrs. Miniver, is a drama of confrontation, between a naive affluence and the specter of war. America encounters Europe, in a mood reminiscent of Henry James. The Farrellys are the epitome of cocktail-party liberalism. When Kurt informs them that "I'm an anti-Fascist and to answer your question, no that does not pay well", Fanny replies ingenuously, "But we are all anti-Fascists." As the film progresses, she will learn the real meaning of that term. Another impoverished European, Romanian Count Teck de Brancovis (George Coulouris), and his wife Marthe (Geraldine Fitzgerald), a family friend, have also taken refuge with the Farrellys. The audience learns (before the Farrellys) that Teck is a Nazi collaborator, eager to curry favor with high-level Fascists by revealing Kurt's whereabouts. As the Count's identity becomes clear, Sara confronts Fanny:

> Sara: It was careless of you to have a man like that in this house! . . . the world has changed, Mama and some of the people in it are dangerous. It's time you knew that!

Although Kurt is the more active partner, Sara articulates the primary moral and political messages of the film.

DeBrancovis finally attempts to blackmail Kurt and Muller is forced to kill him. The protected world of the Farrellys collapses, as they must take a stand. Fanny risks her security and protects Kurt so he can escape to Germany to continue his mission. Inspired by Sara's courage, Fanny declares: "It's a fine thing to have you for a daughter, Sara. I would like to have been like you." The Mullers' visit has permanently transformed the Farrellys. At the end of the film Fanny counsels David: "I understand very well. We will manage. I'm not put together with flour paste. And neither are you — I'm happy to learn."

The generational tables turn as Sara Muller (Bette Davis) serves as courageous role model to her mother Fanny Farrelly (Lucile Watson). Kurt Muller (Paul Lukas) looks on, in Herman Shumlin's Watch On the Rhine (1943).

As Kurt leaves (to face probable death), and her elder son, Joshua (Donald Buka) later decides to follow, Sara displays her bravery and commitment to freedom. She is a dedicated comrade willing to forego her own happiness to fight Fascism. Although Sara is not Kurt's equal, neither is she the "little wife," blindly supportive of barely understood "causes." Like her movie counterpart, Anna, in Hitler's Children (1943), Sara is a thoroughly dedicated and informed anti-Fascist with a commitment to human dignity that is as strong as that to her family.

Watch on the Rhine despite its "staginess," is a powerful cultural document of the Popular Front, that sector of Hollywood and American society (like Hellman and screenwriter Dashiel Hammett) who were leftist as well as anti-Fascist. Sara Muller is, thus, symbolic not only of wartime womanhood in general, but of women on the left, comrades yet not equals. The "woman question," as Browder put it, had not yet come to the fore. Yet neither were women in and around the Communist Party a "backward force," asserting the primacy of family over politics.

The strong feminine presence in Watch on the Rhine is hardly accidental. The inspiration for Muller's character (and, probably Sara's as well) was female: Hellman's friend Julia, a dedicated anti-Fascist, murdered by the Nazis:

> ... by 1938 I had been through the life and death of my friend, Julia, and had been to Spain during the Civil War and had been moved by men willing to die for what they believed in.
>
> I moved the play (Watch on the Rhine) to Washington, placed it in the house of a rich, liberal family who were about to meet their anti-Fascist son-in-law ... who had fought in Spain. He was, of course, a form of Julia.(13)

Yet the social climate of the time, as well as the left, prompted even an outspoken, independent female writer to create a male protagonist. It was not until 1977 that Julia would have her own film.

Sara Muller, however, Popular Front ideal, embodied power and commitment, yet in the service of family and human dignity, rather than for herself or her sisters. For female audiences, Sara inspired pride in womanly bravery. And for Communists and "fellow travelers," she symbolized the unequal yet vital and often underestimated role of women on the left.

SINCE YOU WENT AWAY: AN AMERICAN MRS. MINIVER

Claudette Colbert as Ann Hilton joined the ranks of Hollywood's valiant heroines-in-waiting in John Cromwell's lengthy and lavish 1944 United Artists adaptation of Margaret Wilder's homefront saga, Since You Went Away. The first image appearing on the screen is that of a large suburban home, with the following words superimposed upon the screen: "This is a story of the unconquerable fortress: The American Home ... 1943." As strains of "No Place Like Home" echo, the image dissolves to that of a window with a gold star in its center. This is the home of a GI. Yet Captain Timothy Hilton has gone to war. This is Mrs. Hilton's story.

Our first glimpse is of a woman alone, returning to her home with sadness and strength. Fortyish, furcoated Ann Hilton radiates a strong maternality suffused with softness and sensuality. As she walks around her house, after leaving Tim at the station, she mourns his absence. We enter her thoughts, as Ann sadly gazes at his pictures and other mementoes (narrating in voice-over):

> Ann: This is the moment I've dreaded . . . coming back to our house alone. . . . Darling, Darling, I've tried to understand, I've held myself together through all our goodbyes . . .
>
> I'll try to remember what you said — that this will be the greatest adventure we ever had, even though we had it separately.

Like Ma Joad, she gazes into the mirror, seeking solace in her past. In close-up, Ann looks in the mirror flanked on either side by a photo of her husband. Ann exclaims in voice-over dialogue with an absent Tim: "But I have no courage, Tim . . . You know I have no courage and I have no vision . . . and already I'm so very lonely." Her actions, however, belie her words. Amid her private reverie of doubt, teenage Jane Hilton (Jennifer Jones) and twelvish Brig (Bridget — Shirley Temple) arrive home. She summons her courage to greet her daughters; the distraught wife becomes the resilient mother.

The first scene presents a dichotomy between the private and public persona of Ann Hilton. Privately, she is sad, afraid, and incomplete; publicly she is cheerful, brave, and resilient. As the narrative unfolds, her public and private selves grow closer together, as both Ann and her daughters come of age. And the absent father, though he remains vital to their lives, recedes into the background of the narrative.

The Hilton women begin physically and emotionally to fill the space left by Tim's absence. Ann moves out of her bedroom, Brig and Jane "double up," their old maid Fidelia (Hattie McDaniel) moves back, and the family rents a room to a gruff-but-gentle retired colonel (Monte Wooley, in a classic Oscar-nominated performance). The tearful woman of the first scene has become (at least outwardly) a cheerful and competent homemaker.

Ann's life grows more complex as Tony Willett (Joseph Cotten), a family friend, comes to visit. Ann meets Tony as she's having a drink with gossipy divorcée Emily Hawkins (Agnes Moorhead) at the Paradise Cocktail Lounge (scene of several interesting war vignettes). As the two women discuss the strains of war, a pair of male hands slips over Ann's eyes. The audience (and Ann) wonders, "Is it Tim?" As Ann turns around, a roguish Tony exclaims, "Tim! Does it always have to be Tim?" Foreshadowed by this scene, sexual attraction and ambiguity surround Ann and Tony's relationship. Tony, on leave from the service, stays with the Hiltons. He and Ann spend a lot of time together. As they attend a dance in a crowded converted aircraft hanger, the band plays "Together," Ann and Tim's song. A saddened Ann clasps Tony, closes her eyes and whispers "Tim." As the couple drive home together, they are clearly tempted — by the full moon, their mutual loneliness and attraction.

(close-up on Tony)

Tony: I was just thinking how much fun it would be . . . to be a heavy, synthetic rubber heel

Ann: It would be synthetic, Tony.

Tony can only fill Tim's space in fantasy.

Ann Hilton is more overtly sexual than Kay Miniver, Sara Muller, or Ma Joad. However, subscribing to both the code and dominant American values, Ann resists temptation, remaining the ideal war wife, even when Tim becomes missing in action. Yet her sexuality is acknowledged and affirmed.

The Hilton women (Claudette Colbert, Jennifer Jones, Shirley Temple) receive "bad news" with courage in John Cromwell's Since You Went Away (1944).

The major subplot focuses on the maturing of Jane Hilton. Jane is first depicted as a flighty mooning adolescent; Jennifer Jones, fresh from her role as the wide-eyed saint in Song of Bernadette (1943), succeeds in evoking audience annoyance at Jane's immaturity. However, as time progresses, Jane grows more like Ann as she falls in love with Smollett's shy grandson, Bill (Robert Walker) and convinces her mother to let her become a nurse's aide at a V.A. hospital. The mooning teenager becomes a committed, serious young woman; the camera captures a uniformed Jane (in medium shot) serving ice cream to rows of legless and paralyzed veterans.

Jane's courage, like Mrs. Miniver's, is put to the test when she learns that her fiancé, Bill, died in action at Salerno. Her mother counsels her:

Ann: Jane, I'm terribly proud of the way you've grown up. . . . I like to think that you have that kind of courage, too.

Jane channels her grief into hospital work. And as she matures, she becomes unafraid to defend her beliefs. In one of the film's most compelling scenes, Jane confronts Emily Hawkins:

Emily: Nurse's aide! What a revolting idea for an unmarried girl of your age! Well, our whole code of living seems to be ignored these days. But possibly, it's none of my business.

Tony: That's right, Mrs. Hawkins — it is none of your business.

Emily: I meant no offense to you, Jane. I just feel that well brought up young girls shouldn't have such intimate contact with all sorts of . . .

Jane: (emphatically) All sorts of boys who've lost their arms and legs?

(camera moves in close-up to Jane's face — strong and angry).

They're young too, lots of them. But they're not too young for that, Mrs. Hawkins, and I don't think breeding entered into it, either.

(Reaction shot cuts to Colonel)

Colonel: Bravo, Jane.

Emily: I don't want to debate with you, Jane. But surely there are women who are more suited to . . .

Jane: Yes, there are women more suited. And women like you who might help, Mrs. Hawkins. You think you're doing your part if you attend a canteen dance for your own pleasure.

We're not V-girls. We're simply helping with the wreckage.

(Laughing and crying)

Please don't worry if our precious, well-bred hands come into contact with those mangled bodies. We'll survive even if they don't!

From this encounter, the generational tables turn and Ann is inspired by Jane's bravery to become a welder. The scene shifts from the chintz-and-lace Hilton home to a grimy war factory.

(David O. Selznick hired Josephine von Miklos, author of <u>I Took a War Job,</u> as a consultant on technical details in the war factory.(14)) As overalled female welders appear on screen, Ann narrates in voice-over (from a diary she keeps for Tim):

> <u>Ann</u>: Tremendous changes have taken place in the pampered woman who was your wife. It's even hard for me to realize that I'm studying to be a lady welder.

Ann writes of the different women she encounters at the plant, women like Russian immigrant Zofia Koslovska (Nazimova).

The last scene, also set in winter in the Hilton home, parallels the first. In the opening scene, Tim has just left; by the closing scene he is about to return. Yet, whereas the Ann Hilton we first encounter seems defined by his absence, the woman of the last scene, while overjoyed at his homecoming, is much more complete in herself. <u>Since You Went Away</u> closes on a religious note, as the Hilton women together face the future with the same courage they brought to the war years. As "Little Town of Bethlehem" echoes, this message appears, superimposed on the screen:

> Be of good courage, and
> He shall strengthen
> your heart, all ye
> that hope in the Lord.

<u>Since You Went Away</u> enjoyed enormous box office success, and mixed critical acclaim. It was nominated for five Academy Awards (Best Picture, Best Actress, Best Supporting Actor and Actress, Best Black and White Cinematography) and received one (Best Score of a Drama or Comedy). However, it has been viewed by critics, feminist and nonfeminist alike, who saw it as simply a paean to domesticity. While Ann and Jane Hilton are traditional in orientation, like Kay Miniver, they represent an evolution from "earth mother" Ma Joad. And, most importantly, they are complete persons within themselves. Furthermore, they have sexual and emotional desires with which they must cope alone. For war wives, girlfriends, and widows, experiencing the challenge of defense work, single parenting, and unmet sexual needs, heroines like these provided inspiration.

> Davis' stoic wife . . . and Claudette Colbert . . . emerge as heroines of epic dimension. They learn to live <u>without</u> their men. Their survival (is) not as hysterical embittered martyrs, but as womanly, capable models.(15)

FROM TRADITIONAL MOTHER TO INDEPENDENT DAUGHTER: A TREE GROWS IN BROOKLYN, I REMEMBER MAMA, AND LITTLE WOMEN

Some maternal dramas of the late war and postwar transition reflect a signficant thematic evolution. In movies such as A Tree Grows in Brooklyn, I Remember Mama, and Little Women, traditional mothers raise independent daughters oriented toward creativity and self-expression rather than solely nurturance. These films possess several common features: historical setting (turn of the century America − A Tree Grows in Brooklyn, I Remember Mama; Civil War America − Little Women); a matriarchal family (due to poverty, ethnic tradition, and father's alcoholism − A Tree Grows in Brooklyn; due to poverty and ethnic tradition − I Remember Mama; due to war − Little Women); strong female bonding; an independent and career-oriented daughter. The gentle feminism of these films can be explored further by analyzing a classic one in depth: I Remember Mama.

I REMEMBER MAMA: MOTHER AS MUSE

George Stevens' RKO film I Remember Mama (1948), adapted from Katherine Forbes' autobiographical best-selling novel, Mama's Bank Account (also serialized and adapted for Broadway), is the ode of a young writer to her muse: her mother.

Katrin Hansen (Barbara Bel Geddes, in an Oscar-nominated performance) narrating the film in flashback, tells her story in gratitude for the inspiration provided by Mama (Irene Dunne, also in an Oscar-nominated role). In the first scene of I Remember Mama, the camera focuses in medium shot on Katrin, an attractive, self-possessed young woman typing "The End" upon a printed page.(16)

Katrin: For as long as I can remember the house on Larkin Street had been home. Papa and Mama had both been born in Norway, but they came to San Francisco because Mama's sisters were here. . . . But first and foremost I remember Mama.

Like A Tree Grows in Brooklyn, this film is set in a turn-of-the-century urban immigrant world; the city is San Francisco and the family Norwegian. Mama, Marta Hansen, is fortyish, an attractive, sensibly dressed woman with upswept blond braids. Like her movie counterparts, her sexuality is muted, her mood, sacrificial and family-oriented. Her husband, Lars (Philip Dorn) is an intermittently employed carpenter, a loving spouse and father. Yet, although Papa is the breadwinner, he is neither the center of the family nor the primary inspiration for Katrin's writing. Ethnic tradition and strength of personality, as well as poverty, sustain Marta's matriarchy. Yet, unlike Ma Joad, she doesn't appear uncomfortable with her power.

Although household labor is sex typed, Mama's unpaid work merits equal or greater value than Papa's paycheck. And it is Mama who cleverly manages family finances, inspiring some of the most amusing and touching scenes. The first segment, called "Stretching the Wage," sets its tone. Katrin introduces the scene in voice-over narration: "It was like a ritual — those Saturday nights. Mama would sit down at the kitchen table and count out all the money Papa brought home in the little envelope." The Larkin Street home is "poor but honest," cleanly and carefully furnished. The kitchen, Marta's domain, is heart and center of domestic activity. On Saturday evenings, as the Hansens (Marta, Lars, Katrin, Christine, Nels, and Dagmar) gather around the dinner table, Mama and Papa would conclude a weekly litany:

Papa: Is all, Mama?

Mama: Is good — we do not have to go to the bank.

Mama's "bank account" seemed to stand between the Hansens and poverty. At their weekly meetings, the family would always discover the needed cash; someone would "do without" or find part-time work. And luckily, once again, they would not have to go to the bank. Luckily, because the bank account was a fiction, sustained by Mama to create security for her family. And, as the audience discovers in the conclusion, only Marta has had to live with the knowledge of their desperate poverty. "Stretching the Wage" sets a model for the filmic segments to follow: the family experiences a crisis and only through Mama's cleverness and wisdom is it resolved.

In "The Aunts," I Remember Mama's second segment, the audience meets Marta's female kin, her three sisters. Marta, like other mothers in similar films, finds her relationships to her sisters ones of strain as well as closeness. The middle sister, in more ways than one, Marta mediates between Jenny and Sigrid (Hope Landin and Edith Evanson), older, nosy, catty, and intolerant, and Trina (Ellen Corby), younger, timid, and unassertive. The visual iconography of the four sisters symbolizes their personalities. Jenny and Sigrid, bossy and overbearing, are overweight and conventionally unattractive women of late middle age. Trina looks mousy and unconfident, more an awkward aging adolescent than a mature woman of 42. (Corby's compelling performance won her a Golden Globe Award and an Academy Award nomination.) Marta, however, is physically appealing as well as tolerant and cooperative. Stevens clearly chose to express their personality differences and family roles by appealing to popular filmic codes of femininity.

Marta's conflicts with her older sisters intensify when Trina tells her that she plans to marry funeral director Peter Thorkelson (Edgar

Bergen), a man as shy as herself. Trina enlists Marta's support in approaching Jenny, Sigrid, and Uncle Chris (Oscar Homolka), the absent and titular patriarch of the clan. (Although Marta clearly heads both her immediate and extended family, lip service, at least, is given to Chris' rule.)

When Marta informs her older sisters, they double over in laughter of surprise and ridicule. Marta sternly orders them not to mock Trina; they ignore her and refuse. Here Marta exercises her ingenuity and power as she carefully plays her trump card. She asks Jenny if she'd like it known publicly that her husband tried to run away and reminds Sigrid of her wedding night when she had to be brought home to her mother. Yet Marta, unlike her older sisters, does not gossip:

> Marta: I do not tell these stories for spite, only that they do not laugh at Trina.

Marta emerges as a powerful, clever mediator, a defender of rationality, tolerance, and justice. Mama is depicted as a flexible immigrant willing to adapt "old country ways" to new surroundings. Neither abandoning nor denying her heritage, Marta learns from and adapts to American culture.(17)

The theme of tolerance is further explored in another episode focusing on Uncle Chris' death. Chris, an alcoholic, blundering, bossy but basically good-natured old man, lives on a Nebraska farm. Like Marta, Chris has a bittersweet relationship with the aunts; he loves them but finds them bossy and offensive. The chief source of tension between Chris and his older nieces springs from his relationship with Jessie Brown (Barbara O'Neil), housekeeper and common-law wife. The aunts refuse to call Jessie by name; the terms shameful and that woman are all they can say. When Chris visits San Francisco, Jenny and Sigrid fail even to acknowledge Jessie. For them, the only acceptable love relationship is a legal one. Marta, however, is more tolerant. Though not necessarily advocating Chris' lifestyle, she is accepting of Jessie, respecting the love between the elderly couple. Ironically Chris reveals now to Marta that he finally married Jessie, yet was too annoyed with the aunts to bother telling them.

Young Katrin, present with Mama at her great-uncle's death, learns tolerance — for different lifestyles as well as for life's frailties and inevitable end. The aunts again provide the negative example.

> Jenny: All this expense to watch a wicked old man die of the D.T.s.

It is predictably Marta who reveals the truth: Chris had not squandered his money at a bar, but rather, had donated it to help crippled children, among them his own great-nephew, Arne (Tommy Ivo). Chris, who limped from an injury suffered as a child in Norway, was determined that other poor youngsters would not face the same fate.

Marta introduces 13-year-old Katrin to the reality of death by insisting that she accompany her to see Chris for the last time.

> Marta: I like you to know what death is like so you are not frightened of it — ever.

Marta treats Katrin not as a child to be shielded from life's harsher realities, but as a developing adult who must learn to face them with courage.

The most powerful sequences of I Remember Mama are those in which Katrin explores her relationship to Mama and ultimately, to herself. Like many real-life working-class daughters, Katrin often found her mother too busy to just talk. The film visually counterposes Katrin's reverie with Marta's endless toil. As her daughter reflects in a voice-over flashback, Mama appears in a montage of images washing windows, hanging laundry, sewing:

> Katrin: I don't think I can ever remember Mama unoccupied. It wasn't often I could get her to talk about herself and her life in the old country.

These work-visions dissolve to a long shot of mother and daughter strolling arm-in-arm down Market Street. Their body language speaks the camaraderie of friends coupled with the protectiveness of parent toward child.(18)

This sequence focuses on the meaning of maturity. Katrin is eager to be seen as an adult, symbolized by permission to drink coffee.

> Katrin: Mama, when can I drink coffee?
>
> Marta: When you are grown up.
>
> Katrin: When I'm 18?
>
> Marta: Maybe before that.
>
> Katrin: When I graduate?
>
> Marta: (Wisely smiling) Comes the day you're grown up, Papa and I will know.

As they stroll along, Katrin's consumer dreams contrast with Marta's ideals of family and ethnic tradition:

> Katrin: When I'm rich and famous . . . I'll buy you just lovely clothes: white satin gowns with long trains on them and jewelry. I'll buy you a pearl necklace.

Marta: (Looking down and touching her necklace in an amused way) Better I like my solya.

Katrin: (puzzled) But, Mama, wouldn't you like to be rich?

Marta: I'd like to be rich the way I'd like to be ten feet high. It's good for some things, bad for others.

Katrin: Didn't you come to America to get rich?

Marta: No-o-o-o (emphatically) . . . we come to America because they were all here, the others. It's good for families to be together.

The symbols of coffee and the solya re-emerge as Katrin prepares for graduation, and is rehearsing to play Portia in a school production of The Merchant of Venice. The camera captures Katrin, gazing into the mirror; narcissism envelops her. Her self-absorption causes sharp conflict with her younger sister, Christine (Peggy McIntire). As the girls walk down Market Street (scene of several "morally instructive" family encounters), Christine reproaches her:

Christine: It's all I've heard for weeks — school play, graduation, going on to high. You don't give a thought to what's happening at home. All you and your friends can think about is the presents you're going to get. You make me ashamed of being a girl. (Emphasis mine.)

Katrin is too preoccupied to respond, however. She has her heart set on the perfect graduation present: a comb set of "genuine celluloid." Christine informs her that Mama has planned another gift — the solya.

Katrin: You mean that old silver thing she wears that belonged to Grandmother? What would I want with an old thing like that?

Christine: It's an heirloom. Mama thinks a lot of it.

Christine scolds her for her "selfishness"; Papa Hansen was out of work and times were especially hard. Yet, ultimately, the necklace's significance was more than economic, symbolizing Katrin's connection to Mama and Norwegian culture. The antique silver solya contrasts sharply with the showy plastic comb set.

However, Katrin, to her surprise, receives the coveted dresser set. Yet, almost immediately, she notices the ever-present solya missing from Mama's neck. An angry Christine informs her that Mama sold her necklace to buy the set. A guilty Katrin sells the set, redeems the solya and returns it to her mother. Although angry at Christine, Marta is pleased with Katrin and convinced of her maturity. Marta presents an appreciative Katrin with her solya, while Lars pours his woman-child a steaming mug of coffee. Katrin has successfully completed a rite of passage into early womanhood, allying her more closely with Mama and her ethnic culture.

In the film's final segment, as Katrin completes high school, Mrs. Hansen emerges as her muse. Up to this point, Mama has supported assertion and achievement in her children, particularly her daughters. Katrin plans to complete college and write, Christine is forthright and outspoken, and little Dagmar dreams of becoming a veterinarian. Never does Marta mention marriage or motherhood as obstacles to a career.

In this sequence, Katrin announces, after receiving an obviously disappointing letter: "Mama, I'm not going to college. The only point was to become a writer and I'm not going to be one." Her best story has been rejected — for the tenth time.

Lars, after listening to his daughter's despair, describes a newspaper article he read, "Woman Writer Tells Key to Literary Success" by Florence Dana Moorhead. Katrin quickly skims the article. Moorhead's advice is quite simple: be sincere. Marta suggests that Katrin send the author some of her work.

> Katrin: You seem to think that writing's like cooking or something. All you need to have is a recipe. It takes a lot more than that — you've got to have the gift for it.

> Marta: You have to have the gift for cooking, too. There are things you must learn even if you have the gift.

Katrin's immaturity and disrespect for Marta are again criticized. The worlds of the homemaker and writer are not so far apart; they both demand skill, practice, confidence, ingenuity, and courage. And Mama has experienced and conquered some of the same psychological blocks Katrin must surmount.

Marta, who cannot read well, asks her son Nels (Steve Brown) what else the article says. He informs her that Moorhead's second major interest is gastronomy. When Mama learns that gastronomy means 'eating,' her strategy unfolds.

In the next scene, as Mama meets Florence Dana Moorhead, the film visually juxtaposes working-class and aristocratic images. Up to this point in I Remember Mama, the setting has been strictly working class: the Hansen home, Chris' farm, the hospital ward, and Market Street. This scene offers a striking contrast. In an exquisitely composed shot (through a mirror), Mama's immigrant simplicity collides with the hotel lobby's ornate, velvet, and chandeliered splendor. Moorhead (Florence Bates) epitomizes popular stereotypes of the female aristocrat. Overweight, top-heavy, and haughty, she is perfectly at home in crystal and velvet. At first Miss Moorhead informs Mrs. Hansen imperiously that she has no time for unpublished work. Yet Marta has strategized carefully. In a close-up of the two women on the lobby couch, Mrs. Hansen exerts the same clever leverage of power that worked with her sisters.

> Marta: I saw your picture in the paper. It's a picture of a woman who likes to eat good.

Marta makes a "deal": if Moorhead will read some of Katrin's stories, Mama will give her a favorite recipe. And, as usual, Marta wins. As the hotel scene ends, the audience has observed a successful power play, bridging the cultures of rich and poor women.

The frame dissolves – to a despairing Katrin at her attic desk, convinced that her barely begun career is over. Mama arrives home and is frank: Moorhead thought that Katrin's work was not good because she did not write about herself.

> Marta: You must write about things you know. But she says you have the gift.

Katrin, at first, does not listen. She insists that she cannot write because she "hasn't been anywhere or seen anything." Mama suggests that Katrin write about her own San Francisco.

Mama's wisdom proves true in the next segment. The frame of Katrin in the attic dissolves to a shot of an envelope from the "Stuart Literary Agency." Katrin's story, "Mama and the Hospital," will be published and she will earn $500! The film ends as it began with Katrin's voice-over narration: (Katrin: But first and foremost I remember Mama.) The frame dissolves to a back-lighted shot of Mama in close-up, peering through her curtained windows. The centrality of Marta's image – in the window as well as the frame – visually expresses her influence on Katrin.

The emergence of the traditional mother-independent daughter in late war-postwar women's films is a significant clue in the reconstruction of female social history. The world of films like I Remember Mama, A Tree Grows In Brooklyn, and Little Women is far removed from that of Life With Father. Although these dramas are domestic, the family that is idealized is matriarchal. Men are either absent from or peripheral to the household. Through strength of character, as well as the gaps created by male absence, women grow in maturity, status, and power, bonding together as sisters, mothers, and daughters. Although men may reappear in the filmic conclusions (A Tree Grows in Brooklyn, Little Women), they do not displace the heroines from power. The most striking aspect of these films, however, lies in the second generation: the promise of independence personified in the writer-daughter.

Why did women favor this type of film? Several interpretations suggest themselves. First of all, the female kin world of these maternal dramas mirrors the feminine universe of wartime America.

Eleven million men were away at war, leaving lovers, wives, mothers, sisters, and daughters to fend for themselves. These films portray a traditional domesticity, while celebrating a resilient, even if temporary, matriarchy.

The historical settings are intriguing. Perhaps audiences were tiring of contemporary variations on Mrs. Miniver or Since You Went Away. In addition, research shows that Americans grew weary and cynical in the late war years. The postwar era threatened readjustment problems for veterans and their families. The appeal of nostalgia, the desire for a simpler, more golden time may have endeared women and Hollywood studios to these films.

The female kin bonds, however, are central to decoding the meanings and discovering the appeal of these films. Each movie presents two primal relationships between women: as sisters and as mothers and daughters. Whereas these bonds are familial in nature (appealing to a broader audience and less threatening to Hollywood), their symbolic value extends to female friendships and love relationships as well. The sister bonds in these dramas prove complex. Sisterhood is the source of both joy and pain, sameness and difference. The differences remind each sister of roads not taken, choices not pursued. The range of female personalities in these filmic families subtly critiques determinist notions of female socialization. The appeal of sisterhood as a theme is universal to women. Sisters share a common language and stock of memories no one else can know. Each sister relates to the other as her reflection, one of the only persons in the world to grow up female in the same family.

Elizabeth Fishel in her study Sisters (1979) suggests that the female reader-viewer relates to Little Women for example, as a "fifth sister," a voyeuristic member of the March family. Little Women, for Fishel, as well as other feminist scholars, is quintessentially a parable of sisterhood:

> Little Women is undoubtedly the most popular and powerful model women have for thinking about sisters: a charmed story which for generations has transcended the limitations of its sentimentality. It is still as intrinsic to the mythology of most American girlhoods as slumber parties, dress-up clothes and fantasies of Mr. Right.

> But, even deeper than this, and more seductive to starry-eyed readers lies the fundamental core of unity in the March family, the solidarity of an essentially female household where Father has gone to war and Marmee has become the head of the household. . . . The novel is titled Little Women, after all, to underline the unity of the sisters — both within the family and without, and, years ahead of its time, becomes a parable of matriarchal power and of sisterhood.(19)

For women in the 1940s audience, the theme of female bonding had great appeal. As GIs left for war and over 7 million women migrated across America, female support networks became more crucial than ever, for love, moral support, and practical assistance — at work and in the community. Films like Dalton Trumbo's Tender Comrade (1943), for example, portray a sisterly model of female friendship. In this movie, a group of war wives take up residence together, sharing the joys and heartaches of homefront America.

The appeal of the female filmic universe may have had other roots as well. The psychic worlds of the sexes in wartime were sharply divided, as young women adjusted to new and more powerful roles at home, while their husbands, fathers, brothers, and sweethearts faced danger in battle. When the conflict ended, women plummeted in power and prestige, while returning men, facing serious adjustment problems, starred as America's heroes. It is likely that women preferred movies of female bonding that celebrated their own achievements.

But what of the traditional mother-independent daughter theme? Wartime social-work literature provides a clue, describing an earlier transition to adult and often more stressful roles for adolescent girls with mothers at work and younger siblings at home. As America's women were growing up younger and faster, popular magazines began to print "scare" stories, warning working mothers of dangers to their female children — drinking, sex, "bad" company. Antifeminists like Marynia Farnham would warn mothers that working outside the home causes both a loss of femininity in themselves and their daughters.(20) Films like A Tree Grows in Brooklyn, I Remember Mama, and Little Women reflected the "pressure to grow up" for young girls during the war era, and provided an antidote to hysterical antifeminist assertions that powerful mothers destroy their daughters. The maternal heroines of these films are not working mothers; they labor primarily at home. However, they are very busy, without time to spend leisurely with their offspring. Like many mothers in defense, time to talk with their children is often "stolen" from housework. Francie Nolan (A Tree Grows in Brooklyn) and Katrin Hansen both openly express disappointment that their mothers are not more available. However, the model of power and ingenuity provided by the mothers compensates for the scarcity of time. And the daughter-heroines become neither delinquents nor dominatrixes. They grow to become mature, self-assertive young women primarily focused on careers. These films express a subtle and oblique feminism, softened by a mood of generational progress. The gains of the war years are communicated in the characters of the daughters.

It is easy to speculate why this model was acceptable to Hollywood in the 1940s. Openly feminist films had little precedent; fear of code violations and "bad box office" made the film industry wary. Some in Hollywood saw their role as supporting the "official ideology" of temporary female "emancipation." However, wariness was not the industry's alone. In 1936, for example, Hollywood produced a drama about a nineteenth-century suffragist, A Woman Rebels, starring Katharine Hepburn. Despite Hepburn's potential star appeal, the film became a box-office flop. Audiences were ready for Ma Joad and Stella Dallas, but not Susan B. Anthony. The feminism of Francie Nolan, Katrin Hansen, and Jo March expresses itself as individualism. They do not confront the social and sexual division of labor; they must simply find the confidence (and material) to write. Not surprisingly, their workplaces are domestic and their values traditional. This vision of feminism fit nicely with the American dream of individualism and upward mobility.

The evolutionary feminism of these films paralleled an evolution in female consciousness in the war era, challenged by traditionalism. However, the traditional mother-independent daughter theme may have fascinated female audiences because it dramatized a perhaps yet-unspoken question: How would women's wartime experience affect the next female generation?

GOING IT ALONE: VARIATIONS ON A MATERNAL
THEME – NOW, VOYAGER – FROM MATROPHOBIA
TO SELF-SACRIFICING MATERNALITY

> Sometimes tyranny masquerades as mother love.
> Dr. Jaquith, in Now, Voyager

Now, Voyager, Irving Rapper's 1942 Warners' adaptation of a novel by Olive Higgins Prouty (author of Stella Dallas), represents a significant variation on the maternal theme. The voyage alluded to is that of Charlotte Vale (Bette Davis, in an Oscar-nominated role) who frees herself from a tyrannical mother to choose a lifestyle both maternal and untraditional.

The contemporary setting is among the most aristocratic of women's film interiors: a mansion in Boston's haughty Back Bay. Fortyish Charlotte, plump, repressed, and bespectacled, is the casualty of the Vale family. Renowned psychiatrist Dr. Jaquith (Claude Rains) has been summoned by Charlotte's sister-in-law Renee Beauchamps (Ilka Chase), to visit the nervous and disturbed Charlotte. Mrs. Vale (Gladys Cooper), an elderly dominating aristocrat, objects: Vales simply don't have nervous breakdowns. She sees her daughter as her possession, an unwanted "late life child" whose duty is to be her mother's companion in old age. Charlotte's mother, beneath her icy exterior, delights in the idea of an eternal baby whose function is to serve her. Early on, Jaquith becomes aware of the roots of her illness.

When Charlotte comes downstairs and realizes that a psychiatrist has come to see her, she becomes agitated. Yet she agrees to speak with Jaquith, simultaneously desiring to open up and shield herself. The first shots of Charlotte convey the image of "maiden aunt" (a term she uses to describe herself). Plump, bespectacled with unflattering hairdo, clothes, and shoes, Charlotte exudes repression and unhappiness. Yet, beneath the surface, anger, intelligence, and creativity abound.

> Charlotte: Am I introverted, Doctor? When I was 17, I came in once after midnight. The tread on the stairs hasn't been fixed yet.

Taking Jaquith into her confidence, Charlotte shows him her room, a secret den of pleasures forbidden by her mother — liquor, cigarettes, and racy novels. Most intriguing is Charlotte's obsessive hobby: carving tiny ivory boxes. As Charlotte and Jaquith are captured in medium shot, she leans against the window symbolizing her entrapment. As she reveals her inner world to Jaquith, Charlotte begins to answer his unspoken question (How did she become the way she is today?) Perusing an old album, Charlotte remembers a time 20 years ago on a cruise.

The Charlotte of this flashback scene is radically different (Davis' physical transformations in this film are compelling): twentyish, slim, fashionable, a far cry from "Aunt Charlotte" with her stealthy sips of sherry and obsessive carving. Her mother, however, seems just as anxious to control her, stating that Vales don't associate with common people. She also admonishes Charlotte to wear her glasses; Mrs. Vale seems threatened by her daughter's budding sexuality. Despite her mother's domination, however, Charlotte manages secretly to fall in love with a young naval officer, a man obviously below her class. Yet her happiness was brief. Mrs. Vale discovered the two necking in a cabin, and separated them. The officer would later receive a disciplinary censure from his superior (and, the movie implies, Charlotte knuckled under to her mother's authority).

The film flashes forward to Aunt Charlotte in the present:

> Charlotte: What man would even want me? I'm my mother's servant.

Jaquith is sympathetic and admiring of her craft. Praise is rare for Charlotte, and she responds warmly by presenting him with a carved box. She reveals, however, that her hobby also offers an outlet for anger, showing Jaquith a box destroyed by angry stabbings of her knife as her mother called from downstairs.

As Charlotte asks Jaquith for help, he suggests she spend some time at Cascade, his sanitarium. She accepts his offer, despite Mrs. Vale's protestations.

After a few months at the Sanitarium, Charlotte begins to improve. The audience is never sure exactly what happens at Cascade (other than a brief shot of Miss Vale weaving at a loom), but Charlotte emerges, thinner, calmer, and seemingly freer of maternal tyranny.

Dr. Jaquith and Renee, however, realize the irony of the situation. Charlotte seems well enough to go home, but "home" is the perpetrator of her illness. Never having been employed, Charlotte suffers the peculiar dependency of the rich: she is bound to Mrs. Vale financially. Renee comes up with a solution: she will send her on a 6-month Latin American cruise. Charlotte's healing will continue, but she will have to manage alone, an ocean away from the protection of Jaquith and Renee. The doctor recognizes this as he sends her forth on her journey by quoting Whitman:

> Dr. Jaquith: Now, voyager, sail thou forth to seek and find.

The Charlotte of the cruise ship is different from the three "Charlottes" encountered so far (Aunt Charlotte, young Charlotte, recuperating Charlotte). She is glamorous, slimmer, with elegantly upswept hair. Her glasses are noticeably absent. Charlotte is still unsure of herself, however, and one wonders if she will backslide into her old, perhaps "safer" identity.

Charlotte keeps to herself, until asked to share some accommodations with architect Jerry Durrence (Paul Henreid). She becomes Jerry's companion, and helps him shop for his children. His younger daughter, Tina (whom he calls an "ugly duckling") intrigues her. Seeing a parallel with herself, she asks Jerry, "Does Tina know she wasn't wanted?" As she becomes sympathetic to Tina, he becomes closer to Charlotte. She confides in him that she has just had a breakdown. As she shows him a family photo, he wonders aloud — "Who's the fat lady with heavy brows and all that hair?" She answers that it was she.

Their friendship turns to romance when the couple became stranded on a mountain together after a taxi accident (implying, of course, that they're lovers). However, Jerry is married (though unhappily) and, though he loves Charlotte, will not abandon his family. Isabel, Jerry's wife, is depicted as ill and obsessed by martyrdom and jealousy (a parallel with Mrs. Vale). Charlotte agrees that she and Jerry should not meet again.

Although her shipboard romance ends sadly, Charlotte has developed a sense of herself as an attractive woman who could love and be loved. The disaster of her earlier cruise finally reversed itself. Charlotte seems to have broken free.

However, the real test occurs when she returns to Back Bay. As she arrives home, Mrs. Vale is eager to reassert control immediately. She orders Charlotte around, telling her what to wear

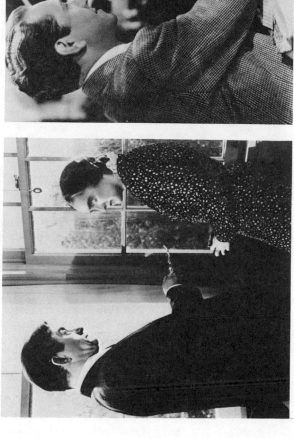

Left: The repressed "Aunt Charlotte" (Bette Davis) meets Dr. Jaquith (Claude Rains) for the first time in Irving Rapper's Now, Voyager (1942).
Right: Jerry Durrence (Paul Henreid) in the famous cigarette lighting scene with the "new" Charlotte Vale (Davis).

and how to act. "A late child's duty," Mrs. Vale reiterates, "is to her mother." Charlotte, however, will have none of it, although her mother first falls down the stairs, and later threatens to disinherit her.

Although Charlotte continues to live at home, she and her mother have an "armed truce." Yet loneliness and a desire for children make Charlotte restless. When Elliot Livingston (John Loder), a wealthy widower with two sons, proposes, she agrees to marry him, although she isn't in love. However, she realizes her true emotions when she accidentally meets Jerry again at a party. He tells her that his daughter Tina (plot contrivance!) is seeing Jaquith, and that he still loves her, although he cannot leave Isabel. Face to face with her real feelings, she ends her engagement.

This decision shocks and angers Mrs. Vale. How could her daughter give up what every aristocratic woman dreams of: a respectable marriage? Charlotte is brave enough to tell her mother what Jaquith said long ago: "Sometimes tyranny masquerades as mother love." Yet Mrs. Vale does not feign illness this time: she dies of a heart attack.

Her mother's death precipitates a crisis for Charlotte. Consumed with guilt and convinced that she caused her mother's death, Charlotte goes again to Cascade. While there, she develops an intense bond with troubled young Tina Durrence (Janis Wilson), who is puzzled by her devotion.

Tina: Why are you so good to me?

Charlotte: Because somebody was good to me when I needed it.

Charlotte (unknown to Jerry) becomes a surrogate mother to Tina, accompanying her shopping, taking her camping, etc. Tina, in turn, chooses a special name for Charlotte: Camille.

When Jerry learns of Charlotte's bond with Tina, he feels ashamed and asks her not to sacrifice anymore. Charlotte Vale, however, views it differently. Tina is both a reflection of herself as a girl and a surrogate daughter. And while she will never marry Jerry, her relationship with Tina is an expression of their love. As Steiner's romantic score echoes, Jerry and Charlotte gaze out of the window and light a cigarette (cigarettes are the source of much sensuality in this film!) and reflect on their "arrangement":

Jerry: Will you be happy, Charlotte?

Charlotte: Don't let's ask for the moon. We have the stars!

Rapper's tale of liberation from maternal domination and fulfillment through vicarious motherhood became a run-away hit of 1942. "It Can't Be Wrong," the song celebrating Jerry and Charlotte's "illicit" love, boomed out over wartime radios. And men began imitating Henreid's sensual style of lighting two cigarettes and giving one to their partners!

Now, Voyager may have appealed to wartime women for a variety of reasons. First of all, it asserts that "it's never too late" for a woman to "come of age," to become more confident and independent. Charlotte's metamorphosis symbolized, in the mythology of melodrama, the transformations in the female audience. Its openness toward mental illness reflected a growing tolerance in American society, as well as a rather uncritical romance with psychoanalysis paralleled in other 40s films such as Snake Pit, Since You Went Away, Possessed, and Spellbound.

Charlotte's liberation from maternal domination may have inspired some real-life daughters to do the same. Davis, who fought for the role of Charlotte Vale and personally worked on the screenplay, received hundreds of letters from daughters of possessive mothers who identified strongly with Charlotte, and many from mothers admitting similar mistakes with children.(21)

Though wealth seems a necessity for Charlotte to enjoy her lifestyle, upper-class status is linked with repression and domination. Michael Wood (1975) has interpreted this as a way of symbolically equalizing social classes for audiences:

The message is not so much that the rich have far more troubles than we do, as that they had better have more troubles than we do, if we believe there is any fairness in the world.(22)

Charlotte's romance with Jerry and "adoption" of Tina supports as well as challenges traditionalism. The security of marriage for its own sake does not appeal to Charlotte; "true" love is her desire. Breaking off her engagement probably meant abandoning her last chance at a conventional life and the respect of her peers. Yet she also seems content in Jerry's shadow, neither desiring nor demanding more than she receives (Is masochism her rebellion against her mother?). Tina, as a surrogate child, provides her with the chance to be the kind of mother she never had. As the mature "other woman," and vicarious parent, Charlotte has chosen her own style of loving and working (with Jaquith), a style that meshes uneasily with independence and self-negation.

Female audiences could relate Charlotte's experience to various aspects of war-era lifestyles: love outside of marriage, marriage outside of love, motherhood outside of marriage. Charlotte is not depicted as a homewrecker, but as a woman who falls in love with the wrong man at the wrong time. "Compromise" is the mood of the last scene, as Charlotte seems content to abandon dreams and seek satisfaction in what she can realistically attain. The compromise theme (particularly compelling in a "coming of age" film) may have appealed to female viewers whose wartime insecurities intensified needs for love and parenthood, while limiting opportunities for achieving them in traditional ways. "Let's not ask for the moon when we have the stars" (Davis to Henreid) may have provided solace to the mother without a husband, the war wife with an illicit lover, the single Rosie with a married GI lover. If Davis could still look herself in the eye, perhaps so could they.

UNREQUITED MOTHER LOVE: TO EACH HIS OWN

Director Mitchell Leisen thought the theme of this film hopelessly old-fashioned. But Olivia de Havilland (returning to the screen after a protracted contract battle with Warners) and writer Charles Brackett overcame his resistance, persuading him to make To Each His Own, a classical drama of unwed motherhood and a top-grossing film of 1946.

The film opens on a wartime New Year's Eve in a London blackout, with two middle-aged air wardens, a brusque, assertive American (de Havilland in an Oscar-winning performance) and a crusty Briton (Roland Culver) on duty. Trenchcoated Miss Norris seems all business:

> Miss Norris: I don't relish being treated as an incompetent. I happen to run a munitions factory with 1500 employees.

Mr. Desham retorts: "No woman ought to be allowed on a post like this." But, soon, he proves the buffoon, almost falling off the roof, only to be saved by Norris. As they break the ice, and begin to become friends over coffee, they both realize that they had been behaving like caricatures of their real selves. Desham calls them both freaks, middle-aged outcasts in a holiday world of young people and families.

"Middle aged people come in two varieties — the ones who never cared and the ones that cared too much," he says. It's clear soon where he places himself: his wife and son died in the flu epidemic of World War I and he hasn't "settled for" love since. Josephine Norris claims her story is of no possible interest. Yet this filmic foreshadowing prepares us for what will follow: Norris' brusque exterior is merely a cloak for a very caring and maternal woman.

As Desham and Norris talk, an old friend of hers, Bill McNair, comes by and mentions that Gregory Piersen will be in town. As her face lights up and she rushes off (leaving Desham), we (and he) assume that she is going to meet her lover. That assumption is both right and wrong.

We next encounter Jody Norris as a "waiting woman," pacing the train platform as she searches for Gregory Piersen. Her plump, lined face embodies desperate anxiety. Another waiting woman commiserates, and tells Jody she's waiting for her flyer-boyfriend: "You can't imagine what it's like to be in love with a flyer!" Her face in shadow, obscured by her hat, grows sad and reminiscent, as the film flashes back.

It's 20 years earlier, the set is well lit, but it's still wartime — World War I. Jody Norris is much younger, with short curly hair and a white blouse, serving soda at her father's drugstore to two beaux, Alec Piersen (Philip Terry) and Mack Tilton (Bill Goodwin). Jody seems uninterested in them, however; it's true love that she's after. Although Alec warns her that he'll marry his next choice, Corinne (Mary Anderson), Jody is unmoved — she'll wait for the real thing.

As movie conventions go, however, that doesn't take long. Captain Bart Cosgrove (John Lund) a renowned flyer, visits Piersen Falls on a nationwide tour. However, before he addresses the crowd, he suffers a minor accident and is brought to the drugstore to recuperate. As a sentimental score resounds, Jody meets Cosgrove, as he is lying down, and she serves him food and drink. As we watch Jody in white ministering to the flyer, images of Florence Nightingale suggest themselves, woman as healer and nurturer.

Cosgrove is worn-out and cynical, but addicted to flying, "the way a drunk likes liquor. . . . Flying's for the wild ones," he says, "with nothing to come back to." Bart depicts himself as spending free time with "a bottle of cognac and any girl we can grab." Jody, however, brings out other needs in Cosgrove, needs for a saner, more civilized way of life.

> Cosgrove: I get sober once in a while. I get moments when I know there's something else. A girl comes into a quiet room and lights a lamp . . .

Later that night, Jody and Cosgrove go flying in his plane. Cosgrove pretends to run out of gas, but later, because he really cares about her, tells Jody it's a trick to make her spend the night with him.

> Cosgrove: Love — the way you think about it is a lifetime job. And I've got no lifetime.

Jody replies surprisingly, "How much time do you think I can be sure of? I only have until dawn, too." As Cosgrove leaves (and later writes Jody), we sense that their night together has civilized him; perhaps Jody will find true love.

But not before she "pays" for her night of pleasure. In the next scene, an expectant neighbor-woman meets a pale and queasy bride Corinne at the Norris drugstore. Jody serves them both tall glasses of milk. Daniel Fapp's cinematography captures well the divisions between the women. On one side of the counter, Corinne and her neighbor exchange knowing smiles, bonding in the sisterhood of pregnancy, while, on the other, Jody looks uncomfortable and excluded. As the women leave, Jody pours a glass of milk, and drinks it – alone.

Excluded from the joy of legitimate pregnancy, Jody hides her condition, and consults a doctor in New York. He tells her that, indeed she is expecting a child, but that she should not continue her pregnancy because she is suffering from potentially fatal peritonitis. Jody agrees to have the operation. A very acceptable alternative, a therapeutic abortion (though the word is never spoken on film), promises to return her life to normal.

Yet, back at home, Jody learns (from an old man in the store) that Bart has been killed. She reverses her decision: "I don't care what the Doctor said. I don't care if I do die. That baby's going to get its chance for life." Her elderly father is kind and nonjudg- mental.

Flashing forward to a New York City hospital ward, the camera moves in close-up to Jody and her son, both thriving, as the doctor tells her she can go home tomorrow. Jody looked pained: "home" is the last place she wants to go. She asks nurse Daisy Gingras (Victoria Horne), a tough Eve Arden type, if she knows anywhere she could board her child for a few weeks.

Gingras: Who do ya think you're fooling?

Jody: Does everybody know?

Gingras: Lissen, a girl like you comes into a hospital, no visitors, no flowers – to an old timer like me that adds up to just one thing.

Jody: Does everybody know?

Gingras: No – and I'm not tellin 'em. You sinned – you pay for it for the rest of your life. I don't collect on those payments. . . . I'll take the baby over at my place.

Jody: Would you, Miss Gingras?

Gingras: My name is Daisy. The more I hear of them cozy little towns, the better I like the Bronx.

Daisy expresses traditionalism (and an adherence to code standards) and sisterly support. The women hatch a plan: Daisy will keep the child for a few weeks, and then leave it on a Piersen Falls doorstep. The friendship between the streetwise city woman and small-town girl will endure throughout the film.

The plan, however, backfires. After Daisy leaves the child on the Bellingham's doorsteps, they give the baby to Corinne Piersen, whose own child died. Jody is dissuaded from claiming the baby by her father who claims the infant will be a "marked child." We now know the mystery of Gregory Piersen.

Jody becomes a surrogate aunt to little Griggsy, living for the days when she could see him, caught in an uncomfortable triangle with Corinne. Fapp's cinematography again captures the divisions between women: Jody at the edge of the frame, Alec, Corinne, and Griggsy bonded as a family. Finally, the uneasy alliance explodes as insecure Corinne learns that Jody is the mother and orders her not to see Gregory again.

Meanwhile, Mack Tilton asks Jody to marry him. She refuses (hinting about a "special someone"), but goes to New York to work at his business, Lady Vyvyan Cosmetics. Her motivation is obsessively maternal: she will earn enough money to raise Griggsy herself. Jody succeeds in making Lady Vyvyan a leading cosmetics firm (it had previously fronted for a still), yet still meets Griggsy on the sly, appearing as a "nice lady" at circuses and other public events.

The tensions of maternal love: Jody Norris (Olivia de Havilland) and Corinne Piersen in Mitchell Leisen's To Each His Own (1946).

A few years later Jody's chance to be Griggsy's "real mother" finally arrives. The Piersen's pianola factory goes bankrupt and prosperous Miss Norris is on hand to loan them money — if only she can have her son. Corinne, now with two children of her own, sadly agrees; Jody takes 4-year-old Griggsy to New York.

Yet Griggsy misses his home, and doesn't mesh with Aunt Jody in the way that she hopes. In missing his early childhood, she lost the real bond of motherhood. With unselfish maternal love, Jody returns Griggsy to Corinne.

The film flashes forward to the present, as Jody hopes against hope finally to be a real mother. She meets him (John Lund, again) and tells him she's "Miss Norris," but, though polite, he barely recognizes her and is distracted by looking for his fiancée. He accepts Jody's hospitality, but can't stay with her, because his leave is shortened. Gregory feels affection for her as the Aunt Jody of his childhood — and wonders why her tie to him is so strong.

To Each His Own has a fairytale ending, as Jody finally realizes her dream. Lord Desham hears her story and uses his influence to extend Griggsy's fiancée's leave and relax the marriage regulations. After the couple marries (with an approving Jody and Desham looking on), Griggsy takes Jody's arm — "I think this is our dance, Mother." Jody finally realizes a mother's joy — to dance at her son's wedding.

As sentimental and contrived as this film is, it clicked for postwar audiences. The woman alone, outside traditional family life, was portrayed powerfully by de Havilland. Her strength of character, nurturance, and integrity linked her with other women's film heroines. True, she paid for her sins, but she also emerged as a competent, resourceful woman. As Marjorie Rosen (1973) has asserted,

> Perhaps these women (in Bette Davis' Old Maid and To Each His Own) paid . . . by voluntary exile from traditional family life, but they also matured as warm, loving and independent people. Neither resorted to hysteria; neither declined into withered, jumpy old ladies.(23)

As in Now, Voyager, women who transcended the traditional bounds of morality in wartime found sympathy in films like this. And for many women, this film confirmed the feeling that motherhood is often difficult and unrewarded. In this and other films of the war era (Tomorrow Is Forever), separation from a son is the source of maternal disappointment.(24)

The erotic tone and overinvolvement of Jody's relationship with Griggsy is apparent. Perhaps this reflected a tendency (conscious or not) of some wartime mothers to eroticize and prioritize their sons in the absence of adult men. Whether or not women actually romanticized their sons, they were drawn to filmic fantasies centering on that theme.

The storybook ending is pure wish fulfillment. For every unrequited love, there is a second chance to make it right. For audiences dealing with the persistent loose ends of wartime daily life, this thought was comforting indeed.

DARK MIRROR: MILDRED PIERCE – OBSESSIONAL MOTHER-EVIL DAUGHTER

A powerful mother-daughter bond again appears in Michael Curtiz' Warners' production of Mildred Pierce (1945). Yet the mood and meaning of this film differ sharply from that of most other maternal dramas.

In Mildred Pierce we leave the historical settings, well-lit interiors, and sunny streets for the dim and seamy underside of contemporary Los Angeles, the world of film noir.

> Her is a world where it is always night, always foggy or wet, filled with gunshots and sobs, where men wear turned-down brims on their hats and women loom in fur coats, guns thrust deep in their pockets.(25)

Our first introduction to the heroine occurs not at a happy family gathering, but a murder. After the credits play over a tide-washed beach, the screen image fades into a car outside a house, on a gloomy, rain-drenched night. We hear multiple gun shots. The film jump cuts to the living room: a middle-aged man (Zachary Scott) falls down a spiral staircase, clutching himself and rolling on the floor, uttering one word: "Mildred." The camera pans to bullet holes in a mirror, and a car drives off. The question mark of the film lies in the missing shot of this sequence: Who fired the gun?

This scene dissolves to the Santa Monica Pier, a rain-drenched wharf of shadow and light. The camera follows an attractive, dark-haired, fur-coated woman (Joan Crawford in an Academy Award-winning performance) down a boardwalk. Hands in her pockets, she gazes down sadly and invitingly at the swirling dark water below. Is this Mildred? And is she the murderess? And will she also kill herself? Darkness and ambivalence surround our introduction to the female protagonist.

The tension is broken by the sarcastic intervention of a policeman, who walks up to the distraught woman and raps the iron railing with his nightstick.

Policeman: What's on your mind? (Mildred doesn't answer – just stares)

Policeman: You know what I think? I think maybe you had the idea of taking a swim. That's what I think.

Mildred: (Apathetically) Leave me alone.

Policeman: If you was to take a swim, I'd have to take a swim. Is that fair? Just because you feel like bumping yourself off, I should get pneumonia? Never thought about that, did you?

(Mildred turns away and shakes her head mutely.)

Policeman: O.K. Think about it. Go on now – beat it. Go home. Before we both jump in.

Mildred walks back down the pier.

The audience soon learns that she is indeed the infamous Mildred. As she passes a cafe, Wally Fay (Jack Carson), an old friend, raps on the window, calling her name. Appearing distraught, she enters the bar. As Mildred talks to him, it becomes clear that they share a checkered past. As noir cinematography casts light and shadow on their faces, references are made to broken business partnerships and unrequited lust (Wally's). Images of murder, seamy sex, and crooked business deals color these first scenes.

As the night draws on, Mildred, bitter and overwrought, appears to succumb to Wally's advances. Seductively she invites him to her beach house: "There's better stuff to drink at the beach house, Wally."

As they arrive at the house, Mildred continues to tease Wally: "Maybe I find you irresistible. . . . You make love so nicely, Wally." Mildred goes into the bedroom, seemingly to change her dress. As Wally relaxes in the living room, Mildred quickly exits by the back door, leaving a shocked and humiliated Wally to find the "stiff." Wally escapes through a window, only to be discovered by two more sarcastic policemen, whom he then leads to Mildred.

At the police station, more of the mystery unravels. The corpse is Mildred Pierce's second husband, Monte Beragon. Later that night she is summoned by police from an elegant mansion to identify the body and undergo questioning. As Max Steiner's score sets the scene, her daughter, Veda (Ann Blyth), her friend and business partner Ida Corwin (Eve Arden), and first husband, Bert Pierce (Bruce Bennett) all appear on the scene. The atmosphere feels like a noir "This Is Your Life, Mildred Pierce."

Detective Peterson, as sarcastic as his counterparts, announces that he's cracked the case: Bert Pierce, owner of the gun, is the killer. Mildred cries out desperately: "I tell you Bert didn't do it! I know he didn't." So does the audience. This murder is far from being solved, leaving all the major characters, especially Mildred, shadowed by suspicion.

This first sequence introduces the major characters and poses questions to be answered by subsequent flashbacks. Our initial feelings colored by ambivalence and suspicion, the audience is set up as a kind of jury, to judge Mildred's life.

After this enigmatic beginning, we are introduced, in flashback, to the world of Mildred Pierce. Narrated by Mildred this sequence is sunnier, fully lit, reminiscent of better times. Icing a cake, she comments:

Mildred: I was always in the kitchen. I felt as though I'd been born in a kitchen and lived there all of my life, except for the few hours it took to get married. I married Bert when I was 17 and never knew any other kind of life. Just cooking, washing, having children.

The camera captures an aproned thirtyish Mildred in the bustle of domesticity, about 10 years younger, less drawn and cynical. Like her maternal movie counterparts, Mildred Pierce is a martyr-mother in a daily struggle with poverty. Her cheery but small suburban California home spells effort to become solidly middle class. Bert Pierce, an unemployed insurance agent, like other fathers in the maternal drama, is peripheral to his family, as he cannot support his wife and the children in the style to which they are accustomed. Bert's weak, ineffectual character simply cannot match Mildred's strength and determination, and she despises him for it. It is her daughters, and not Bert that give Mildred a reason for living. Mildred's flaw, if any, is an obsession for her children, Veda and Kay (JoAnn Marlowe). As Mildred says to Bert, placing another home-baked pie in the oven, "I'll do anything for those kids. Do you hear me — anything!" These words foreshadow the major theme of Mildred Pierce: her obsessional love for Veda.

At the beginning of this sequence, Mildred's world is domestic, her aims traditionally feminine. She bakes and sells pies by the dozen to purchase the "little extras" that will make her daughters "refined" young ladies: party dresses, piano, and voice lessons. The film's stance toward Mildred seems more sympathetic. The hard-boiled woman at the police station is, underneath the surface, just another dedicated homemaker.

Yet Mildred's relentless drive pushes her uncomfortably out of her social class and pushes her jobless, ineffectual husband into an affair with Maggie Biederhof (Lee Patrick) and out of the home.(26) Like most real-life women in her situation, Mildred was left with little money and few skills to support her family:

Mildred: It didn't take me long that night to figure out that I was broke . . . dead broke. And with Bert gone, it looked as though I'd stay that way.

A relentless survivor, Mildred seeks employment in offices and stores all over Los Angeles. A montage of shot upon shot tells the same grim story; Mildred is told to return later when she has experience.

Montage (series of quick dissolves)

Mildred's voice: (over montage) It wasn't as easy as I thought. I walked my legs off . . . until my shoes were so thin I could count the cracks in the pavement through them.

Dissolve to: Mildred at the Wicket. The man shakes his head.

Mildred's voice: And always, everywhere I went, I heard the same thing.

Man's voice: Sorry — we need someone with experience.

After many unsuccessful attempts, she seeks work doing what she knows best: making and serving food. Mildred finally lands a job waitressing in a busy downtown restaurant managed by the brassy but kind Ida Corwin.

A contrasting montage of shots dramatizes Mildred's struggle to become a top-notch waitress:

(Quick dissolve)

Stack of dishes balancing on Mildred's arm

Mildred's voice: I learned it the hard way. In three weeks I was a good waitress . . .

Quick dissolve

Mildred's legs

Mildred's voice: In six weeks I felt as though I'd worked in a restaurant all my life.

Mildred and Ida soon become fast friends, developing a sisterly and supportive relationship that endures throughout the film. Ida's hard business sense and cynicism toward men give Mildred support and confidence in making the transition from marriage to divorce, from home to work.

However, early in Mildred's career, a tragic flaw foreshadows her doom. Ashamed of her present job and her working-class background, Mildred hides her occupation from the children, hires a maid, Lottie (Butterfly McQueen), and lives well beyond her means. As she narrates, Mildred reveals her deepest fear: "Only one thing worried me, that some day Veda . . . would find out I was a waitress." Mildred's fears prove true when Veda discovers her uniform and reacts with characteristic revulsion at the "smell of grease": "My mother — a common waitress!" In a rare loss of Crawford-Pierce control, Mildred slaps Veda across the face. Although they both apologize, the rawness of the moment fails to subside. Mildred, however, is, in general, too involved with her own dreams of mobility to notice that her eldest daughter is becoming a monster whom only increasing amounts of material goods can satisfy.

Kay Pierce, unlike Veda, does not care much about upward mobility. A comic tomboy, she is criticized by Veda for looking like a peasant. However, fairly early in the film, Kay tragically dies of pneumonia (at the home of Bert's lover, Mrs. Biederhof), leaving Mildred grieving, guilty, and overinvested in Veda.(27)

Whereas Mildred suffers personal loss, she begins to enjoy economic gain. Ida and Mildred buy property from playboy Monte Beragon to open a restaurant (with the help of the somewhat sleazy, but ever-present Wally Fay), and achieve phenomenal success. They are decent, cooperative, hard-working businesswomen, as compared to the spineless manipulative men upon whom they often, at least initially, depend. Although Mildred's status is quite unconventional for a woman, her motives (like Jody Norris) remain traditional. Mildred knows no bounds in sacrificing for her child. And Veda, now a precocious teenager, has not been untouched by her mother's meteoric rise. Her insatiable greed has grown in greater proportion than Mildred's business.

By the time "Mildred's" is the well-known name of a restaurant chain stretching across L.A., Mildred, now divorced, is involved with Beragon. Though she is clearly attracted to Beragon, Mildred is never deeply in love. Monte represents the "leisure class" who need not taint themselves with the smell of grease to earn a living. He has few redeeming qualities. Monte is a wealthy do-nothing ("With me, loafing is a science") and a playboy. (Mildred notes caustically the array of female swimsuits in his closet: "Too many sisters. They all seem to be my size.") The audience senses, however, that Monte is, like her business, more for Veda than herself. And such is the case, more than Mildred can at first imagine. After a loveless, economically pragmatic marriage, Veda falls in love with Monte, who represents a lifestyle of endless consumption. Both Veda and Monte use Mildred, while despising her lack of class. In the following response to Mildred, Monte reveals his true feelings:

> Monte: Yes, I take money from you. But not enough to make me like kitchens or cooks. They smell of grease.

Hardworking Mildred Pierce has become a tragic pawn in the hands of both her lover and daughter.

As the film flashes forward in midstream to the police station, new evidence surfaces. Mildred, it seems, had run from the house while Fay waited. Suspicion clouds her character. Yet now she admits to Monte's murder. Yet we are no more convinced by Mildred than by Bert. The question mark remains, and the film flashes back.

Mildred and Beragon end their relationship; Veda runs away from home to become a nightclub singer (filmic code for prostitute?). Mildred travels to Mexico to forget, but feeling distraught and abandoned, schemes to bring Veda back. Although she does not love Monte, Mildred asks him to marry her. He is more than willing to accept Mildred's money and play mother and daughter off against one another in a grotesque triangle. Yet, Monte is equally uncommitted to Veda. When she asks him to leave Mildred, he refuses and Veda shoots him in revenge. Mildred Pierce has come full circle; the missing shot has been filled in. Veda shot Beragon.

When Mildred learns the truth, she rushes to protect Veda and tries to frame Wally. When this fails, Mildred is even willing to confess herself. Yet, finally, justice prevails. It is Veda, not Mildred, who is behind bars, as the film concludes. Mildred leaves the jail with none other than her ineffectual first husband, Bert. Is Mildred, too, back at start, having tried and failed at independence?

Mildred Pierce is an ambiguous film, whose characters and narrative structure differ radically from the classic maternal drama. Unlike Ma Joad or Marta Hansen, Mildred is disgusted by poverty, revolted by the taint of grease (a recurrent image), desperately trying to pass as middle or even upper class. Although Mildred herself is depicted as a slightly obsessed paragon of virtue, her "dark mirror" Veda reflects the insidious side of social mobility. And any analysis of the portrayal of womanhood in Mildred Pierce must consider these two women together as well as separately. This approach is necessitated by the visual imagery of the film which constructs the Mildred-Veda relationship as a double image mirror. In one interior scene, for example, Mildred and Veda face one another, in a soft-focus, close-up, two shot. Staring intently into each others' eyes, both women wear black, with their hair pulled back severely from their faces. As the camera captures their interaction, there is an unsettling mirror effect. Mildred is Veda is Mildred is Veda.

Eric Rhode suggests that Veda was created by novelist Cain and re-interpreted by director Curtiz as an indirect critique of Mildred:

> In order to keep Mildred's reputation untarnished, the violence of her ambition is displaced onto her daughter Veda, so that Mildred may seem to be motivated purely by a well-meaning desire to serve this adolescent child. The interest of both the film and the James M. Cain novel . . . is that neither of them denies this displacement.(28)

Mildred may be implicitly criticized through Veda on a number of counts: (a) her shame at her working-class past; (b) her rapid mobility; (c) her materialistic values (she gives Veda "things," but rarely teaches her moral lessons); and (d) her untraditional achievements as a woman.

The mother-daughter relationship in Mildred Pierce can be read on other levels as well. The world of Mildred Pierce is matriarchal, both female and business-oriented. The men in the film are not only peripheral. By and large, they represent negative role models, objects to be avoided, manipulated, or dominated by the women. Mildred's strongest attraction is for her daughters, not her husbands or lovers. A number of shots at the beginning of Mildred Pierce capture Mildred hugging Veda and/or Kay while an excluded, angry and impotent Bert looks on. A thinly veiled eroticism and narcissism colors Mildred's obsession for Veda:

The obsession with the daughter (Ann Blyth), with its erotic implications, is the most fascinating aspect in the movie, since it is a veiled expression of self-love and takes on the aspect of narcissism.(29)

Is Mildred Pierce warning women against excessive self-love? Or lesbianism? Or incest? Or, perhaps, it is making a statement about overmothering, a role that leaves little room for the self.

Mildred is overinvested in her child, leaving little boundary between Veda and herself. While some critics might interpret this as another postwar "damned if you do, damned if you don't" message to American women, it deserves more careful examination. In recent feminist scholarship, a major barrier to female autonomy has consistently been identified: the overidentification of mothers and daughters.(30) The fact that maternal overidentification was hard to accept in so self-sufficient a character as Mildred made it perhaps all the more compelling.(31)

Molly Haskell analyzed the Veda-Mildred relationship differently: as reaction formation, the taboo of maternal hatred masquerading as its opposite!

Mildred Pierce (Joan Crawford) bonds with Veda (Ann Blyth) as an excluded Bert (Bruce Bennett) looks on in Michael Curtiz' Mildred Pierce (1945).

The sacrifice of and for children — two sides of the same coin — is a disease passing for a national virtue, and a constant theme in films that preach one thing, and for anyone who is listening, say another. Whether the totem is challenged, as in the women's films of European directors like Ophuls and Sirk (Reckless Moment, There's Always Tomorrow, All That Heaven Allows) or played straight and heartwarmingly (as in Penny Serenade, Mildred Pierce, To Each His Own, all three versions of Madame X, The Old Maid and That Certain Woman), the spectacle is of a woman owned by her children or consumed by her maternal zeal.

Like all obsessions this one betrays a fear of its opposite, a hatred so intense it must be disguised as love. (Emphasis mine.)(32)

In analyzing the complex possibilities of audience response, it is hopelessly reductionistic to view the film as a simple patriarchal formula: single working mother begets monster daughter.

We must also examine the other significant female bond in the film: that between Mildred and Ida. Although the mother-daughter relationship is obsessive and exploitative, their bond is strong and supportive. Loyal friends and good business partners, they are neither neurotically obsessed with nor dominating of each other. Both women are strong and independent, yet genuinely care about and cooperate with each other. Ida offers a positive alternative to the ineffectual dishonest males we meet in this women's film noir. However, the Ida-Mildred relationship is distinctly noneroticized, and Ida's strength and appeal are somewhat undercut by her cynicism toward herself as well as men:

Eve Arden's role in Mildred Pierce also tells us much. In the film she plays her characteristic role of the smart, cheerfully bitter woman, sidekick to the heroine and running commentator on the cruelties and stupidity of men. . . . Independent, witty, intelligent, a true friend to her own sex and of all women the most apparently "complete" within herself, she is made to talk constantly and longingly of men, to deprecate her own powers of attraction . . . to bemoan her "incompleteness". . . .

There is something as disheartening as it is brave in her acceptance of the status quo, for she is using her brains to deprecate their importance and downgrading her friendships with women as second-best arrangements.(33)

It is Ida who speaks the most naked (and darkly comic) truth of the film: "Alligators have the right idea; they eat their young."

Mildred Pierce has been highly debated among feminist film critics. Its meaning in 1945, as today, was ambiguous. Mildred Pierce sharply contrasts with other maternal dramas. A darkness shrouds female success; economic gain is paralleled by maternal failure. Furthermore, a deeper ambivalence surrounds Mildred as a character from the very beginning; the narrative of Mildred Pierce is "wrapped" in a murder mystery.

Mildred Pierce is both a women's film and a film noir; its multiauthored script testifies to both of these influences.(34) Any interpretation must recognize its complex and contradictory levels of meaning. It is most probably not an accident or coincidence that, in Mildred Pierce, a top-grossing and Academy-award winning film of 1945, female business success is narratively linked to motherly failure.

Mildred Pierce may have been created by a patriotic Hollywood (consciously or unconsciously) to warn women of the hazards of independence and prepare them for postwar demobilization. Female audiences may have flocked to see the film for related and somewhat different reasons. Many wartime working women experienced guilt and confusion over their changing roles. In a society that failed to provide adequate childcare or supportive services, working mothers feared the present and future effects of their employment on children. Many a mother may have identified with Mildred's grief and horror at Veda, using the film as a vehicle for their own guilt and confusion.

Tragedy, however, is not the only mood of Mildred Pierce. Between the suspicion of the first segment and the tragedy and resignation of the last is a tale of female success and supportive female bonding. At the same time that Mildred was a tragic figure, she was also a winner and survivor. It is safe to assume that women who watched the film probably identified with and responded to both. The rather unconvincing ending of Mildred Pierce is hardly feminist, yet neither is it clearly patriarchal.(35) Mildred leaves with Bert, but why? Is it because weak, ineffectual Bert is symbolic of all men? The reunion of the Pierces occurred on screen at the same time as millions of GIs returned home. Mildred's ambiguous reunion with Bert might be seen as a parallel to that of the war wife and her GI mate. Yet the mood was not strongly romantic, only mutedly upbeat. Mildred had lived in several worlds, that of the poor man's wife, the independent divorcée, and the playboy's bride; none had spelled true happiness. Perhaps, in the land of the blind, Bert Pierce is the one-eyed king. One of the few films noir to feature a female heroine, Mildred Pierce cast doubt and darkness on both the wartime success of working women and the promise of the feminine mystique.

CONCLUSION: FROM MA JOAD TO MILDRED PIERCE

The strong mother is a staple of the 1940s women's film. Yet her changing image and relationship to her sisters and daughters reflects, through the conventions of Hollywood, the transformed nature of women's lives during and after the war. Ma Joad, Sara Muller, Kay Miniver, and Ann Hilton are nurturers, displaying strength in traditionally feminine ways. Although they rarely transcend woman's place, they embody personality traits encouraged by contemporary feminists: power, courage, physical stamina, and perseverance. For American women adopting new roles, these films may have provided assurance that a gain in social power need not mean a loss of femininity. And, Hollywood, buffeted by currents of conservatism and social change, embodied those tensions within the films it produced.

In popular maternal dramas of the later 1940s such as A Tree Grows in Brooklyn and I Remember Mama, the traditional mother remains, yet her ingenuity, persistence, tolerance, and power make her the muse for writer-daughters. Assertion for family, in these films, transforms itself in the next female generation into assertion for self. The feminism of these films is gradual and evolutionary, and does not demand the breakup of families or the displacement of men. Yet feminist influences, representing both emergent and residual cultural currents, are nonetheless present in the writer-daughters. As the war drew to an end, much discussion centered on the impact of the war years on the generations of women to come. Would wartime women in defense be remembered, as Lola Weixel of Connie Field's documentary The Life and Times of Rosie the Riveter expressed it, as "The New Woman?"(36) Would the new-found independence of wartime women grow or diminish as GIs returned, and would the female war experience translate into further gains in the lives of their daughters, literal and figurative? Adapted from novels and plays written by women from their own experience, films like I Remember Mama convey a strong sense of female power and community as well as pride in immigrant and working-class culture.

The "woman alone" is the focus of three films with a maternal theme: Now, Voyager; To Each His Own; and Mildred Pierce. These films express both traditional and alternative conceptions of femininity to appeal to audiences caught in the tide of shifting morals and difficult life choices. To Each His Own and Now, Voyager convey sympathy for women who must love and parent at a distance. For war workers like Lyn Childs (in Field's film) who had to leave their children behind to take defense jobs, these films probably provided comfort, solace, and hope of a positive future.

Mildred Pierce, however, reflects a much bleaker vision. Fears of female domination, emasculation, and daughterly desertion pervade this film. Its cynical mood and camera style mock the sunny optimism of the maternal drama. Fear, ambivalence, suspicion, and guilt surround female power in Mildred Pierce. This film reflects the conservative backlash as well as the commonly felt underside of the new female power. However, its message is hardly univocal. In the midst of mother-daughter tragedy, we see recurrent images of female strength and resilience as well as positive bonding between women.

Through the prism of Hollywood mythology, these films offer rich insights into the wartime world of American women, and the variations and challenges posed to the dominant ideology of sacrificial motherhood. First and foremost, as Katrin Hansen said, "I Remember Mama." And every woman in the audience was invited to become a daughter.

NOTES

(1)   See Nancy Chodorow, The Reproduction of Mothering: Psychoanalysis and the Sociology of Gender (Berkeley: University of California Press, 1978); Dorothy Dinnerstein, The Mermaid and the Minotaur: Sexual Arrangements and Human Malaise (New York: Harper and Row, 1977; Adrienne Rich, Of Woman Born: Motherhood as Experience and Institution (New York: W.W. Norton, 1976); Jessie Bernard, The Future of Motherhood (New York: Penguin, 1974).

(2)   Christiane Viviani, "Who Is Without Sin? The Maternal Melodrama In American Film: 1930-39," Wide Angle, 4, 2, (1981): 4. Also see Ellen Elizabeth Seiter, "The Promise of Melodrama: Recent Women's Films and Soap Operas," unpublished Ph.D. dissertation, Northwestern University, 1981, for a discussion of the appeal of melodrama for female viewers.   Seiter viewed melodrama as expressing contradictions in female experience which it does not and cannot necessarily resolve. On the other hand, Serafina Kent Bathrick, in "The True Woman and the Family-Film: The Industrial Production of Memory," unpublished Ph.D. dissertation, University of Wisconsin, Madison, 1981, contended that maternal dramas or "family films" primarily function as an ideological ally of patriarchal capitalism, adjusting women to domesticity through nostalgia.

(3)   The film received widespread critical acclaim. The Grapes of Wrath won two Academy Awards: John Ford for Best Director, Jane Darwell for Best Supporting Actress. It was also nominated for three more (Henry Fonda for Best Actor, Nunnally Johnson for Best Screenplay, and for Best Picture). In addition, The Grapes of Wrath was named Best Motion Picture and John Ford Best Director by the New York Film Critics. The National Board of Review cited it as among the ten best American films of 1940, and named Jane Darwell and Henry Fonda as among the best performers.   The

American Film Institute survey (1977) listed The Grapes of Wrath as fifth in the list of top ten American films of all time.

(4)   Toland's cinematography, aided by Ford's gift for lighting, has been compared by Warren French and others to the photography of Dorothea Lange and Walker Evans. The beauty of Ma Joad clearly contradicts dominant Hollywood codes of femininity. For further discussion of Toland's cinematography, see Eric Rhode, A History of the Cinema (New York: Hill and Wang, 1976), pp. 416-18. Jane Darwell's portrayal of Ma also bears similarity to the white tenant farm women interviewed in Margaret Jarman Hagood's Depression study Mothers of the South: Portraiture of the White Tenant Farm Woman (New York: Norton, 1977, orig., 1939).

(5)   The film's ending is much more optimistic than that of Steinbeck's novel. In the novel, Rosasharn, deserted by her husband and having delivered a stillborn baby, nurses a starving man. The novel's end conveys a sense of desperation coupled with the resilience of female nurturance. However, code standards would never have allowed the scene and Ford and Zanuck desired a more upbeat ending than Steinbeck had provided. See Mel Gussow, Don't Say Yes Until I Finish Talking: A Biography of Darryl F. Zanuck (Garden City, N.Y.: Doubleday, 1971). In other respects as well, the novel and the film differ markedly. See Warren French, Filmguide to The Grapes of Wrath (Bloomington: Indiana University Press, 1973).

(6)   John Ford was of Irish heritage. Very likely his conception of Ma Joad was drawn from the tradition of strong mothers within Irish Catholic peasant culture.

(7)   Peter Roffman and Jim Purdy, The Hollywood Social Problem Film: Madness, Despair and Politics from the Depression to the Fifties (Bloomington: University of Indiana Press, 1981), p. 126. Also see Russell Campbell, "Trampling Out the Vintage: Sour Grapes," in The Modern American Novel and the Movies, ed. by Gerald Peary and Roger Shatzkin (New York: Frederick Ungar, 1978), pp. 107-118 for a more open-ended reading of the politics of The Grapes of Wrath.

(8)   The novel much more explicitly conveys Ma's sense of her matriarchy as temporary and somewhat illegitimàte. Also, see Hagood's Mothers of the South for discussion of the contradiction between patriarchal ideology and female power in rural Depression America.

(9)   Michael Anderegg, William Wyler (Boston: Twayne, 1979), p. 118.

(10)   Bosley Crowther, New York Times, June 5, 1942, p. 23:1.

(11)   M. Joyce Baker, Images of Women In Film: The War Years (Ann Arbor: UMI Research Press, 1980), p. 33.

(12)   The Grapes of Wrath and Watch on the Rhine are both women's films and films of interest to both sexes. In fact, both films (unlike most other women's films) have strong male protagonists. However, an almost equally powerful heroine appears in Grapes of

Wrath as the hero's mother, and in Watch on the Rhine as his wife. For this reason, I consider these two films to be women's films.

(13) Lillian Hellman, Pentimento (Boston: Little, Brown, 1973), pp. 186-87.

(14) M. Joyce Baker, Images of Women In Film: The War Years, p. 102.

(15) Marjorie Rosen, Popcorn Venus (New York: Coward, McCann, Geoghegan, 1973), p. 205. However, one must also note that, not surprisingly, divorcée Emily is cast as a callous social climber. For a "reading" of this film as patriarchal discourse, see Michael Renov, "From Fetish to Subject: The Containment of Sexual Difference in Hollywood's Wartime Cinema," Wide Angle 5, 1 (1982): pp. 16-27.

(16) Serafina Bathrick in "The True Woman and the Family Film: The Industrial Production of Memory," notes that "the mise-en-scene which includes window, desk and typewriter does more than that to suggest a 'homecoming;' for the quaint Victorian window closely resembles the front of a B-17 bomber" (p. 228).

(17) While some critics might contend that Kris, Jenny, Sigrid, Trina, and Peter present negative and/or narrow stereotypes of immigrants, Marta is very clearly not presented as a model of homogenization or ethnic assimilation. As illustrated in a filmic segment to follow (the sequence of the solya), Marta Hansen represents an ethnic pride as well as an ability to adapt to and learn from her American experience.

(18) See Erving Goffman, Gender Advertisements (New York: Harper, 1976). Goffman discussed the arm-in-arm position as a visual sign in a pictorial system ordering dyadic relationships. He defines the "arm-lock" as a "tie-sign" usually depicting a male and female in a sexual relationship. This "tie-sign" is asymmetrical — the woman usually leaning on the (taller) man for guidance and protection. However, he notes that the sign is also employed in the dramatization and portrayal of other (usually unequal) relationships — father/daughter, grandparent/grandchild, etc. In this scene of I Remember Mama, it visually indicates both the closeness and inequality of Katrin and Marta. Katrin is looking up to Marta for guidance and support. However, although this physical sign connotes a relational hierarchy, it also suggests a more equal relationship then the "shoulder-hold" (one person's arm around the other).

(19) For a further discussion of Jo as feminist model see Elizabeth Fishel, Sisters (New York: Bantam, 1979), especially Chapter 4, "Sister Roles: Sisters as Little Women," pp. 71-92. Also see Sarah Elbert, A Hunger for Home: Louisa May Alcott and Little Women (Philadelphia: Temple University Press, 1983) and Nina Auerbach, Communities of Women (Cambridge: Harvard University Press, 1978).

(20) See Ferdinand Lundberg and Marynia Farnham, Modern Woman: The Lost Sex (New York: Harper, 1947).

(21) Whitney Stine (with Bette Davis), Mother Goddam (New York: Hawthorn, 1974), p. 168.

(22) Michael Wood, America in the Movies (New York: Basic, 1975), p. 106.

(23) Rosen, p. 269.

(24) Martha Wolfenstein and Nathan Leites, Movies: A Psychological Study (New York: Atheneum, 1977), pp. 130-131.

(25) Wood, America in the Movies, p. 98.

(26) See David Thomson, America in the Dark: The Impact of Hollywood Films on American Culture (New York: Morrow, 1977), p. 217.

(27) Kay dies after an outing with Bert, in which he fails to heed Mildred's warning that she may be getting sick. While there is no heavy-handed criticism implied in the film, nonetheless, Kay's death is clearly linked to the Pierces' divorce and Mildred's over-worked status as a single parent employed outside the home.

(28) Eric Rhode, A History of the Cinema: From Its Origins to 1970 (New York: Hill and Wang, 1976), pp. 405-06.

(29) Molly Haskell, From Reverence to Rape (New York: Holt, Rinehart and Winston, 1973), p. 179.

(30) See Chodorow, The Reproduction of Mothering; Dinner-stein, The Mermaid and the Minotaur.

(31) See Marjorie Rosen, Popcorn Venus: Women, Movies and the American Dream (New York: Coward, McCann, Geoghegan, 1973), p. 208, for a somewhat different view of the "overidentifica-tion" theme.

(32) Haskell, From Reverence to Rape, p. 169.

(33) Ibid., pp. 180-81.

(34) Catherine Turney and Ranald MacDougall were the major screenwriters; other scriptwriters included Margaret Gruen, Albert Maltz, Louise Pierson, Thames Williamson. See Alfred J. LaValley, Mildred Pierce (Madison: University of Wisconsin Press, 1980). LaValley calls this film "a bad fusion of the women's movie and film noir" (p. 29).

(35) For a discussion of the unconvincing nature of the ending, see Sidney Rosenzweig, Chapter 8, "Aprons and Minks," Mildred Pierce, Casablanca and Other Major Films of Michael Curtiz (Ann Arbor: UMI Research Press, 1982).

(36) See Connie Field, The Life and Times of Rosie the Riveter (Emeryville, Calif.: Rosie the Riveter Film Corp., Clarity Produc-tion, 1980).

Chapter 4

VIVE LA DIFFERENCE: Career Woman Comedies of the 1940s

If I want to be a strong woman, I've got to wear shoulder pads. Why Katharine Hepburn and Joan Crawford taught me that.

Ann S., age 36, homemaker

The advantage man enjoys . . . is that his vocation as a human being in no way runs counter to his destiny as a male. He is not divided . . . the emancipated woman . . . refuses to confine herself to her role as female, because she will not accept mutilation; but it would also be a mutilation to repudiate her sex. . . . To renounce a part of her humanity.

Simone de Beauvoir, The Second Sex
(New York: Bantam, 1970) pp. 641-42

A laugh is a reverse gasp.

Raymond Durgnat, The Crazy Mirror: Hollywood Comedy and the American Image (New York: Dell, 1969) p. 33

Can women "have it all" — career, love, family? Does success on the job spell loss of femininity? The theme of femininity versus achievement dominates contemporary women's magazines and fiction. Though many women today are more feminist than their foremothers, the issue of having it all is not new. In the 1940s, with its reordering of the sexual landscape, the question became crucial. Career woman dramas gave it symbolic life on the screen.

137

Career heroines – young, brash, attractive, and assertive – originated as flappers and working girls in films of the 1920s and 1930s. Employed in a variety of "women's jobs" (modeling, sales, clerical, and service work), most flappers proved hopeful, energetic, and assertive, even in the face of boredom and low pay. Yet their optimism usually sprung from hopes of early retirement and upward mobility through marriage. Mary Ryan (1976) remarked of such films as Subway Sadie (1926) and The Girl from Woolworth's (1928): "The working girl of the twenties cinema won her retirement through the promptings of love and trusting submission to her man."(1) While these films do reflect some pessimism about living "happily ever after," femininity took precedence over achievement.

By the Depression, the affluent flapper vanished from the screen; sacrificial mothers and downtrodden working girls took her place. With the advent of sound and the Production Code as well as the maturing of the women's film, working-girl movies became a Hollywood staple. Spoken dialogue facilitated the depiction of a more complex interpersonal world, while code-prescribed limits on cinematic sexuality inadvertently promoted the "career heroine."

The 1930s working girl, star of many A and B films, both compared and contrasted with her 1920s counterpart.(2) "Golddiggers" still proved popular; We're in the Money (1935) and Golddiggers of 1937 featured likeable heroines comically scheming to snare rich men. Like prostitutes, golddiggers are cynically pragmatic about the relations between the sexes. For one heroine (Golddiggers of 1933), "Either you work the men or the men work you."

However, alongside the golddigger, emerged the "superwoman," who views work not as a means to a "good marriage," but an end in itself.(3) As lawyers (The Law in Her Hands), businesswomen (Traveling Saleslady), reporters (Mystery of the Wax Museum), or doctors (Mary Stevens, M.D.), these heroines face the hostility of threatened husbands, lovers, and male co-workers. While the femininity-achievement conflict creates tension, that tension proves both positive and negative, however. These embattled superwomen seem to have far more exciting lives than their homebound sisters. However, dominant Depression ideology – in the studios and audiences – prevailed in the (usually) conservative endings.(4) Classic superwoman Rosalind Russell has noted:

Except for different leading men and a switch in title and pompadour, they were all stamped out of the same Alice in Careerland. The script always called for a leading lady somewhere in the 30s, tall, brittle, not too sexy. My wardrobe had a set pattern: a tan suit, a gray suit, a beige suit, and then a negligee for the seventh reel, near the end, when I would admit to my best friend that what I really wanted was to become a dear little housewife.(5)

CAREER HEROINES IN 1940s WOMEN'S FILMS

The 1940s saw the flowering of the filmic superwoman, her assertiveness symbolized by shoulder pads. Typically she is a middle-class professional: a writer (My Sister Eileen, Old Acquaintance); an executive (Roughly Speaking, Take a Letter, Darling); a politician (Lady from Cheyenne, The Farmer's Daughter); a nurse (Cry Havoc, So Proudly We Hail); a teacher (The Corn is Green, Remember the Day); a reporter (His Girl Friday, Woman of the Year); a psychiatrist (Spellbound); a dancer (Dance, Girl, Dance); or a lawyer (Adam's Rib). Rarely is she a welder or riveter, and then usually her motivation is middle-class patriotism (e.g. Meet the People and Since You Went Away), rather than working-class necessity. And rarely does the camera enter the factory. The glamorized ambiance of the law office, the newsroom, the bustling hospital constitutes the universe of working woman dramas.

Some of these films, while set in the workplace, are thematically similar to maternal dramas. The teacher in The Corn is Green (Bette Davis) and the psychiatrist in Spellbound (Ingrid Bergman) are "professional mothers" whose careers enable them to nurture psychologically needy men. Like Ma Joad, they may be culturally acceptable as strong heroines since they use their skills to empower men. A maternalized form of achievement makes peace with traditional femininity in these films.

Some of the most enduringly popular 1940s career woman films, however, are neither maternal workplace dramas nor classic "compromise" films. Comedies such as His Girl Friday (1940), Woman of the Year (1942), and Adam's Rib (1949) for example, feature heroines in a comic, competitive, sexually charged dynamic with male lovers/co-workers. It is both within and against the couple relationship that the heroines define themselves. From His Girl Friday (1940) to Adam's Rib (1949), we can trace a progressive evolution in the presentation of the femininity-achievement conflict.

Another top-grossing feature, the Freudian-inspired musical comedy Lady in the Dark (1944), however, approaches the issue very differently. The heroine, a successful editor, is haunted by a longing for dependency. Perhaps the most antifeminist movie of the era, Lady in the Dark presents images of womanhood that conflict sharply with the superwoman ideal.

Through describing the thematic evolution from His Girl Friday to Adam's Rib, this chapter contrasts their narrative patterns to that of Lady in the Dark. Perhaps most importantly, the career woman comedy raises a critical question: Why do both the most and least feminist films of the decade portray the dynamic of femininity versus achievement?

HIS GIRL FRIDAY (1940)

I'm a newspaperman.

Hildy Johnson

Howard Hawks' screwball comedy opens at a hyperactive pace in a busy contemporary urban newsroom. Stopping to chat briefly with harried switchboard operators, fast-talking, smartly tailored Hildy Johnson (Rosalind Russell) has a mission: to inform her ex-spouse and editor that she is remarrying and leaving the newspaper world forever.

As soon as Hildy confidently strides into Walter Burns' (Cary Grant's) office, a comic rapid-fire verbal duel is underway. Walter, the ultimate con-man, is put on the defensive. In what Hawks called "the fastest on-screen dialogue in history," Hildy informs him that she's changing her life. In a mere 24 hours, Hildy Johnson will become Mrs. Bruce Baldwin, wife of an insurance agent, living contentedly in upstate New York.

As Walter pleads with Hildy and follows her, pacing rapidly about the newsroom, she asserts:

Hildy: You wouldn't know what it means to be respectable, to live a halfway normal life . . .

He doesn't treat me like an errand boy, either, Walter. He treats me like a woman.

Walter: He does, does he? How did I treat you – like a water buffalo?

Hildy: He's kind, he's sweet, and he's considerate.

Walter: Hmmm, hmmm . . .

Hildy: He wants a home and children.

Walter: Sounds more like a guy I ought to marry. What's his name?

As the camera moves from medium shot to close-up and back again, Walter (literally) is falling out of the frame, visual comedy underscoring the zaniness of the dialogue.

Despite his acid tongue, however, Walter is desperate. It is quite clear that he wants Hildy back – as his wife and reporter. And, although he seems traditionally masculine in many ways, he will resort to "feminine" wiles to win back his ex-wife.

Hildy, too, is complex. Although her new-found domesticity is traditionally feminine, her assertiveness is "masculine." She seems totally in control as she barges into Walter's office, telling him she is leaving the newsroom with its locker-room misogyny forever. Yet Hildy's preference for domesticity, however, is contradicted by her appearance. Rosalind Russell, with her bold manner, determined features, and crazily striped business suit, is very much the professional woman.(6) It's almost impossible to imagine Hildy (as one male reporter comments later in the film) "singing lullabies and hanging out dydies."

Beneath Hildy's confidence in her reborn housewifery, however, lies deep ambivalence. If she's so sure of her choice, why has she come back personally to see Walter? As Stanley Cavell suggests, Hildy may be returning for a "last fix" of Walter.(7) As we watch Russell and Grant revel in their verbal sparring match, they seem quite at home together in that newsroom. Walter asserts confidently to Hildy, "We've got something between us nothing can change." As he runs a race against time (Hildy's wedding is only a day away), he is determined to prove this statement true.

Walter, as unscupulous as he is loving, devises a plan. Convicted murderer Earl Williams (John Qualen, in a classic role as a down-trodden proletarian) is about to be hanged. A good newspaper interview (as only Hildy can do!) might save Williams.

Walter convinces Hildy to do the story in the context of an awkwardly hilarious luncheon date involving Walter, Hildy, and her fiancé Bruce (Ralph Bellamy). True to form, Walter invites himself along for lunch and uses the opportunity to ridicule Bruce and charm Hildy.

> Walter: She deserves all the happiness, Bruce — all the things I can't give her . . .
>
> You're going to live with your mother?
>
> Bruce: Just for the first year.
>
> Walter: That will be nice . . . a home with mother. In Albany, too.

A reaction shot shows a smirking Hildy; she knows what Walter's up to. But it's clear she's also enjoying it.

Although Bruce is a classic milquetoast, his appeal for Hildy is easy to understand. It would be hard to imagine the chivalrous Bruce slamming doors on Hildy, abandoning her on their honeymoon for a "hot" story, or smirking as she struggled with a heavy suitcase. Yet Bruce is as boring as he is dependable.(8)

While we begin to understand Bruce's appeal, Walter clearly wins the lunchtime confrontation. Baldwin is unknowingly humiliated by a clever Burns who jokes snidely about Hildy and Bruce traveling together on an overnight train before the wedding. When Bruce soberly replies that mother will chaperone, the victory is Walter's. A lifetime of Bruce is rapidly becoming less attractive to Hildy. And as Walter kids Hildy about their shared past (Walter: "Want my fingerprints?" Hildy: "No thanks, I've still got those"), a sense of intimacy re-emerges. As Stanley Cavell has noted, "the pair communicate . . . in a lingo and tempo, . . . about events present and past, that Bruce can have no part in."(9) Hildy, tempted by a last chance to ply her trade, agrees to do the story and leave later for Albany.

As Hildy starts the story, she re-experiences frustration as a woman in the male world of journalism. In the grimy pressroom, hard-boiled cynicism dominates among her card-playing male colleagues who comment sarcastically on everything from world politics to the female body. "Stairway Sam" even gazes up women's dresses! Opportunism dominates; the "hot angle" takes precedence over the truth. Even Hildy, interviewing the pathetically confused prisoner, exploits the situation (albeit for humanitarian reasons) by suggesting murder motives rather than allowing Williams to reconstruct the crime.

Hildy Johnson (Rosalind Russell) encounters the cynical masculinity of the press room in Howard Hawks' His Girl Friday (1940). Louie is played by Abner Biberman.

In the pressroom, Walter Burns' ethics dominate. Hildy, a classic token, loses power, her feminine attire appearing humorous and incongruous at work:(10)

When she runs after Warden Cooley, her skirt pulled up around her knees and her high heels making her totter precariously, we realize to what degree the humor of the film depends on our assumptions of how women normally behave.(11)

Yet Hildy is no victim. Energetic and competent, she stands head and shoulders above many male reporters and has won their respect. As a woman, she approaches her work with heightened sensitivity, treating Williams' distraught girlfriend Mollie Malloy (Helen Mock) with more compassion than her male colleagues can muster.

> Mollie: They ain't human.
>
> Hildy: I know. They're newspapermen.

Yet Hildy never demands that the newsroom become equally a "woman's space." Her answer is retirement to the home. In a particularly exasperating moment (one of Walter's tricks has landed Bruce in jail!) Hildy decides to quit:

> I'm gonna be a woman, not a newsgetting machine. I'm gonna have babies and take care of them and . . . watch their teeth grow, and, and — oh dear, if I ever see one of 'em look at a newspaper again, I'm gonna brain 'em.

Yet Hildy is "hooked" by Walter and the exciting bustle of the pressroom. When shots ring out (Williams has escaped), Hildy can't leave. As she calls Walter Burns to "tell him I need him," with Bruce hanging on another line, it sounds like Hildy is escaping, too — from her conversion to domesticity. Only Walter can really share her passion for her work.

In a series of comic vignettes (one of which includes the gagging and kidnapping of Bruce's mother), Hildy and Walter are reuniting as a couple. As Bruce barges into the pressroom to confront Hildy and Walter (who are hiding Williams in a rolltop desk), he asks naively:

> Bruce: Can you tell me where my mother was going?
>
> Hildy: She couldn't say.

Hildy has adopted Walter's 'trickster' style. Bruce leaves, angrily. Dull as he is, he can see that he's now the outsider.

After more madcap misadventure, Williams lives, but Walter and Hildy are arrested for harboring a criminal. After their release, they reminisce about old times: the theft of a stomach off a coroner's table and their unwed sexual adventures at the Shoreham Hotel. "We could have gone to jail for that, too," laughs Walter.

In less than 24 hours, Hildy is reunited with Walter, a Walter who acts more gentle but is as much a trickster as ever. Yet, it is not primarily Walter who persuades Hildy. It is experiencing herself in a relationship that is both intellectual and sexual. As Molly Haskell has noted,

> Grant . . . shakes her into the realization of her true
> nature. . . . It is as a newspaper reporter rather than as a
> wife and mother that she discovers her true "womanliness,"
> which is to say, simply herself.(12)

In the screwball tradition (with similarities to <u>Philadelphia Story</u> and <u>Bringing Up Baby</u>) <u>His Girl Friday</u> celebrates the madcap battle of the sexes rather than the security of stable family life. This "comedy of remarriage," as Cavell has termed it, seeks "to turn marriage itself into romance, into adventure . . . , to preserve within it something of the illicit."(13) The traditional and avant-garde blend in an uneasy alliance.

Although Hildy and Walter share an unusual and alternative relationship, their marriage is far from equal. As the film title (and ending) suggest, Hildy is a classic, Hawksian woman, a token in a man's world.(14)

> In the crucial confrontation between editor and reporter, a
> long tracking shot done in one continuous take, Walter
> restrains Hildy. . . . She backs away from him, but he guides
> her as if in a dance, prodding her, turning her, physically
> dominating her, all the while weaving a hypnotic spell with
> his ceaseless talking. . . . She concedes, she cries.(15)

Although Hildy opts for a career, the standards she must meet are masculine. As Hildy admits, "I'm a newspaperman."(16)

WOMAN OF THE YEAR (1942)

The duelling couple appears again (Hepburn and Tracy, in the first of their nine features) in this George Stevens film. The woman is Tess Harding (Hepburn), star wartime political reporter for a major New York City newspaper; her male foil is Sam Craig (Tracy), leading sportswriter on the same journal. Their filmic relationship (like that of Russell and Grant) begins in hostility and rivalry.

In the opening scene, Sam Craig, in a bar with some male cronies, explodes with rage at Harding who has suggested abolishing baseball for the duration of the war. Although he has never met her, Sam, with his down-to-earth, man on the street air, is determined to fight back. She has challenged his territory. A barroom friend advises caution: "She's the number 2 dame in the country, next to Mrs. Roosevelt." Undaunted, Sam attacks Tess in his column; their relationship begins as a war of the pen.

Sam meets Tess in the next sequence, as he visits her office and encounters her rather effeminate and rudely efficient secretary, Gerald (Dan Tobin). Tess appears to be a superwoman – brilliant, businesslike, and efficient. Yet the first visual introduction to her is a very sensually composed shot of first her shapely stockinged legs and then of her attractively suited body. A current of sexual attraction quickly passes between the warring pair. The differences between them — Tracy, embodying a working-class and not overly handsome masculinity; Hepburn, displaying an upper class and sometimes brittle aristocratic femininity — would create the electricity for their success on the screen:

> They came together at a time when their careers were foundering; misfits in the Hollywood mold, they were not in any way typical romantic leads. Hepburn had grown older, the face that once blushed in gracious concession to femininity now betrayed in no uncertain terms the recalcitrant New England spirit. And Tracy, too short and dumpy for conventional leading roles, hadn't found the woman who could lure him from the rugged masculine world he inhabited. Out of their complementary incongruities, they created one of the most romantic couples the cinema has ever known.(17)

In Harding's office, Craig feels unsophisticated. Gerald treats him rudely and Tess buzzes about, speaking several different languages simultaneously on the phone with world leaders. Craig attempts to turn the tables by inviting Tess to a ball game. She accepts, and in the next scene, Sam hilariously plays teacher to her neophyte. Yet the power balance doesn't last long. She invites him to her home for what Craig assumes is a romantic evening. When he arrives, however, Sam suffers a grave shock. He's been asked to a party with diplomats and celebrities from around the globe. Conversations whizz by in a dozen tongues, and Tess as hostess virtually ignores Sam. As power shifts toward Tess, audience sympathy slants toward Sam. The superwoman seems to have a "superego."

The twists and turns of their sexual power play create the context for sustained comedy. Their sarcastic rapid-fire dialogue occurs in classic Hollywood two-shots, visually emphasizing the dynamic between the characters, rather than the environment around them.(18) The Harding-Craig relationship, like that of Johnson-Burns, presents a complex, untraditional sharing of sexual roles. Sam's work is traditionally masculine, yet so is Tess'. However, Tess, more explicitly feminist than Hildy, is no token. She has an important role model in a feminist aunt (Fay Bainter), and addresses women's groups on female emancipation. In one of the film's most hilarious scenes, Sam comes to meet Tess, who's addressing a women's luncheon. He unexpectedly walks out onto a stage full of females. As Tess ardently proclaims that "women of the world are faced with a changing place, no longer in the home but also the line of battle," Sam falls over his feet, a veritable bull in a china shop, token male in a world of women.

The rocky romance quickly escalates into a marriage proposal. Tess accepts but doesn't allow matrimony to cramp her style. Like Walter Burns, work comes first, even on her wedding night, when she hosts a group of political refugees. Ever eager to reassert his power, Sam asks several friends over for a party. Tess quickly gets the point; they declare a truce and the guests depart.

Their marriage is as unconventional as their courtship. As Karyn Kay (1977) has noted,

> She is the important news reporter, he, the simple sports writer. He mopes when she ignores his new hat or forgets a dinner appointment. He wants children; she doesn't. He cooks; she can't.(19)

Yet strain intensifies after they wed and Sam considers Tess insensitive and egotistical. The last straw occurs when Harding, chair of a refugee committee, adopts Kris, a Greek orphan, without consulting her husband. Tess, in desiring to present the correct public image, is callous to both Sam and the confused boy. As she is about to be named "Woman of the Year" at a banquet, Sam acidly retorts, "You want to know something? The 'woman of the year' is no woman at all!" He returns Kris to the orphanage and leaves Tess.

Sam's departure is a rude awakening for Tess. She begins to question her values and personality style. At the wedding of her aunt and her widowed father, Tess asks her aunt about life as an emancipated woman. Her relative replies: "You can't live alone forever. I'm tired of winning prizes – they're cold comfort. For once, I'd like to be the prize."

Tess resolves that she, too, will change. With the "Gibson's Housewives' Cook Book," she rushes over to Sam's now-bachelor flat to prepare the perfect breakfast. In a supposedly hilarious episode, Tess bungles even the simplest culinary task. Coffee boils over, waffles explode, and toast pops all over the floor. Tess, paragon of efficiency at work, is a disaster at home.

Up to now, Tess' "reborn domesticity" seems not a permanent state, but an understandably guilty reaction to her previous insensitivity. When Craig awakens, he enters his kitchen and can't believe his eyes. He asks Tess incredulously: "Are you going to cook and sew?" Although she replies, "Yes," Sam remains unconvinced. And, understandably, since the "new Tess" lacks the dynamism of the superstar columnist. Craig doesn't seem to want a hausfrau, merely a more sensitive mate. "Can't you be Tess Harding Craig?" he asks her in compromise.

However, just as Woman of the Year seems about to conclude on a more egalitarian note, Gerald arrives, to ask Tess to cover the launching of a ship. As she wavers, Sam escorts Gerald out the door. Offscreen, a loud crash resounds. Craig proudly returns to announce, "I've just launched Gerald." An ambiguous film unconvincingly ends on a clear note of male dominance.

Woman of the Year presents the femininity-achievement conflict in ways both similar to and different from His Girl Friday. Harding and Craig, like Johnson and Burns, find that a mutual passion for work and interpersonal competition invigorate their relationship. Yet, unlike Hildy, Tess is a woman whose career involvement, rather than her token status, seriously undermines her sensitivity. Whereas one might argue that the portrayal of Tess merely critiques workaholism and not feminism, one must ask why Tess, and not Sam, is depicted so negatively. Woman of the Year presents a dual message: public achievement both heightens and threatens the identity of a woman.

ADAM'S RIB (1949)

Seven years later, Hepburn and Tracy appear again, portraying a slightly older and more settled but still embattled pair of lawyer-spouses. Although there are similarities to both His Girl Friday and Woman of the Year, the presentation of characters and resolution of the narrative are much more egalitarian.

Adam's Rib, shot on location, and inspired by a true story, begins on a late afternoon in contemporary downtown Manhattan. A distraught young blonde woman (Judy Holliday) paces nervously, chewing compulsively on a candy bar, obviously waiting for someone. A gleam of recognition in her eye tells the audience that a particular man (Tom Ewell) leaving an office building across the street is the one she wants. She stalks him through a crowded subway and up to the second floor of a brownstone. Comedy punctuates this scene as she clumsily removes a gun from her purse, anxiously scanning the instruction manual. She bursts through the door to discover Ewell embracing a negligee-clad young woman (Jean Hagen), as jazz blares in the background. Crying hysterically "my dear husband" she fires several times. As Ewell falls, wounded, she embraces him.

Although little dialogue has been spoken, the audience knows that it has witnessed an act of female revenge. A newspaper headline appears boldly on screen: "WIFE SHOOTS FICKLE MATE IN PRESENCE OF LOVE RIVAL."

The film cuts to the next morning in the posh uptown duplex of lawyers Adam (Tracy) and Amanda (Hepburn) Bonner, preparing to go to their respective offices. The Bonners seem the closest friends, warm lovers and sexual equals. Affectionately, they call each other "Pinky" (his with a "y," hers with an "ie"), and joke in bathrobes and slippers. Yet their cameraderie begins to wane as they both read the newspaper feature story. Doris Attinger shot and wounded her husband Warren at the home of his lover Beryl Caighn. Amanda and her maid have a similar immediate response:

> Maid: Hot Dog! Woman shot her husband!
>
> Amanda: He was playing her fast and loose so she caught him out and popped him a few 32 calibers . . . . Serves him right, the little two-timer!

Adam, however, is outraged. Mrs. Attinger shows nothing but "contempt for the law."

As the Bonners drive to work, Amanda asserts that Doris Attinger will suffer the inequities of an unwritten law that exonerates a man, but not a woman, of a crime of passion. Hard-headed Adam, however, contends that "crime should be punished, not condoned," no matter what the extenuating circumstances. As they discuss the Attinger case, visual comedy underscores the dialogue and plays on traditional conceptions of sexual roles. As Mrs. Bonner weaves in and out of traffic, stopping suddenly, a male taxi driver exclaims "Lady drivers!"

As Amanda arrives at her office, her secretary, like the maid, is taking vicarious pleasure in the crime: "Look at that, he two-timed her and she popped him one!" Doris Attinger has conquered female passivity and martyrdom and, abstractly right or wrong, inspires admiration from other women of all classes. Amanda is excited and obsessed by the shooting, viewing it as a symbol of the double standard. But it is Adam's sexism that persuades her to take the case. In a phone conversation, Adam, who informs her that he will represent Warren Attinger, responds in a classic male manner to Amanda's feminism: "You just sound cute when you get causy." For Amanda, it's the last straw; she decides to defend Doris.

In the next scene (in one of several exceptionally long takes), Amanda Bonner meets the imprisoned Doris Attinger. Elite feminism encounters the common woman's revenge. Doris presents a deceptively naive and comic first impression. Bleached blonde, somewhat inarticulate, and confused, Doris contrasts sharply with the tailored, polished Amanda. She refuses a cigarette Amanda offers her: "It's not feminine." And Doris, with her exaggerated "Brooklyn-ese," seems quite gullible and suggestible at first.

> Amanda: Occupation?
>
> Doris: No occupation.
>
> Amanda: Housewife.
>
> Doris: That's right — housewife.

Yet Mrs. Attinger proves more complex and strongly motivated than her appearance initially suggests.

> Amanda: Let's start with the day of the accident.
>
> Doris: No accident! I wanted to shoot him.

As Amanda asks her to reconstruct the day of the crime, Doris pours out a tragi-comedy of physical abuse, philandering, confusion, overeating, and revenge.

> Amanda: And what did you do?
>
> Doris: I had a cup of coffee. . . . So then I bought some chocolate nut bars and kept eatin' all of them until he come out . . . and then I followed him.
>
> Amanda: After you shot him, how did you feel?
>
> Doris: Hungry.

Judy Holliday, in her first major screen role, creates a character type she would play again (in another Cukor-Kanin-Gordon film, The Marrying Kind): the "dumb blonde who isn't so dumb."(20)

Doris is portrayed comically but with dignity. Although distraught, Doris is far from mad; "It was no accident . . . I have three children — she was breaking up my home." However, her intent was not murder. Doris merely wanted to scare the lovers and end the affair.

The relationship between lawyer and client is portrayed with comic sympathy. A wide cultural gap separates Amanda, with her Ivy League air, from Doris, with her working-class slang. Yet, interestingly enough, Attinger is the actor and Bonner the defender. And, rarely does Amanda elicit laughter at Doris' expense.

> Cukor and company acknowledge the most fundamental intellectual, spiritual and economic inequality between the educated elite and the less privileged and less imaginative members of lower-middle-class America; but they never deprive them of their dignity or deny them joys and sorrows.(21)

When Amanda arrives home that evening to host a dinner party, she informs Adam that she will be on the other side of the courtroom. He drops a tray of drinks! Amanda is testing a basic commandment of traditional marriage: "Thou shalt not challenge thy husband's authority in public." As Mrs. Bonner refuses to put up the "united front," she places her marriage in jeopardy. From this point on, Adam's Rib alternates between court and home, as the war of the sexes spills over from one into the other.

Amanda constructs her defense around the proposition that women are, in all spheres, equal to men. At first she and Adam even flirt with each other in court, maintaining an air of good-natured conflict and mutual respect. Cooking together and joking after their day in court lends vitality to their marriage:

His virility acts as a buffer to her intelligence; she is tempered by him just as he is sharpened by her.(22)

However, the Bonners' cameraderie begins to unravel as their courtroom battles become front-page news. Adam asks Amanda to drop the case: "It's going to get . . . messier day by day by day." Yet she refuses, aggravating him further. Their neighbor Kip (David Wayne), a somewhat effeminate songwriter, becomes enamoured with Amanda and her defense. Adam reacts in classic male posture.

> Kip: I'm on your side. You've got me so convinced I may even go out and become a woman.

> Adam: And he wouldn't have far to go, either.

Kip writes a Cole Porterish tune for the occasion, "Farewell Amanda," which becomes the theme song for the film.

The Bonners' dispute breaks into open conflict when Amanda dramatizes her feminism by parading in a series of outstanding women — from prizewinning chemists to taxi drivers to lumberjacks. The piece de resistance, however, occurs when she orders wrestler Olympia LaPere (Hope Emerson) to hoist Adam on her shoulders and parade him around the courtroom.

Adam feels that not only he, but the law itself, is being ridiculed. He is discovering a new side of Amanda, a side he doesn't much like or respect. And furthermore, he's reached his limit with her feminism, reacting in classical male backlash:

> Adam: I'm old fashioned. I like two sexes. All of a sudden I don't like being married to what's known as a 'new woman.' I want a wife, not a competitor.

Declaring that Amanda has lost respect for the law and their marriage, Adam moves out near the end of the trial. As he clumsily slams the apartment door, "Farewell Amanda" is heard on the record player.

Amanda finally wins the case, after a brilliant cross-examination of Warren Attinger and an impassioned final appeal to the jurors. She asks the women and men of the jury to imagine Warren Attinger as a woman, Doris Attinger and Beryl Caighn as men. Doris and Beryl's images dissolve to portray them with mustaches and short dark hair. Warren, in this filmic fantasy, looks very much the female impersonator in Doris' hat (actually Amanda's) and blonde wig. Mrs. Bonner asks her jurors what their judgments would be if the genders were reversed. The fantasy exercise wins the case for Amanda: doesn't our society find the cuckolded husband more forgivable than the betrayed wife? Adam, with his recourse to abstract standards of justice, fails to convince the jury.

Adam, however, wins in a second round. One night he returns home to find Amanda and Kip innocently embracing. Adam points a gun; Amanda shrieks, "nobody has the right." Her husband smiles, "That's all sister, that's all I wanted to hear," and puts the gun in his mouth. It's licorice, just a joke. But Adam proves his point: no one has the right to threaten human life under any circumstances.

After winning the philosophical battle, Adam gets Amanda back as well. As the estranged couple meet with their accountant, Adam starts crying. Amanda is deeply moved and goes with him to their country home where they're reunited, sitting on their four-poster bed. Adam admits he faked the "tears," but then, if the courtroom can be a stage, why not the accountant's office as well? The film ends on a note of mutuality: she won publicly, he won privately. Yet, as Amanda praises marital equality, Adam proclaims, "Vive la différence!"

Molly Haskell has called Adam's Rib "a commercial 'feminist' film."(23) Though it may not be feminist, it does stand out as one of the most egalitarian films of its era, and ours. Amanda Bonner is a courageous woman who is unafraid to challenge publicly the very basis of her marriage. Her union with Adam is a mature, seasoned relationship whose passion sparks from equality and difference.

However, the sexual dynamics of the film are not wholly without stereotyping. Amanda plays "emotional female" defense lawyer to Adam's "rational male" prosecutor. As Joan Mellen (1977) has noted,

> Logic becomes the male prerogative, as Tracy is proven entirely correct that Holliday's excuse of passion would allow us all to be murderers, a position in defense of reason which had been thwarted solely by Amanda's resort to the emotional.(24)

And when Hepburn says "No one has the right," you know Tracy has won. And winning the philosophical battle is no simple "eye for an eye." It is the real contest upon which the trial is based.

Yet Amanda's courtroom victory is hardly eclipsed. Myths of female inferiority and passivity are challenged by Doris' revenge, Amanda's brilliant rhetoric, and the impressive array of superwomen on the stand. As Brandon French (1978) has noted,

> While the movie asserts that no one has the right to shoot another human being, the symbolic value of this gesture as a liberation from traditional female passivity is simultaneously affirmed.(25)

Yet perhaps most significant, is the sense that men and women see the world differently. Amanda refuses to categorize morality in absolute terms, while Adam cannot respect or understand the complexity of her ethics.(26)

Although Adam has the last word (symbolically and literally), his edge of power is quite slim. Adam's Rib is a world away from His Girl Friday, and stands out as perhaps the most progressive women's film of the decade.

LADY IN THE DARK (1944)

Liza Elliot (Ginger Rogers), the fashion editor in Mitchell Leisen's top-grossing musical comedy, at first seems just another wisecracking, shoulder-padded executive. Yet first appearances are deceiving.

Lady in the Dark opens in a darkened doctor's office. A female head appears in silhouette, as a white-coated man examines her eyes. Images of feminine vulnerability contrast to masculine expertise.

Doctor: Liza, there's nothing wrong with you physically.

Liza: Why do I have this horrible depression, this panic, if I'm all right?

The doctor suggests psychoanalysis to a skeptical Liza.

Liza: You don't really believe in that hocus-pocus?

Doctor: All of us hide things from ourselves. I believe that's what you've done and that may be the root of your trouble. If you go on this way, there won't be any work.

The mood radically changes, as the setting shifts to the metropolitan offices of Allure, "magazine of fashion" (Liza Elliott is an editor there). Yet the nether-world of dreams spills over into work. Her middle-aged friend and assistant Maggie is supportive, urging her to rest. However, her ruthlessly competitive assistant editor Charlie Johnson (Ray Milland) is threatened by Liza (who has been editor for 10 years). He uses his knowledge of her depression as a weapon against her:

Boss lady, ya gotta minute? You know you're losing your grip. When I was in the third grade, Miss Comfort used to make the boys stand in the corner. By the way you didn't happen to know Miss Comfort, did you?

Johnson clearly wishes he were in Elliott's shoes and never loses an opportunity to try to prove himself and humiliate her. He's convinced that her efficiency masks deep sexual insecurities.

Johnson: You ever see one of these brick houses? When you get close to it, the brick's not really brick at all, but just painted on. That big executive pose of hers is the same thing. Every time I see her I can't resist chipping little bits of it off to see what's underneath.

The troubled editor Liza Elliott (Ginger Rogers) surrounded by her staff at Allure. Charlie Johnson (Ray Milland) is in the background, in Mitchell Leisen's Lady in the Dark (1944).

We next encounter Liza in her posh apartment. Her fiancé and publisher Kendall Nesbitt, a kindly older man, is visiting. Liza and Kendall plan to marry, yet Nesbitt's estranged wife refuses to divorce him, placing their relationship in limbo. Kendall, however, seems more perturbed about it than Liza.

The frame fades out and into the office of young psychoanalyst Alexander Brooks. Liza tells him that, for 6 months, she's been consumed by anxiety and terror, unable to find solace even in work. A frightened Liza agrees to a trial analysis. On the analytic couch, Liza relives the counterreality of her dreams. In the (aesthetically horrendous) dream sequences, the photography shifts to color and the filmic mode to musical comedy. As Liza dances among clouds, she finds a coffin-like box marked "Private, Editor-in-Chief." Out of the box pops a filmy blue gown. As Liza dons the gown and removes her glasses, she looks much more "feminine" and glamorous. She glides through a huge, ornate hall, surrounded by adoring men. Charlie Johnson, however, appears in her dream, as in life, to unruffle her composure; he's painting a portrait of her for a U.S. stamp. As he unveils the picture, her admirers burst out in uncontrolled laughter. The "portrait" is a caricature of a bespectacled Liza at the editor's desk, with upswept hair and pinstriped business suit. Johnson exclaims: "What's the matter, Boss Lady, can't you take it?" As the film fades to black and white, Liza says that she awoke crying.

> Brooks: In reality you are a woman who cares little for feminine adornments. In fact you go to the other extreme. In your dream you were a glamor woman.

> Liza: If I wanted my fill of clothes and glamor I could have it. I'm surrounded by it all day.

> Brooks: Unless there was something in the past, in your memory blocking you. Have you never consciously wanted to be that glamorous, seductive woman?

> Liza: Never!

Brooks suggests that a traumatic episode might have blocked her true desires for "femininity." As the film progresses, the black-and-white work scenes contrast to the color dream sequences, and Liza comes less and less to trust herself and more and more to believe Brooks.

Back at Allure, film star Randy Curtis is capturing the attention of the female staff. All, that is, except the editor. Liza seems nonplussed by Randy (he asks her to dinner), and cannot understand the fawning of the other women: "You think they've never seen a man before." At the same time, Kendall's wife finally agrees to a divorce. Although he seems overjoyed, Liza is anxious and perturbed.

Her anxiety translates itself into a dream (shot in technicolor on gaudy sets) of her wedding to Kendall (Charlie Johnson as priest). However, it is not Kendall, but Randy she embraces. Johnson asks, "Is there anyone who knows a reason why these two should not be married? A female chorus sings, "This woman at the altar — is not the true Liza Elliott." One woman chants: "Tell them about yourself . . . the woman you really want to be, longing to be beautiful, yet rejecting beauty." The next shot is of a terrified Liza atop a huge wedding cake surrounded by prison bars.

The color frame slowly dissolves to the black and white of Brooks' office. He suggests that Liza never really wanted Nesbitt. Rather, he represents a father figure who could protect her from her own sexuality and competition with other women: "Isn't your affection for Kendall Nesbitt based on the fact that he resembles your father?" (The camera pans to Liza's look of shocked recognition.)

Brooks: That you have in fact transferred your love for your father to him. As long as he was married to a woman who wouldn't give him a divorce, you were safe, safe from competition with other women. But the moment you were faced with becoming his . . .

(Liza angrily turns her back.)

Liza: That's horrible — not true!

Brooks: If it's not true, then why do you reject Randy Curtis? . . . Most women would be very interested in Randy Curtis.

Liza: I am not most women . . . . I can think of nothing I'd hate more than a lot of men chasing after me making love to me.

Brooks: Aren't you resisting his invitation because you're afraid to compete with other women? The plain way you dress is a protective behavior. With it, you are not forced to compete. You don't dare it!

Liza: I loathe fancy clothes!

Brooks: That's not true — your dreams deny it!

Liza: (angrily) . . . your interpretation of them!

Brooks: I think we'll find that those interpretations are true.

Liza: (turning her back) We'll find nothing.

Liza terminates therapy, asking Brooks for a final bill. Yet Liza's rebellion will be short-lived.

At work, however, Liza remains as confused as ever. Johnson suggests — in his insulting way — similar insights to those of Brooks. He tells her he is taking an editorship at Town and Country; he's long eyed Liza's job and it's unlikely she will relinquish it.

Charlie: I know your kind. You have magazines instead of babies.

Liza: Why you insolent pup — ill-mannered boor!

Charlie: Rage is a pretty good substitute for sex.

After this scene, Liza tells Kendall she's not ready for marriage. He is angry, but understanding, thinking that Liza is merely experiencing "cold feet."

Liza decides to prove something to herself and Brooks – she goes out with Randy Curtis. Liza even dresses up, if only to see if she can enjoy looking feminine. Randy suddenly becomes intensely infatuated: "You're the only person I want." Yet he is unable to follow through on his desire, as he is constantly interrupted by women requesting autographs. Liza becomes annoyed; echoes of Brooks return. Does she desire as well as fear competition with other women?

Disturbed by recurrent dreams, Liza is back again on Brooks' couch. In her latest dream, she is being charged in court with the "inability to make up her mind as to the kind of woman she wants to be – the executive or the enchantress." Another fantasy involves herself as a young child being yelled at by her father for wearing a blue dress.

After intensive analysis, Liza reveals that she had adored both parents. Particularly she had longed to be feminine like her mother and please her father. However, Liza's mother died when she was 4 or 5. Wishing to please her bereaved father, little Liza put on her mother's blue gown. Yet this only served to exacerbate his grief; Mr. Elliott sternly ordered Liza never again to wear that dress. Blue became a hated color and Liza vowed to focus on school and avoid looking pretty: "If I wasn't going to be anything else, I was going to be tops in my class." This pattern lasted until her late teens when she met Ben. The romance was short-lived, however; Ben's ex-girlfriend returned, displacing Liza.

For Brooks, the puzzle pieces fit neatly:

Brooks: A little girl convinced of her own ugliness sees herself as not as good as other little girls. You build a wall around yourself after that. You are determined that you'd never put yourself in a position to be hurt again – until that one time with Ben in high school. You dropped your defenses and in that crucial moment you received another blow. I think it was then that you withdrew as a woman and would never again risk being hurt as a woman compared with other women. You buried your emotions and all your painful memories . . . you proceeded to escape into a loveless world of work.

Liza: It wasn't loveless; I loved Kendall.

Brooks: No, Miss Elliott. In rejecting Mr. Nesbitt, you proved that you dominated him, and you tend to dominate all men . . .

Liza: (looking ashamed) Well, what's the answer?

Brooks: Perhaps some man who will dominate you (emphasis mine)

Soon after Liza tells Maggie: "I want and need someone to lean on, to take care of me .... I want to live as other women do." Maggie replies, uncharacteristically: "It's what I always hoped for you. I want a big picture of Freud right in my office!"

Then Liza proceeds to choose the appropriate man to dominate her. Curtis seems a likely choice; conveniently he now works at Allure. However, he wants Liza as boss. She knows immediately he is not the "right man":

> Liza: I thought he was a tower of strength... he's frightened and insecure. He needs what Kendall needed — a mother, not a wife.

The next logical choice proves to be her archrival, Charlie. In what may be the most antifeminist ending of a 1940s film, Johnson walks in, and assumes the editor's chair, as Liza falls on the floor. They kiss and Charlie takes charge — of Liza and Allure.

Despite its conservative message, aesthetic deficiencies, and simplistic Freudianism, Lady in the Dark achieved box office success. The late-war dream-world was a complicated one.

HIS GIRL FRIDAY TO ADAM'S RIB:
THE EVOLUTION OF THE CAREER WOMAN COMEDY
AND ITS APPEAL FOR FEMALE AUDIENCES

Hildy Johnson, Tess Harding, and Amanda Bonner portray the new woman — young, contemporary, career-oriented, and sophisticated. All three films associate verbal facility with female power. These women may not be as physically strong as men, but in an argument they can more than hold their own. Female independence is linked strongly to the city, with its possibilities for economic success and personal autonomy. For female audiences, experiencing unforeseen opportunities and migrating to urban centers and war-boom areas, these heroines held powerful promise. Through the codes of Hollywood, female viewers probably experienced vicarious pride in gazing at these stars, a pride similar to that of welder Lola Weixel: "We were going to ... be welders for ever and ever. It was almost an art as well as a skill. It was a very beautiful kind of work."(27) The comic mode of these films may have served to alleviate anxiety experienced by women moving out of traditional roles.

Heterosexual monogamy remained, on screen and in mainstream America, the dominant ideal. However, within the parameters of that norm, an alternative model of marriage emerges in these films. The three couples have relationships that are work-oriented, vital, and somewhat egalitarian. Within the comic mode, they are willing to test those relationships and are unwilling to settle for stagnant stability. The "duelling dyads" in these films have "the capacity to notice one another, to remember beginning, to remember that you are strangers."(28) As weddings and divorces soared in number, the companionate model of marriage became more popular on screen and in society. For lesbian and bisexual audiences, heterosexual fantasy was the only alternative on screen. Yet the flexibility of role typing in these films and the free exchange of masculine and feminine characteristics may have appealed to lesbians as well.

Yet the model presented on screen is hardly one of easy equality. Professional, affluent, and childless, these "supercouples" have advantages many in the audience could hardly hope to dream of. ("Minnie" may have been "in the money," but she also very likely had hungry young mouths to feed as well). Furthermore, the type of equality presented in these films is that of a seesaw – one goes up, the other down. Only the "fittest" perhaps can ride.(29) The dream world of Hollywood producers and writers (some of whom, like Ruth Gordon and Garson Kanin, may have had similar lifestyles) most probably both attracted and alienated viewers.

In all three films, to varying degrees, sexual egalitarianism bows in concession to masculinity. In His Girl Friday and Woman of the Year, the male edge of power is more pronounced, whereas the margin of masculine privilege in Adam's Rib is slimmer. However, all three films present, in a male supporting role, the effeminate counter-ideal, reflecting the misogyny and homophobia of both Hollywood and its audience. Bruce Baldwin and the "poet" Bensinger in His Girl Friday, Gerald in Woman of the Year, and Kip in Adam's Rib represent the "sissy" contrasting to the "real men" (Grant and Tracy) who emerge as the heroine's love choice. As Vito Russo (1981) has commented,

> Open contempt for men who are perceived to be like women was not new . . . in the "feminist" Adam's Rib . . . Kip, a yardstick sissy par excellence, functions as Katharine Hepburn's girlfriend, a high-class Ethel Mertz to her feminist Lucy Ricardo.(30)

In the military mentality of World War II and its aftermath, the glorification of the warrior – on screen and off – is hardly surprising.

In their differences, these films signify the changes in female roles over the decade. Unlike her movie counterpart Kitty Foyle (also 1940), for whom work fills the time between men, Hildy chooses career over domesticity, prefiguring populist politician Katie Holstrom in The Farmer's Daughter and crusading lawyer Amanda Bonner in Adam's Rib, and symbolizing the movement of wartime women into the mainstream of American labor.

However, Hildy is a marginal woman. Unlike the heroines of the maternal drama, Hildy's world is virtually womanless. Alienation from other women and traditional domesticity is the price she (and many real-life professional women of that era) paid for success. As Arlie Hochschild (1974) has noted,

> In entering a male culture, they have left behind if not the female role, at least the female culture. . . . The professional woman is at the "cutting edge" of the female minority group, and is thus more "marginal" than women who live in the more "segregated" world of suburban den mothers, volunteer work and bridge parties . . . in order to maintain a professional identity she must sometimes prove herself different in some ways from what other women are taught to be like.(31)

Tess Harding, yet another reporter-heroine in Woman of the Year, is much less marginal than Hildy. An established columnist, she has her own office with a male secretary and is situated in a women's network. References appear throughout the film to the growing independence of women. For female audiences, the elegant competence of Tess must have been awe-inspiring.

Yet Tess' character was far from unambivalently presented. Hepburn, in classically aristocratic style, portrays Tess as a super-woman – callous and egotistical. She even adopts an orphan for her public image. The portrayal of Tess implies that to succeed in a career is to fail as a woman. The tacked-on "happy homemaker" ending attempts to resolve this dilemma.

The conflicts within the character of Tess partly result from tensions in the film's production between Hepburn and Stevens, and scriptwriters Michael Kanin and Ring Lardner. Hepburn's performance and Stevens' direction stand at odds with Kanin and Lardner's script, whose dialogue depicts the "career woman as a bitch." The battle of the sexes occurred on the movie set as well as the screen.

Why female audiences flocked to a film with such a traditional ending is another matter, however. Star appeal is significant, but neither Tracy nor Hepburn were immune to box office failure. Did women viewers merely tolerate Harding's "conversion to domesticity" because they identified with her more feminist aspects (and because they had no choice)? Unlikely. Rather the appeal of the film may relate to ambivalence and guilt women themselves experienced around issues of public achievement.

Amanda Bonner, on the other hand, seems to experience little conflict between femininity and achievement. Unlike Hildy, she is far from a token. Her achievements, unlike Tess', render her more vital and humanly sensitive. And her relationship with Adam is genuinely egalitarian. Yet she is always a woman, never a counterfeit man.

Adam's Rib, released in 1949, clearly reflects the changes women experienced in wartime. Amanda's courtroom parade of outstanding women mirrors the movement of women into all facets of labor. The evolution of heroines in the career comedy from Hildy to Tess to Amanda suggests that the "achieving woman" on the screen became more acceptable to Americans with women's success in the wartime labor force.

However, 1949 was hardly the year of feminist propaganda. Female defense workers had long been demobilized. And while many were rehired, they were concentrated in the pink-collar ghetto. The "happy housewife heroine" dominated the world of women's magazines.

Yet the mood on screen was different. Amanda Bonner does not stand alone as the only strong movie heroine of 1949. Other popular films such as Pinky, A Letter to Three Wives, The Heiress, and Little Women featured heroines of strong and autonomous will. Adam's Rib cannot be analyzed as simply a leftover, a hanging thread of "cultural lag," a "fluke" or "accident." Rather, it is part of a narrative pattern that was popular among audiences in 1949. The overwhelming (and enduring) popularity of films like Adam's Rib suggests that an emergent current of prefeminist consciousness existed among American women in the postwar era.(32)

LADY IN THE DARK: THE UNDERSIDE
OF THE DREAM OF FEMALE SUCCESS

Lady in the Dark (1944) stands alone as the most antifeminist film of the decade, implicitly critiquing career woman comedies and similar films. In the anxiety and backlash surrounding changing sexual roles in the late war years, it is not surprising that Lady in the Dark was produced. What does need explanation, however, is its popularity among female audiences. Since Lady in the Dark is far and away an aesthetic disaster, its appeal must be accounted for in other ways. The film suggests that achieving women are conflicted not because of the social strains of multiple roles, but because they deny their own bio-psychic nature. Lady in the Dark ends on a note of internal peace, not capitulation.

Confused, anxious, and unhappy, Liza Elliott is a negative projection fantasy; she is the dark side of the feminist dream. The solution to Liza's "divided self" is found on the analytic couch. Through the character of Dr. Brooks, Lady in the Dark dramatizes a biologically determinist Freudianism à la Helene Deutsch and the notorious Lundberg and Farnham (Modern Woman: The Lost Sex). Miss Elliott is nothing more than a masculinized woman, who has chosen a career because childhood trauma blocked her "true" desires for "normal" feminine sexuality and submission.

The popularity of Lady in the Dark cannot solely be attributed to male backlash, or the popularity of musicals. A woman (Frances Goodrich) co-wrote the script (with her husband, Alfred Hackett) and another woman (Alma Macrorie) edited the film. And female audiences helped make it a box-office hit. The appeal of Lady in the Dark and its rabid antifeminism must be attributed, in part, to the conflicts wartime women experienced between femininity and achievement.

As wartime women encountered new and unforeseen opportunities for public achievement, they most probably experienced guilt and fear as well as excitement. Women in transition may have felt as if they were living in three worlds: that of the traditional past, the expanding present, and the unknown future. The "double day" of household and waged labor, in a society that offered little assistance, was structured to produce guilt and ambivalence.

A popular magazine cover (House and Garden, September 1943) featured a divided young woman: on one side, dressed in overalls holding a pitchfork, on the other, wearing a dress, holding the hand of a sad-looking preschool girl. A man stands behind her.

Furthermore, the future was unclear, clouded by hope, anger, anticipation. What will happen when the GIs return? Will women "return home" or to more traditionally feminine occupations? Will the returning vets be threatened by the new woman? And will the new woman be willing or able to re-adopt a traditional lifestyle? And if not, who will care for the children? Who will love her?

The literature of female socialization has consistently documented the psychological effects of the conflict between femininity and achievement experienced by women in patriarchal societies. Fear, anxiety, guilt, and ambivalence often surround the issue of public achievement for women.(33) Amid the turbulence of 1944, Liza Elliott may have served as a convenient dream symbol upon which to project that fear and ambivalence.

Taken together, the first three films suggest a narrative progression with parallels in female consciousness. From His Girl Friday to Adam's Rib, from 1940 to 1949, femininity and achievement become more compatible. Lady in the Dark stands at the opposite pole, suggesting that the nature of femininity is a love of domesticity and submission. What is perhaps most striking, however, is the fact that both the most and least feminist films of the decade center on the conflict between femininity and achievement. As 18 million American women participated in the wartime labor force, their hopes and fears ran high. The films they loved are testimony to both.

NOTES

(1) Mary P. Ryan, "The Projection of a New Womanhood: The Movie Moderns in the 1920s," in Our American Sisters: Women in American Life and Thought (2nd ed.), ed. Jean E. Friedman and William G. Shade (Boston: Allyn and Bacon, 1976), p. 377. Two types of husband seekers appear on film: the golddigger, seeking wealth

and leisure; the woman marrying for love, content with a man of her own class. See also Marjorie Rosen, "Delineating the Flapper," Popcorn Venus, pp. 75-97; Molly Haskell, From Reverence to Rape.

Ryan has noted that this pessimism about men and marriage expresses itself in 1920s films in a few classic ways. First, in movies such as Our Blushing Brides (1930), which featured several female protagonists, one woman met misfortune (e.g., married a gambler, lost her mate to another woman), serving as a distorted mirror image of the other heroines' happiness. Secondly, the interwoven themes of infidelity and female competition ran through these films. In the 1920s, close to 300 movies depicted infidelity. Typically, in these films the "betrayed wife" is aging, having lost some of her physical charms; the "other woman" is a nubile young flapper. The persistence of these movie themes reveals that undercurrents of discontent/disillusionment often rested below the surface of filmic "happy endings."

(2)   Warners, the so-called "workingman's studio," produced many A and B films with career heroines. See (Susan) Elizabeth Dalton, "Women at Work: Warners in the 1930s," in Kay and Peary, ed., Women and the Cinema (New York: Dutton, 1977), pp. 267-82.

(3)   "Superwoman" is the word used in these films (often by jealous males) to describe these heroines. The term is double edged, implying excellence on the one hand, and exception on the other. A superwoman is neither a woman nor a man, but a third sex, a rare being. Furthermore, it connotes a negative perception of the female sex as a whole. As the lover of Mary Stevens, M.D. responds caustically: "A woman couldn't. But you, well, you're a superwoman." For further discussion of superwoman imagery, see Dalton.

(4)   For exceptions to this pattern, see, for example, Dorothy Arzner's Christopher Strong (1932) or Mark Sandrich's A Woman Rebels (1936). See Jeanine Basinger, "Ten That Got Away," pp. 61-72; Karyn Kay and Gerald Peary, "Interview with Dorothy Arzner," in Women and the Cinema, ed. Kay and Peary. Also see Claire Johnston, The Work of Dorothy Arzner: Towards a Feminist Cinema (London: British Film Institute, 1975); Molly Haskell, From Reverence to Rape; Marjorie Rosen, Popcorn Venus for further discussion of films that do not conform to popular stereotypes.

(5)   Russell, quoted in Dalton, pp. 272-73.

(6)   Molly Haskell, From Reverence to Rape (p. 134), commented that Pauline Kael, in The Citizen Kane Book, noted that newspaperwomen in films of this era were modeled on Hearst's star reporter, Adela Rogers St. Johns. In His Girl Friday, Russell's suit was allegedly copied from one of St. Johns' outfits.

(7)   Stanley Cavell, Pursuits of Happiness: The Hollywood Comedy of Remarriage (Cambridge, Ma.: Harvard University Press, 1981), chapter 5.

(8)   See Tom Powers, "His Girl Friday: Screwball Liberation," Jump Cut, no. 17, April 1978, for discussion of the contrast between Walter and Bruce.

(9)   Cavell, p. 167.

(10)   Jane Marie Gaines and Charlotte Cornelia Herzog in "Hildy Johnson and the Man-Tailored Suit: The Comedy of Inequality, Film Reader, pp. 232-246, have noted Hildy's tokenism in a number of different ways. First of all, her attire is masculine. Secondly, and perhaps most importantly, the other female characters in the film are depicted in either or both a powerless or negative way. The other female workers at the newspaper are all cast in stereotypic roles (e.g. telephone operator). The two supporting female characters (Williams' girlfriend, Molly and Bruce's mother) are defined by their relationship with men and are both somewhat hysterical. Bruce, in his bumbling gentleness, can also be read as symbolizing the feminine in contrast to manly Walter.

(11)   Powers, "His Girl Friday: Screwball Liberation," p. 26.

(12)   Haskell, From Reverence to Rape, p. 135.

(13)   Cavell, Pursuits of Happiness, p. 186. Also see Haskell, From Reverence to Rape, for a similar interpretation.

(14)   Hawks has worked in a variety of genres (Westerns, dramas, adventures, comedies). However, his films exhibit similar themes and characters and display a fascination with masculine traits in both sexes. Hawks is noted for his strong female characters and balanced depiction of couple dynamics (Grant-Hepburn, Grant-Russell, Bogart-Bacall). As Leigh Brackett, his female screenwriter, notes, "Hawks' gallery of women is unmatched for the depth of characterization, and more important, the strength and intelligence they exhibit . . . . The balanced tension between the men and women in the film gives it a special psychological relevance." (James Monaco, How to Read a Film, p. 244). Also see Robin Wood, Howard Hawks (New York: Doubleday, 1968); Joseph McBride (ed.), Focus on Howard Hawks (Englewood Cliffs: Prentice-Hall, 1972); Claire Johnston, "Women's Cinema as Counter Cinema," in Notes on Women's Cinema, ed. Claire Johnston, Screen, Pamphlet Z.

The screenplay of His Girl Friday is particularly well suited to the creation of a token masculine woman. The Ben Hecht-Charles MacArthur play The Front Page (New York: Covici-Friede, 1928), from which His Girl Friday was adapted, featured the Hildy Johnson character as a male. Charles Lederer and Ben Hecht (uncredited) worked on the screenplay. However, before one concludes that Hildy Johnson is merely a man in drag, we need to remember that Rosalind Russell helped create the "wisecracking professional women" in the 1930s and early 1940s as well. The Russell persona can be interpreted as a cultural image of the 1930s and 1940s drawn from a variety of sources and in this film, filtered through the creative imagination of Hecht, Lederer and Hawks.

(15)   Powers, pp. 26-27.

(16)   Molly Haskell, in From Reverence to Rape, argued the opposite position: "Russell does not become an imitation male, she remains true to the two sides — feminine and professional — of her

nature, and as such promises to exercise a healthy influence on the hard-boiled, albeit male, world of criminal reporting." While I would agree that Hildy does not totally compromise herself, neither is she able to "remain true to both sides of her nature." Walter's physical dominance, the use of masculine language, and her own adoption of a cynical and exploitative style of reportage, are testimony to this. Karyn Kay, in "Part Time Work of a Domestic Slave, or Putting the Screws to Screwball Comedy, in Women and the Cinema, ed. Karyn Kay and Gerald Peary (New York: Dutton, 1977) takes the opposite position from Haskell, analyzing the ending as a "taming of the shrew" classic in screwball comedies. My analysis is situated some-where in the middle of Haskell and Kay.

(17) Haskell, From Reverence to Rape, p. 227. In Woman of the Year, Hepburn not only acquired the rights to the screenplay, but demanded from MGM's Louis B. Mayer that Tracy play the male lead. For the next twenty-five years, Tracy-Hepburn would be classic lovers on and off screen. See Tony Thomas, The Films of the Forties (Secaucus, N.J.: Citadel Press, 1975).

(18) The classic Hollywood or Academy Aperture two-shot was a visual hallmark of 1930s and 1940s American cinema. Before widescreen projection, the classic Academy aspect ratio allowed for shots in which two characters, and not their environment, dominated. Typically, frame form was closed, well lighted, and actors situated within a balanced composition. Visually, the two-shot is well suited to express both sexual vitality and role equality.

(19) Karyn Kay, "Part Time Work of a Domestic Slave or Putting the Screws to Screwball Comedy," in Kay and Peary, ed., Women and the Cinema, p. 321.

(20) Brandon French, On the Verge of Revolt: Women in American Films of the '50s (New York: Frederick Ungar, 1978) called Ms. Holliday's style "somnambulistic naivete," and compared it to the deceptive innocence of Marilyn Monroe. Other "women's films" of the era (A Tree Grows in Brooklyn; The Shocking Miss Pilgrim) also play on and question the "dumb blonde" stereotype.

(21) Haskell, p. 226.

(22) Ibid., p. 227.

(23) Ibid.

(24) Joan Mellen Big Bad Wolves: Masculinity in the American Film (New York: Pantheon, 1977), p. 172.

(25) French, On the Verge of Revolt, p. 8.

(26) See Carol Gilligan, In a Different Voice: Psychological and Women's Development (Cambridge, MA: Harvard University Press, 1982).

(27) Lola Weixel, quoted in Miriam Frank, Marilyn Ziebarth and Connie Field, The Life and Times of Rosie the Riveter (Emeryville, CA: Clarity Educational Productions, 1982), p. 17.

(28) Cavell, p. 216.

(29) See French, p. 32.

(30) Vito Russo, The Celluloid Closet: Homosexuality in the Movies (New York: Harper & Row, 1981), p. 67.

(31) Arlie Russell Hochschild, "Making It: Marginality and Obstacles to Minority Consciousness," in Women and Success: The Anatomy of Achievement, ed. Ruth B. Kundsin (New York: Morrow, 1974), pp. 194-96. Also see Rosabeth Moss Kanter, Men and Women of the Corporation (New York: Harper & Row, 1977).

(32) I am using the term prefeminist to indicate a consciousness that may simultaneously and/or contradictorily value female strength and autonomy as well as domesticity and submissiveness. Gramsci's notion of common sense is useful here as well.

(33) A full discussion of the literature on femininity and achievement lies beyond the scope of the narrative. My assumption is that negative emotions associated with female achievement are equally affected by both psychological and social factors.

See Matina Horner, "Toward an Understanding of Achievement-Related Conflicts in Women," Journal of Social Issues 28, 2 (1972): 157-175; Karen Horney, Feminine Psychology (New York: Norton, 1967); Mirra Komarovsky, Women in the Modern World: Their Education and Their Dilemmas (Boston: Little, Brown, 1953). See Debra Kaufman and Barbara L. Richardson, Achievement and Women: Challenging the Assumptions (New York: Free Press, 1982) for an excellent discussion of the various social and psychological theories concerning barriers to female achievement.

Chapter 5

"THE WEEDS GROW LONG NEAR THE SHORE": Madness, Suspicion, and Distrust in Popular Women's Films of the 1940s

Lord, I really don't think no man love can last
They love you to death then treat you like a thing of the past
There's nineteen men living in my neighborhood
There's nineteen men living in my neighborhood
Eighteen of them are fools and the one ain't no doggone good

Bessie Smith
"Dirty No Gooder Blues"
Empress Music, 1929

Flowers and presents all turn to dust . . .
I never met a man I could trust . . .

Bathroom graffiti
Middlesex Community College
Bedford, Mass., 1979

Why does he keep telling me I'm sick, hopeless?
Is this some kind of <u>Gaslight</u>?

Barbara Gordon
<u>I'm Dancing as Fast as I Can</u>
(New York: Bantam, 1979), p. 71.

"You can't trust a man." "Men only want <u>one</u> thing." "Every man's got a wandering eye." Most women have, at one time or another, offered or heard such advice, shared in the secretive intimacy of female friendship and kin networks.(1) Feminists are, however, not the first to offer such warnings. Grandmothers, mothers, aunts, sisters, and friends, traditional and nontraditional women alike, have spun countless cautionary tales — of abandoned or abused lovers, and wives who trusted too much, and listened too little, to their own wary instincts and the wise counsel of their female confidantes.

Suspicion, hostility, and distrust — of women toward men — are hardly new. Perhaps the culture of pain, defensiveness, and distrust is as old as patriarchy itself. However, it has primarily survived as undercurrent rather than maincurrent, coexisting with, as well as challenging, a dominant ideology stressing nurturance of and loyalty to the "right man." Because of their potentially volatile and subversive effects, these mistrustful feelings have often been belittled, suppressed, denied, confined to private solitary moments, or shared in the often misunderstood female realm of gossip. And although most women in American society, for example, have probably experienced or shared these sentiments, they rarely express them in the presence of men. Or if these emotions are articulated, their impact is often undercut by humor ("I was only kidding around").

Rarely has the culture of distrust been the subject of academic study. Despite this fact, however, the annals of modern history, sociology, psychology, and fiction suggest its prevalence. And contemporary feminism impels us to discover its manifestations and effects. This powerful psychic undercurrent appears in the works of authors as diverse as Sigmund Freud, Karen Horney, Theodore Reik, Mirra Komarovsky, Phyllis Chesler, Joyce Ladner, Barbara Gordon, and Ntozake Shange. From the Gothic novel to the sociological community study to the psychoanalytic case study to the auto-biography to the blues, a persistent message resounds: across age, race, class, and ethnic lines, women do not trust men.(2)

World War II provided fertile ground for the "culture of distrust." With many young men far away, the future uncertain, and the war seemingly endless, distrust and cynicism flourished. And distrust came home — home to the intimate, sacred world of love and family relationships, home to America's silver screen. As GIs fought in Normandy and Bataan, homefront women avidly watched another kind of war on film, that of frightened wives fighting for their lives against murderous husbands.

IN SUSPICION AND DISTRUST:
THE WOMEN'S MOVIE ENCOUNTERS THE FILM NOIR

Popular films of feminine suspicion in the war era, with roots in Gothic fiction and radio and stage melodrama, were very different from the maternal drama or career woman comedy. Lighting was dark and shadowy, settings domestic and claustrophobic, camera angles distorted and unsettling. Flashbacks and flashforwards punctuated twisted, complex, and ambiguous narratives. Although the theme of distrustful wife-murderous husband was not new to the silver screen, the social climate and cinematic style of the 1940s allowed it to flourish.

The women's film of suspicion and distrust spoke the cinematic language of film noir. Literally, "black film," film noir is a term coined by French critics to describe a popular movement in 1940s and 1950s American cinema. Too encompassing to be labeled a genre, film noir is more a pervasive style of cinema than a clearly demarcated set of movies.(3) Films noir are defined, first, by what they are not, and that is "classic realist texts" in the Hollywood tradition. Until World War II, American cinema employed an ordered and predictable grammar, a set of codes and conventions symbolizing order, rationality, and intelligibility: relatively bright or "Hollywood" lighting, closed frame composition, undistorting cinematography, and linear narratives. Film noir stood Hollywood on its head, abandoning traditional filmic language for the symbols of alienation, chaos, irrationality, moral decay, and ambiguity.

The origins of film noir are multicultural, with roots on both sides of the Atlantic. With advances in film technology and the influx of German refugee film artists, expressionistic cinematography — evoking angst, alienation, and threat — moved into the Hollywood mainstream. That distinctive camera style initially merged with themes and narratives drawn from American social realism, as well as the hard-boiled, cynical, urban detective fiction of writers like Dashiel Hammett, James Cain, and Raymond Chandler. The popularity of Freudianism in the 1940s also allowed for the exploration of the unconscious. These influences fused to create film noir, which implicitly critiqued the culture in which it thrived. Reflecting the influence of both disillusioned refugees and left-wing film workers, it conveyed an unrelenting cynicism toward the basic institutions of society. And the weariness and despair of late 1940s America created an eager audience. Film noir enjoyed a short but intense life. Film historians date the earliest film noir to be about 1941 (Suspicion or The Maltese Falcon) and the latest to be 1958 (Touch of Evil), although nouveau noir films continue to be made today. Although critics dispute the length of its history, most agree that the heyday of film noir occurred from about 1944 to 1948.(4)

The typical film noir protagonist is male: weatherbeaten, urban, and alienated: a detective (The Maltese Falcon), an insurance agent (Double Indemnity), or even a war-scarred vet (The Blue Dahlia). Through the twists and turns of an often ambiguous narrative, he encounters crime, moral decay, and a femme fatale for whom he has a fatal obsession. In films like The Maltese Falcon (1941), Double Indemnity (1944), Woman in the Window (1944), and The Postman Always Rings Twice (1945), the face of evil is female: "The dark lady, the spider woman, the evil seductress who tempts man and brings about his destruction."(5) Although these female characters are cast in stereotypically negative ways, they are more autonomous and dynamic than many traditional heroines. As E. Ann Kaplan suggests in Women in Film Noir (1978), perhaps these villainesses imply the threat of growing female autonomy. Furthermore, she has asserted, these films are open to "progressive readings" by feminists, and should not be dismissed as mere misogyny. However, in the classic film noir, female characters, while powerful, are not central. Whereas these films are certainly significant to the study of women in cinema, they cannot be considered women's films. It is rather to a related variety of noir-influenced film, that I turn at this point — the women's film of suspicion and distrust.

Film noir left its mark on all Hollywood cinema, including the women's film. Mildred Pierce, as discussed earlier, represents a tenuous marriage of the women's film and the film noir. Another uniquely feminine variant of noir arose, simultaneous with the emergence of the classic noir narrative. Featuring victimized, mad, or terrified women, and usually set in ornate, claustrophobic interiors, these films express paranoia and distrust in love and family relationships. In the noir women's film the threat is close to home and usually male.

Variations on two melodramatic narratives emerge in war-era noir women's films: (a) portrayal of a female protagonist with an undifferentiated sense of distrust, alienation, and madness (Possessed); (b) depiction of a heroine whose suspicion and distrust are aimed (usually correctly) at a specific target: her husband (Suspicion, Gaslight, Sleep, My Love). In a third related popular film (the sarcastic comedy, A Letter to Three Wives), feminine suspicion focuses on adultery and adopts a contemporary face. Although A Letter to Three Wives is a comedy and stylistically less a noir women's film, it is colored by the feminine paranoia peculiar to this era. The next section analyzes the popularity of these narratives, addressing the following question: Why is filmic suspicion most desired by audiences when muted or garbed in Gothic melodrama?

A DIFFUSE DISTRUST: POSSESSED (1947)

The weeds grow long near the shore.

Louise Howell, upon
Pauline Graham's death in Possessed

Beautiful woman — talented, frustrated, like all the others we've seen.

One psychiatrist to another,
describing Louise Howell in
Possessed.

The opening scene of Curtis Bernhardt's Possessed reflects the mood of the preceding quote: a profound sense of dislocation, madness, and confusion. As Schumann is played hauntingly in the background, a nameless woman, fairly young and attractive (Joan Crawford), walks trance-like along the rain-drenched streets of contemporary Los Angeles. One thing "possesses" her: David. Distracted, yet frantic, she walks up to strange men, calling them "David." They turn away in pity and disgust. Her disorientation intensifies as she is almost hit by an oncoming bus. Finally, she walks into a coffee shop, where some of the patrons ask: "Are you sick?" "Are you drunk?" She cannot articulate her pain: "David" is all she can say. The proprietor calls an ambulance and she is taken to the hospital.

Up to this point, the film conveys an overwhelming, yet unarticulated, sense of dislocation. Little dialogue is spoken. The camera moves slowly, from close-ups of Crawford's haggard, distraught face back to the dreary and slick pavement. Waxman's haunting score intensifies the aura of dread and alienation. This sequence depicts most powerfully a woman who has lost her center, her sense of self.

> The madwoman roaming the streets in the film's first sequence becomes a perfect expression of the end of the line, the total confusion and centerlessness for a woman in whom existence has replaced essence.(6)

All we know about this woman is that she is profoundly disturbed and obsessed with David. Significantly, the audience knows the name of the man (who, in some unknown way, is linked to her confusion) before we know her own.

In this opening sequence, Crawford is, by her mystery, simultaneously no woman and Everywoman. The Everywoman image also appears in the opening scenes of two other postwar Warners' films: Mildred Pierce (1945) and The Unsuspected (1947). The audience, somehow, knows; it has seen this woman before.

> The scene is accompanied by suitably menacing music. A distraught woman, nightmare written all over her face, paces the dark, wet streets of a city, hounded and bewildered by the sound of trams and automobiles, by the sheer presence of people and walls and shops and newsstands. She collapses and is taken to a hospital.(7)

The diffuse madness of the first sequence becomes more clearly defined as the plot unfolds. The dazed woman is taken to a hospital. There male doctors question her, attempting to understand her unusual behavior. Hollywood's (and America's) infatuation with psychiatry becomes apparent in the portrayal of these physicians.

One is young, the other older, both oozing medical mystique. The older psychiatrist remarks that she is not unusual: "Beautiful woman – talented, frustrated – like all the others we've seen." The Everywoman theme emerges again as femininity is linked to invalidism. The doctors mumble to one another about American civilization producing neurotics, and categorize her condition (in almost humorous "psychoanalyese") as a "nontraumatic stupor." She calls out "David" again. The psychiatrists notice a wedding ring, and see that her clothes bear the label of a Washington, D.C. department store. As they question her, she can only reply, haltingly, "I feel . . . ." What she feels and why are still a mystery. She is incapable of articulating her pain. The psychiatrists, who will emerge as heroes of the film, opt for "narco-synthesis," the injection of a serum (sodium pentothal?) to "unlock" her repressed thoughts and emotions. The treatment is successful, making the psychiatrists responsible for her story, the crux of the film. And this detail is significant, since ultimately, it is to them, and not herself, that the nameless woman will be indebted.

She becomes agitated, screaming that she must "get away from them," and hears someone playing Schumann in the background. Like Mildred Pierce, the film flashes back to an earlier and seemingly happier time. Unlike the drawn and distraught patient, the woman is younger, happier, more attractive. No longer a mysterious obsession, David is a living person, seated at a piano playing Schumann. The set shifts from the bleak, barren hospital room, to a fairly cheery living room. A conversation between Louise Howell (Crawford) and David Sutton (Van Heflin) provides clues to her disorientation:

> Louise: "I love you" doesn't describe how much it hurts sometimes. Before I met you I just existed. David, I want a monopoly on you.

> David: Don't bring the subject around to marriage again. I like all kinds of music, except a little number called "promise me." It's a duet and I want to play solo. Why is it that when a man gets interested in his work, or a book or something, a woman always has to start acting like a woman? See that curve? It's a parabola. Now that's something a mathematician could fall in love with.

> Louise: Why don't you love me like that? I'm much nicer and a lot more interesting. I have no pride. I've never had anything I wanted in the whole world except you. I used to be cold, shut in. I can't go back on the outside of other people's lives looking in.

> David: Knowing you has been wonderful, but sometimes you hang on me too hard. Sometimes I get the feeling you are choking me to death. Everyone wants to be loved but no one

wants to be smothered. I don't know what you want but I have to keep moving. <u>Blame it on the army, blame it on the war, blame it on anything you want. I can't love you the way you love me.</u> (Emphasis mine.)

Echoes of Simone de Beauvoir ("men live for work, women for love") reverberate throughout their dialogue. Louise's madness becomes more understandable. David, dedicated to work and "moving on," seems about as accessible to her as the strangers she approached on the street. Though clinging and dependent, Louise is portrayed sympathetically. As a response to David's unwillingness to marry as well as larger social forces beyond her control (World War II), Louise's "nontraumatic stupor" seems quite understandable, even commonplace.

After her break-up with David, Louise returns to her home and workplace, the summer residence of the Grahams. Up to this point, the audience receives no inkling of Louise's occupation (if any), although David's career (as mathematician/architect) is a central focus of conversation.

Louise's job, however, is of a quite different and classically feminine nature: as a private duty nurse. Her patient, wealthy, middle-aged Pauline Graham is a chronic invalid. The nature of Pauline's sickness, however, remains (like Louise's later "mental illness") vague. The audience never sees Mrs. Graham; she exists as a disembodied voice, projected out of a gloomy bedroom. (Some scenes occur in the bedroom with camera on Louise, as Pauline speaks to her.) Mrs. Graham, like the nameless woman in the hospital, is another Everywoman, a haunting symbol of female madness. Pauline consumes herself with jealousy and suspicion, believing that each nurse hired by her husband is really in love with him. Pauline's eerie voice provokes the audience to question: What made her so ill? Hints of "female invalidism" and "empty nest syndrome" suggest themselves.

While both Pauline and Louise suffer from emotional illness (in differing degrees), they cannot communicate. Pauline can only see Louise as her rival.

Louise's despair mirrors itself in Mrs. Graham. When Pauline later commits suicide, we see her for the first time: as a bedraggled corpse lifted from the lake. She lies dead, a nonperson. Yet, symbolically, as a disembodied voice, she has never been a real person. Louise, upset and guilty over Mrs. Graham's (probable) suicide, talks with police who surmise that she accidentally fell in and became trapped by the choking weeds. Louise identifies clearly with Pauline, as she dramatically remarks, slowly and deliberately, as the camera pans to the dark, murky weeds: "The weeds grow very long near the shore." The home (homefront?) is hardly without danger; its waters are inviting, yet they stifle and thwart growth. The "weeds," undergrowths of despair and depression, threaten women, especially the homebound. And sometimes kill them.

From this point on, Louise grows more and more like Pauline, almost as if she were filling the dead woman's role. As disorientation turns to paranoia, the film's viewpoint shifts, first subtly, then dramatically. At first, Louise's behavior seems an exaggerated, but understandable response to the loss of David and the death of Pauline. As the film progresses, she seems more and more mad, while David appears increasingly sane and reasonable.

After the funeral, the Grahams return home to Washington, D.C.; Louise accompanies them as nursemaid for young Wynne. David visits (in "accidental" plot convention!) since he's doing architectural work for Mr. Graham. When she sees David, Louise clings to him and makes excessive demands, although their relationship is clearly over. In this scene, she appears quite <u>irrational</u>. She decides to quit her job in a fit of rage (and probable desire to avoid David). In a surprising (and somewhat hackneyed) twist of plot, kindly Dean Graham (Raymond Massey) proposes to Louise (was Pauline really so paranoid about Dean?). She accepts, in implicit resignation that she'll never marry the elusive David. And after all, Louise surmises, it is better to be rich, bored, and married than poor, anxious, and single: "I've never had a great deal — it's tempting; the kind of life I would have if I were your wife." Louise Howell becomes Louise Graham.

After her marriage, her craziness mushrooms. Dean's college-age daughter, Carol, falls in love with David (more plot contrivance!) and Louise (like her "double" Pauline) grows insanely jealous. Her fantasies run wild. The film enters her paranoia: first, running through her fantasy, as if reality and then, running through the actual scene. The audience becomes enmeshed in confusion: Is this real, fantasy, are the two hopelessly intertwined? Yet the film no longer makes sense of her behavior. Rather, she is portrayed, like her late patient, as an incomprehensible madwoman. Although the roots of her delusions lie in unrequited love, her paranoia runs out of hand. She fantasizes about killing Carol, and wonders if <u>she</u> murdered Pauline.

Her mind snaps, no longer able to distinguish the real from the imagined. Dean, a model "supportive husband" (with a second mad wife!) urges her to consult a doctor, assuring her that he (Old Faithful!) will stand by. Though she admires (and may in some ways love) him, Louise is driven to obey the dictates of her (mad) imagination. Finally, she kills David, as the ultimate revenge for his betrayal.

The film ends as it began, flashing forward to a distraught Louise in a Los Angeles hospital. What began as a film evoking the pain and contradiction of postwar womanhood ends as an ode to the mystique of psychiatry. The doctors "sum up" Louise's case, and in so doing, attempt to make sense of this muddled film. The early roots of Louise's psychosis (e.g., her dialogue with David) are forgotten. The doctors diagnose with scientific solemnity: <u>"Such a person is</u>

possessed of devils and it's the psychiatrist who must cast them out."
(Emphasis mine.)

As the doctor-priests "exorcise" Louise's demons, ever faithful
Dean stands by. In 1947, the year of the film's release, New York
Herald Tribune critic Howard Barnes wrote: "Miss Crawford . . . has
obviously studied the aspects of insanity to recreate a rather
terrifying portrait of a woman possessed by devils."(8)

When first analyzing Possessed, the contradictory emotions
initially evoked seem by the ending to be well incorporated into the
mystifying ideology of post-war psychologism. Louise's paranoia has
been reduced to the "possession of devils"; the film's title underscores this theme. Unthreateningly vague, the "devils" seem to
originate in her (or woman's) inherent irrationality, rather than in
larger social conditions affecting post-war womanhood.

Yet Possessed is more complex than such an interpretation
implies. It can be analyzed as not one film, but two. In the haunting
opening sequence, and throughout the first half of the film, Louise
Howell's madness is not a "possession by devils," but an understandable reaction to a common female situation. Interestingly, both
Louise Howell and Pauline Graham, who typify traditional
femininity, become mad. Perhaps that madness symbolically
critiqued the feminine mystique. The disorientation, centerlessness,
and confusion portrayed by Crawford were most probably common
female responses to a decade of rapid and unprecedented role
change. "Who am I — homemaker, defense worker, waiting wife?" —
questioned America's wartime women. As female power eroded in
peacetime, anger, sadness, and confusion intensified. Crawford, in
an Oscar-nominated performance as a mythic Everywoman,
symbolizes feminine rolelessness and confusion. "Beautiful woman —
talented, frustrated — like all the others" says the older psychiatrist
to his younger colleague.

Yet, in the second half, possession becomes the problem,
exorcism the cure. Everywoman is a very specific Louise Howell,
with a paranoia mysteriously her own. Some feminist critics, such as
Marjorie Rosen (1973), dismissed movies such as Possessed, Snake
Pit, Dark Mirror, and Leave Her to Heaven as "tacitly reprimanding
women for indulging their emotional lives at all."(9) Though Rosen
may be partially correct, one must critically examine the contradictory nature of films like Possessed. The dominant effect of the
final sequence may confirm Louise's insanity as incomprehensible.
Why she, "another woman . . . like all the rest," walks in a catatonic
stupor is never really answered. And the final solution to her
possession seems to lie totally in male hands: in the mystique of her
psychiatrists, and the unfailing support of Dean. Yet "ending" cannot
be equated with "meaning." The haunting opening sequence, the
initial dialogue of Louise and David, encourage us to see beyond the
devils to the experience of postwar women in transition. Possessed
cannot be analyzed simply as an ode to patriarchy. A critical tension

maintains itself between the first sequences and the conclusion. Unless one considers audiences as simple enough to comprehend only one message, it is reasonable to assume that Possessed had a dual and contradictory effect upon female viewers.

SUSPICION CONFIRMED: SUSPICION (1941), GASLIGHT (1944), SLEEP, MY LOVE (1948)

> You are inclined to lose things, Paula.
>
> Gregory to Paula Alquist Anton,
> in Gaslight

"Don't trust your husband " is the recurrent theme of a popular cycle of 1940s noir women's films, of both A and B varieties. George Cukor's Gaslight (1944), Alfred Hitchcock's Suspicion (1941), and Douglas Sirk's Sleep, My Love (1948) are classic in narrative and visual imagery. Other popular films such as Hitchcock's Rebecca (1941), Shadow of a Doubt (1943), and Notorious (1946), Peter Godfrey's The Two Mrs. Carrolls (1947), Joseph L. Mankiewicz's Dragonwyck (1945), Robert Siodmak's The Spiral Staircase (1946), Robert Stevenson's Jane Eyre (1944), and Anatole Litvak's Sorry, Wrong Number (1948), though differing somewhat in plot and resolution, also convey the narrative mood of the noir women's film. Gothic melodrama merged with film noir to produce uniquely feminine cine-dramas of suspicion and distrust.

The following "composite plot" reveals classic features of this cycle: a rich, rather naive and sheltered young woman (Joan Fontaine in Suspicion; Ingrid Bergman in Gaslight; Claudette Colbert in Sleep, My Love) marries a man (often older) after a whirlwind courtship. He may be an irresponsible joker (Cary Grant in Suspicion) or a cool, detached (perhaps "European") gentleman (Charles Boyer in Gaslight). At first, he seems the "ideal husband" — loving, protective, and sensitive. Yet a brooding rage lurks beneath his civilized facade. And, after the "honeymoon" (which may last from a month to several years) ends, all is not so rosy. Clues upon clues appear, leading the wife to suspect that her husband is plotting to drive her mad or kill her. Through the skillful unraveling of the narrative, the initial happiness and security of the heroine turn to terror and suspicion. Joan Fontaine, Ingrid Bergman, and Claudette Colbert — stars of these films — have intensely expressive faces that rapidly transform themselves: from security to terror and back again, and again, and again. Melodramatic scores intensify the suspicion-relief cycle. And rich, dark, claustrophobic, and domestic sets add to the mood of paranoia. Lighting is shadowy, and camera angles askew. The home — and the wife's workplace — becomes, not a secure haven, but a trap of terror. These films are marked by a disquieting cycle of climax and anticlimax, suspicion and relief. Is he going to kill her? Or is she crazy? The narrative asks, and re-asks, until the final resolution. The power of this particular type of film can best be captured by analyzing one in depth: Gaslight (1944), by far the most popular and artistic women's film noir. Gaslight was already popular — as Patrick Hamilton's play Angel Street and a 1940 British film — before its MGM release in 1944. The film instantly won both critical and popular acclaim, receiving one Oscar and five nominations, as well as National Board of Review and Golden Globe awards.(10) Variety (November 29, 1944) noted that approximately 2,500 students at Texas State Women's College voted Gaslight among their best-loved films of the year. In common usage, "Don't you gaslight me" came to mean "Don't try to drive me crazy."(11)

The film is set primarily in Victorian London, specifically the fog-shrouded Thornton Square. In the first scene, teenage Paula Alquist (Bergman) leaves her home to live in Italy after the murder of her aunt and guardian, renowned singer Alice Alquist. Tragedy envelops the young woman as she steps into a waiting carriage.

A different mood colors one of the next scenes, that of escape. It is 1885, ten years have passed and a more mature Paula, also a singer, sits in an Italian railroad car talking with the rather verbose elderly Miss Thwaites (Dame May Whitty).(12) Although Paula is geographically far from Thornton Square, this conversation brings her back. Miss Thwaites chatters endlessly about a novel she's reading about a husband who buried six wives in the cellar. Offhandedly, she remarks that a "real live murder" occurred in her own neighborhood. The address she mentions returns us to the scene of the crime: 9 Thornton Square.

Paula leaves the train eagerly, relieved that her ex-neighbor failed to recognize her. Her lover, Gregory Anton (Boyer), awaits her. An aura of menace colors his European finesse. Has she really escaped?

Mystery surrounds Anton from the first. He falls in love with Paula very quickly (in 2 weeks), almost inexplicably. Yet somehow he seems too controlled for blind passion. Paula, however, fails to notice Gregory's "strangeness." She seems madly in love and relieved of fear and loneliness. Paula was very isolated before meeting Gregory, with singing her only outlet, and a fairly private one, at that. For Paula, Gregory fills the emotional void left by her aunt's sudden and brutal murder.

The couple marries, after a whirlwind courtship. Paula seems relieved to have escaped her loneliness: "I haven't been afraid since I've known you . . . . I've found peace in loving you," she tells Gregory.

Paula seems eager, almost too eager, to please her new husband, abandoning singing and agreeing to live wherever he wants. An early shot of the newlyweds vacationing in Italy suggests menace. On the

The Face of Female Terror

Above: The frightened Paula Alquist (Ingrid Bergman) and the controlling Gregory Anton (Charles Boyer) in George Cukor's Gaslight (1944).

Top (facing page): Is the milk poisoned? A terrified Lina (Joan Fontaine) and charming Johnny Aysgarth (Cary Grant) in Alfred Hitchcock's Suspicion (1941).

Below (facing page): Victimized invalid Leona Stevenson (Barbara Stanwyck) in Anatole Litvak's Sorry, Wrong Number (1948).

balcony adjoining their room, Anton stands menacingly behind Paula, smiling and holding her tightly around the neck. A dual image presents itself: is he passionately embracing her? Or is he threatening to throw her off the balcony?

Gregory wants to move to London and persuades his bride, against her initial wishes, to return to the house willed her by her aunt. With marriage, Paula becomes more and more dependent on Gregory. First, she abandons her career and secondly, agrees to reside in a house filled with horrible memories. Powerlessness and isolation foreshadow her vulnerability and danger.

Gregory's evil nature becomes clear to the audience, although not Paula, early on in the film. Cukor's decision to portray Anton in this fashion allows the audience to adopt Paula's viewpoint and intensify their identification with her.

The Thornton Square house and its fog-drenched setting spells threat; the ornate claustrophobia of the Alquist home contrasts sharply with sunny Italy. Huldschinsky's set design — dim lighting, dark velvets and brocades, ornate chandeliers and candelabra — create the sense of a fashionable prison, a plushly-padded cage. As the Antons begin their life together on Thornton Square, tragedy haunts Paula. Alice Alquist's picture hangs prominently in its former place, painfully jogging Paula's memory. She becomes very upset, recalling her discovery of her aunt's corpse in front of the fire.

Paula grows weaker and sicker with time. The gaslights seem to flicker off and on at odd hours, although Gregory and the maids deny adjusting them. At night Paula hears noises above her room, although she knows that no one lives in the boarded up attic, which stores Alice's belongings. In a series of close-ups, Bergman's face transforms itself from a healthy and robust countenance to a timid and frightened one. This is perhaps, as Gavin Lambert has noted in a conversation with Cukor, the most compeling visual imagery in Gaslight. "Gaslighting" could happen to any woman or Everywoman.

> Lambert: You know how blooming and confident the Ingrid Bergman character was at first.

> Cukor: I like the point that she wasn't normally a timid woman; she was healthy. To reduce someone like that to a scared, jittering creature is interesting and dramatic.(13)

The house itself has a persona; it threatens and frightens Paula. Yet, outside her home, she also experiences memory loss and confusion. In a pivotal scene, Gregory presents his wife with a cameo before they visit the Tower of London. While touring the foreboding tower, Paula panics — the brooch is missing. Gregory's smile is evil: "You are inclined to lose things, Paula." She becomes increasingly fearful and confines herself to her home; Paula suspects she is mad. Paula wonders: Am I too fragile to survive living amid painful memories? Or is Gregory — with his wicked mouth — implicated in my "madness"?

While Paula weakens, Gregory grows more powerful. His occupation is mysterious (he mentions "writing music") and requires strange hours. Late at night, he leaves for his studio, returning early the next morning. He fails to inform Paula, even in the slightest, of the details of his work. Gregory assumes command of the household as Paula's "condition" worsens. He hires a new maid, Nancy (Angela Lansbury), and warns her that her mistress is unwell and quite high strung. A coquettish Cockney, Nancy is more than eager to placate her master and disparage her mistress, perhaps later to win his affections (and wealth). Nancy "protects" Paula by telling visitors that "Master says it isn't good for her to see people." As Nancy, a classic 'male-identified woman,' bonds with Gregory, Paula is defined — by herself and the outside world — as an invalid. Anton's behavior, however, is confusing. Sometimes, he plays the sensitive husband, protective of his ailing wife. At other times, however, his lack of either sadness or anger at Paula's condition baffles her. He seems almost glad that she is ill. Paula wonders: is he my advocate or enemy?

Paula becomes frustrated that she is constantly confined to her home. Upon receiving an invitation to Lady Dalroy's reception, she informs Gregory that she wishes to attend. When Anton retorts that she is too ill, she asserts that she'll go alone. Her strength begins to re-emerge. Yet, upon hearing how much she wants to go, Gregory apologizes and agrees to accompany her. He jokes about her suspicion: "You thought I was being cruel — making you a prisoner." Paula experiences an exhausting cycle of suspicion and relief, first distrusting Gregory, then feeling guilty at ever doing so.

In the next scene, Paula is thrilled to be at the reception; her self-confidence is returning. Yet, her composure soon shatters. In the midst of the musical recital, Gregory can't find his watch and asks Paula if she took it. Paula replies in the negative. Gregory doesn't believe her, and searches Paula's purse, discovering the missing watch. She becomes hysterical and ashamed; they immediately leave. Paula now has appeared publicly as the madwoman. Later back at Thornton Square, a distraught Paula mistrusts her own perceptions. Anton's brooding rage erupts into cruel taunts as he tells Paula that she will be like her mother, who died in an asylum "with no brain at all."

Paula is clearly in danger; her imprisonment seems total. She feels "the house" is driving her mad, and cannot escape. Yet, Paula, too, has allies. Her elderly neighbor Miss Thwaites seems the opposite of Paula: plump, street-wise, and inquisitive, keeping "an eye on" Thornton Square. Elizabeth (Barbara Everest), the other maid, is wary of Anton. And the law (conveniently enough!) is also looking out for her interests. Scotland Yard detective Brian Cameron (Joseph Cotten) has long been infatuated with Alice's memory and fascinated by her unsolved murder. Seeing Paula (who resembles her late aunt) on the street rekindled his interest in the case. Cameron discovers that Anton leaves his house at night, only to re-enter its attic through a back entrance. The audience learns what Paula will know later: the strange sounds and flickering lights are <u>not</u> hallucinations. They are the work of Anton: he is trying to drive her crazy. But why? And what <u>does</u> he do for 8 hours every night in the attic?

Cameron realizes that the danger to Paula is real and immediate. When Nancy tells him that her mistress may soon be leaving for a long time, Cameron and the Scotland Yard detectives move in to "save" her. Paula learns from them that "Gregory Anton" is actually Sergius Bauer, Alice's murderer, who has returned to the house to find the jewels he left behind the night of the murder.

At first, Paula resists reality. Yet, in the course of her conversation with Cameron, she grows to accept the truth. She exclaims sadly, "if that were true, then from the beginning there would have been nothing, nothing real — from the beginning."

As Paula regains her strength, she takes control of the situation. When Anton-Bauer is arrested and tied up in the attic, Paula, despite Brian's objections, taunts him as he did her. She doesn't allow herself simply to be "saved" by another man; she enacts her own unique revenge. When Anton begs her for a knife to cut the ropes that bind his hands, Paula retorts, "Well it isn't there. You must have dreamed you put it there."

The last (predictably upbeat) scene, set on the roof, is sunnier; hopefully Paula will leave her past behind. Brian Cameron, symbol of masculine protectiveness and rationality, promises future romance. Yet the threat of Thornton Square remains sharply etched in the audience consciousness.

Why female audiences flocked to see one film like <u>Gaslight</u> is not hard to understand. Boyer's evil charm, Bergman's distraught beauty, Huldschinsky's ornate Victoriana, sweaty palms from nerve-wracking suspense — all that and more for 35 cents!

What does need explaining, however, is the fact that 1940s audiences, particularly women, chose filmic variations on this theme — victimized wife, potentially murderous husband — again and again and again.

In two of the three films previously mentioned, <u>Gaslight</u> and <u>Sleep, My Love</u>, the heroines' suspicions prove true. Their husbands, a criminal and a fortunehunter, respectively, plan to kill them. With the aid of (naturally!) a "good man," they escape. However, the male rescuer is relatively peripheral to the emotional intensity of the narrative. The mood of these films differs radically from that of <u>Possessed</u>. The roots of female madness lie not within, but without — in the identity of threatening men. "Exorcism" is not the answer. Rather, these women must escape or terminate dangerous relationships.

<u>Suspicion</u> (1941) ends somewhat differently. Lina (Joan Fontaine) discovers that husband Johnny (Cary Grant) is not plotting her

murder, but rather his own. However, the visual imagery of the last scene (is Johnny pushing her out of a car?) is contradictory – and for good reason. Hitchcock tacked on this rather unconvincing ending so that the witty, boyish Grant wouldn't be typecast as a murderer. In Francis Iles' novel Before the Fact, Lina's suspicions proved true. It's easy to see why the ending of Suspicion fails to allay anxiety, and why New York Times critic Bosley Crowther wrote: "Out of slight suggestions and vague uncertain thoughts, a mounting tower of suspicion . . . looms forbiddingly."(14) For its dominant effect, rather than its haphazardly added conclusion, I include Suspicion in this cycle of films.

Why did American women flock to these films? Marjorie Rosen has asserted that late 1940s "women in jeopardy" films offer little more than misogynistic fantasy telling increasingly independent women that they are weaker and more vulnerable in nature than they think. Female audiences, in her view: "Merely accepted these films as distracting entertainment, simply unaware of the psychic damage of the content, which violated . . . their very natures."(15)

There may be some truth in this analysis. Misogyny was hardly a stranger to war-era society in which many males (and some females) resented the growing power of women. It is also likely that misogyny sought symbolic expression in popular culture. The "woman as victim" theme may have placated some insecure men and encouraged some women to withdraw from the public sphere.

However, that does not adequately explain audience response. Do women flock again and again to see the same narratives simply because they like punishment or distraction? And why do they choose to "be distracted" by the same narratives? It is not enough to say that audiences escape. We must ask what they escape into.

These films do present compelling portraits of women in jeopardy, images that clashed sharply with the popular icon of a resilient Rosie the Riveter. Yet the heroines are not doormats; they do fight back and often win, sometimes with the help of an (often older) female ally (Gaslight, Spiral Staircase). And these films also embody another, perhaps more significant aspect: anger, suspicion, and distrust toward men. Behind the patriotic message that "our boys" are the best is the fear that they are really the worst. And in a society in which patriotic Rosies met postwar scorn, feminine anger ran deep.

These films evoke the dark side of the feminine experience, the fear of annihilation – mental and physical – by men. On one level, these narratives are a powerful indictment of romantic love. In this wedding and divorce boom era, when many lonely and desperate women married men they hardly knew, these films possessed great cautionary power. Like the tales of a friend or kinswoman ("Let me tell you of the woman who married a man she met on a train – two days later. You'll never believe . . ."), these films warn against "love at first sight," and cautioned woman against domestic isolation. As

Sandra Gilbert and Susan Gubar (1979) noted in The Madwoman in the Attic: The Woman Writer and the Nineteenth Century Literary Imagination, the metaphor of domestic entrapment has appeared in the work of female authors from Jane Austen and the Brontës in the nineteenth century to Sylvia Plath in the twentieth. Symbolizing the paralyzing strictures of domesticity, this metaphor allowed women artists to express their own anger toward patriarchal society. For 1940s female stars and audiences alike, on the eve of the feminine mystique, it is probable that this symbol — of house as prison — performed a similar function. When watching a Gaslight or Suspicion, female audiences often mentally interject "what ifs" — what if she had a close girlfriend, what if her sister or mother were present, what if she had a job, what if she didn't move to a strange place . . . what if . . . could he still threaten her?(16) As popular female vocalists would sing in a "cautionary" song two decades later, "You better shop around."

Wartime separation brought fear and anxiety to millions of young women. Would their husbands, fiancés, and boyfriends return to love the women they are now? Would their men be the "same" — or would war have transformed them? Or would they find, like Paula, that "nothing had been real from the beginning"? As the war drew to a close, newspaper articles revealed a fear of returning vets — would "blood lust" end when they came home?

The issue of wife battering received national attention in the wartime murder trial of a Muncie, Indiana mother of ten, Clara Edwards. Mrs. Edwards shot her drunken abusive husband allegedly in self defense.   When she was acquitted, a courtroom of sympathetic women cheered. Images of rape and family violence haunted war-era women, at the same time that the dominant ideology stressed nurturance of the returning vet.

On the surface, these films are about rich women exploited by criminals and fortunehunters. The heroines, leisured, upper-class women, have very different lives from the majority of the audience. However, below the surface, these films address a much wider group of women in portraying the powerful cultural undercurrent of feminine suspicion and distrust. The heroines of these films — in their historical and cultural differences from the audience — may have given women the psychic space to identify with them and their narrative. In Suspicion and Gaslight, for example, the heroines also are portrayed in a somewhat vague and undifferentiated way, symbolizing Everywoman. This ambiguity of character development may have allowed some women to project freely upon these charac-ters their own fears, insecurities, and suspicions. The fact that films like Gaslight and Sleep, My Love confirm suspicious feelings toward men, without rooting them in postwar social conditions, is signi-ficant. Clearly, when that suspicion is seen as arising not primarily from fortunehunters (good men are often around the corner), but from causes closer to home, Hollywood backs off.   A wartime drama, for example, about a female welder who wonders if her ex-G.I. husband will kill her, would probably have been taboo for a film industry eager to maintain both the war morale and its own profits, and may have been too threatening for many female viewers to accept. It is as cultural undercurrent that these films convey most power. The Victorian or foreign settings, the mysterious characters, the ornate interiors, the shadowy lighting, like the unconscious, speak for the forbidden.(17)

SUSPICION EXPLORED AND DENIED:
A LETTER TO THREE WIVES (1949)

Any resemblance to you or me might be purely coincidental.

Addie Ross, the unseen narrator, in A Letter
to Three Wives (20th Century Fox, 1949)

Suspicion assumes a contemporary face in Joseph L. Mankiewicz's 20th Century Fox award-winning comedy noir, A Letter to Three Wives, adapted from John Klempner's Cosmopolitan short story. Infidelity is the subject of the letter, as three contemporary suburban wives are shocked by its contents. The film captures an atypical day-in-the-life of Rita Phipps (Ann Sothern), Deborah Bishop (Jeanne Crain), and Lora Mae Hollingsway (Linda Darnell).

Who's Addie Ross? In the answer to that question, lies the meaning of A Letter to Three Wives. As in Possessed, the first sequence sets the tone of the film. Addie, the first, and perhaps most significant, female character we meet is, like Pauline Graham, not a person, but a voice-over (Celeste Holm). The symbol of ideal womanhood, Addie introduces the setting and characters. Catty and misogynistic, the undertone of menace in her voice prepares the audience for catastrophe. The camera creeps slowly down the sunny early morning streets of suburbia, cheerful yet commonplace. With bitchy confidence, Addie remarks in voice-over that this town (unnamed) is 28 miles from a big city, the location is Everysuburb, U.S.A. However, "Any resemblance to you or me might be purely coincidental."In this powerful introductory sequence, Addie invites the audience (particularly women) to speculate: is this film really about me?

Addie narrates, as the camera introduces the "three wives" and their mates: the Bishops, the Phipps, and the Hollingsways. Foreboding colors Addie's voice. She knows something these women don't. What is it?

A Letter to Three Wives revolves around the nature of her secret. Suspense is allayed and heightened, as Deborah, Lora Mae, and Rita receive a joint letter from Addie, just as they are leaving on a Saturday afternoon women's club picnic. Expecting the letter to contain an excuse for missing the outing, they are shocked and horrified to read: "You see, girls, I've run off with one of your husbands."

Addie's cruel revelation immediately engenders panic and suspicion in each woman. All three husbands left home early that morning. Each wife wonders: will my husband return? The intricate and expertly done flashback and multiple viewpoint techniques of Mankiewicz (who won Oscars for both scriptwriting and direction) capture the gnawing suspicions of each woman. And the haunting omnipresence of Addie Ross portrays an elusive and unattainable ideal of femininity. The fears of the three women, their solidarity as well as competition with each other, offer important insights into postwar female culture and consciousness.

As A Letter to Three Wives progresses, each segment explores a different wife's reason for suspicion and distrust. Flashing back to a similar first Saturday in May, 3 years ago, Mrs. Bishop is the first to reminisce. A mid-West farmer's daughter, Deborah wed Brad (Jeffrey Lynn) in the Navy. Returning after the war to his upper middle-class Connecticut neighborhood, she worries if their marriage will survive in this new and alien setting. Deborah painfully recalls her first night out at a country club dance with her new husband, fresh out of the Navy. Wearing a cheap, gaudy mail-order dress, she felt out of place, like a farmhand. Meeting Brad's old high school friends, George (Kirk Douglas) and Rita Phipps, was a test of strength of her marriage. Would a wartime romance die in the cold civilian reality of class, language, and cultural differences? Would Brad see (and reject) her for what she really was: an uncouth farm girl? Rita offers Deborah support and advice, helping her dress for the occasion, socializing her to middle-class suburbia. Deborah, however, is confused by her new identity, unsure of who she has become: "Mrs. Bradbury Bishop? Who is she?" Could she know how to be a "good mother" in suburbia? Clearly, in the dominant ideology of femininity, the adjustments were hers to make. Never once does the film suggest that Brad might relocate to her rural community.

The image of Addie Ross, Brad's old flame, haunts Deborah. Symbolizing taste, class, and femininity, wealthy divorcee Addie is everything Deborah "should be" but can't. When Addie sends over a complimentary bottle of wine at the dance, Brad fondly remarks, "That's Addie, always the right thing at the right time." Addie is the mythical woman every other woman is threatened by, no woman can be, and every man wants. Deborah cannot measure up to Addie's ideal, and winds up drinking too much at the dance and looking very foolish. "I wanted so much to be what he wanted, to do what was right — like Addie Ross," mourns Deborah. Has Brad abandoned the clumsy farm girl for the beautiful socialite?

The film flashes forward to the picnic, as the women keep compulsively busy to avoid those dreaded, private moments of suspicion. Their emotions are split, feeling compassion for, as well as competition with, each other. After all, only one marriage is doomed. Sensing these contradictions, Deborah remarks perceptively: "We're beginning to behave like some movie about a women's prison."

Rita's marriage is the next to undergo critical scrutiny. George left that morning, like the others, dressed up, without saying where he was going. Would he ever return? Rita muses about the tensions within their relationship. High school sweethearts, the Phipps seem to have a strong relationship. The specific strains of postwar adjustment do not present themselves in their marriage. Rather the problems portrayed in their relationship reveal an unusual and somewhat progressive treatment of women in 1940s films. As a writer of radio soap operas, Rita earns more than George, a poorly paid high school English teacher. She is also the mother of twins (aged 5 or 6: never shown in the film) and manages her dual role by hiring a maid, Sadie Dugan (Thelma Ritter). She never questions the assumption that home and children are her responsibility. She can hire a maid, but does not expect George to perform an equal share of the household tasks. Yet, while their relationship is not totally egalitarian, it is equal in many other ways. And, in 1949, it stood out as one of the more progressive relationships on screen.

Their conflicts center on Rita's job as a radio soap writer. Yet the tensions between the pair are not only rooted in the threat her career poses to his masculinity, although George nervously jokes about being a "titular head of the house." (And it is certainly not accidental that masculinity is associated with the "high culture"). Their conflict primarily focuses on what Rita's work means to George: the trivialization and commercialization of mass culture. George sees Rita as more crass and materialistic than he, and as having, in some ways, sold out. (As he also lives off her salary, the strength of the argument is dubious.) Their conflict represents an almost classic high culture versus mass culture debate. George is appalled, for example, at the ways in which Rita appeases her bosses, the Manleighs (Florence Bates and Hobart Cavanaugh), whose only concern is that her plays sell ever-increasing amounts of detergent. Rita is aware of her compromise, but sees only one other alternative: the monotony of housework. As she writes as night, when her mothering responsibilities are over, this career is ideal and lucrative. A 9-to-5 job would be much harder to juggle. George prizes his "modern, enlightened marriage," yet expresses genuine horror at the threat that radio poses to those few like himself still devoted to high culture. Whereas George and Rita caricature high and mass culture, their disputes popularize the critical intellectual debates of their time.

George's anger peaks when the Manleighs come to dinner and spend the evening listening to radio serials: "The Confessions of Brenda Brown" (a not-so-subtle dig at Brenda Starr?) and "Linda Gray, Registered Nurse." The Manleighs' conversation is straight

Advertising Age: "Three minutes gone . . . one full commercial . . . After penetration comes saturation." When Mrs. Manleigh asks George his opinion of radio, he replies: "The purpose of radio writing . . . is to prove to the masses that a deodorant can bring happiness, a mouthwash guarantee success and a laxative attract romance." (George's critique of radio — and implicitly, much of women's popular culture — is an indirect statement by Mankiewicz that A Letter to Three Wives is a clear cut above those cultural forms.) After the Manleighs leave, George confronts Rita: "Seven years ago I made the most perfect marriage . . . to an independent, understanding woman. I don't want to be married to Linda Gray, or Brenda Brown." Their problems are compounded as Rita, in the rush of writing deadlines, forgot his birthday. Addie, meanwhile, sends George, of all things, a classical album he's wanted with a cryptic note: "If music be the food of love, play on." Though the flavor of this segment is comic, it fails to dispel Rita's suspicion. "Is it George?" "Is it George?" (The soundtrack resounds.)

In the last of Mankiewicz's multiple viewpoint sequences, we enter the Hollingsway household. Serious strain between the couple has been suggested in previous scenes. Yet Lora Mae defensively stated at the picnic: "I don't know if Porter ran off with Addie and . . . I don't care." However, after this bold assertion, the phrase "Do I care?" reverberates through her mind, as dripping water resounds annoyingly in the background. Of the three, Lora Mae seems the toughest, coldest, least in need of support. Yet appearances, as we've been learning throughout this film, deceive.

The film flashes back to the beginning of their relationship. Lora Mae Finney is Irish, from the "wrong side of the tracks," living with her mother, Ruby (Connie Gilchrist), and her sister, Babe (Barbara Lawrence). Humorously and graphically, the filmic code portrays their poverty. As trains go by outside, every pot, pan, fork, cup, and saucer vibrate loudly in the kitchen. Lora, a department store salesclerk, has begun dating her boss, boorish Mr. Hollingsway, divorced and at least 10 years her senior. Mrs. Finney worries for her daughter's virtue: "Remember — you're my daugher and a decent girl." Yet, for Lora, Porter may provide a welcome road out of her class. In 30 years, she doesn't want to be like Ruby, 50, poor, alone, and living in the shadow of the El. And chances for advancement out of the ranks of sales are slim. Furthermore with few eligible men on the homefront during the war, Porter had not only solid middle-class status, but perhaps little competition.

Porter and Lora Mae's relationship begins as a curious blend of mutual opportunism and genuine affection. Porter desires female companionship and sex; Lora wants the security of marriage and an escape from poverty. Marriage to Porter spells a step up on the class ladder, a step she is unlikely to make on her own. Yet Addie had stepped into Porter's life as well (more plot contrivance). Lora notices her picture (unseen by the audience) on Porter's piano:

Lora: She sort of looks like a queen.

Porter: Like a queen ought to look.

Addie, the unattainable ideal, haunts each woman in a way unique to her own life. Porter agrees to marry Lora (who plays "hard to get") but the strains in their relationship remain. In the beginning of the film, Lora had accused the now much more successful department store magnate, "You don't spend half an hour a week at home." Has he run off with Addie?

Through the three segments, the audience experiences both the specificity and commonality of these marriages. Up to this point, A Letter to Three Wives suggests that, for a wife in any relationship from the strongest (the Phipps) to the weakest (the Hollingsways), suspicion and ultimate distrust of one's husband is possible.

The three women differ sharply, of course. Deborah is a true believer in the feminine mystique, wondering only if she is inadequate. Rita, however, is a rebel, and does not want to abandon writing for full-time domesticity. Lora on the other hand, is an opportunist, pragmatic exploiter of the feminine mystique. Marriage can provide a lifestyle she is unlikely to achieve herself. Though these women differ in character, they are united by both friendship and the spectre of Addie. No woman is exempt from the power of mythic femininity that Addie represents.

The conclusion of A Letter to Three Wives, however, like that of most women's films, softens and compromises its critical character. After a more intense build-up of suspicion through some suspenseful twists and turns of the narrative, Porter reveals that he planned to elope with Addie. He considered Lora a fortunehunter who had no longer loved him. Yet, after consideration, he realized how much he really loved his wife, and decided to stay. In a very confusing and unexpected ending, the Hollingsways "kiss and make up."(18)

Each woman, however, sobered by her Saturday of suspicion, becomes determined to "work at" her marriage. A Letter to Three Wives concludes on a fairly conservative note. As the film came close to affirming fully their (or even one of their) sense of distrust, it backs off. It cannot carry through with the critique of femininity it initiates. Yet neither is the surprise ending completely reassuring. After all, the letter had not been simply a cruel joke; it did reflect reality. If it had not "touched home," the women would have ignored it, laughed, and regarded it as a prank. Likewise, the emotions evoked throughout the film do not simply vanish in a sigh of relief. The power of the letter (and the film) lies in the fear and suspicion it evokes.

A Letter to Three Wives hit home for postwar female viewers. Infidelity was a sore subject for waiting women, so sore that Hollywood dared not portray it until peacetime (Klempner's original story was set in a war-effort club). Joseph Goulden described a pervasive female jealousy: "an unmeasurable factor in the bring-our-boys-home sentiment was traditional feminine jealousy . . . the woman at home heard enough dire warnings to stimulate any imagination."(19) In sarcastic comedy, A Letter to Three Wives revealed gnawing doubts and long-held insecurities. In its comically chilling portrait of suburban strife, A Letter to Three Wives is ahead of its time, prefiguring the writing of authors like John Cheever and Betty Friedan.(20) Perhaps, from its inception, the postwar suburban dream, built on forced female demobilization and domestic isolation, was riddled with fear and contradiction. If one were simply to analyze this film as counseling feminine adjustment, she or he would ignore both the deep distrust expressed toward men and the anger and envy acknowledged toward the unattainable Addie. No woman is exempt from the power of Addie, not the conformist (Deborah), the rebel (Rita), or the opportunist (Lora Mae). For Addie is both the price of the feminine mystique and a potential source of its rejection. A Letter to Three Wives prefigures the feminist critique by portraying the impact of idealized femininity on real women. This film foreshadows the words of de Beauvoir written 4 years later:

> The myth of woman . . . substitutes a transcendental Idea, timeless, unchangeable . . . endowed with absolute truth. Thus, as against the dispersed, contingent and multiple experiences of actual women, mythical thought opposes the Eternal Feminine, unique and changeless.(21)

Addie Ross is the filmic symbol of the Eternal Feminine, personification of male fantasy and female oppression.

THE POWER AND POTENTIAL OF UNDERCURRENT

Madness, suspicion, and distrust infuse the noir women's film. Garbed in melodrama, undercurrents of hostility toward individual men and patriarchal society surface in the safety of a darkened theater. Movies like Gaslight and A Letter to Three Wives provided outlets for female anger rooted in the demobilization of Rosie the Riveter, the multiple strains of wartime separation, and a broader historical oppression of women, manifesting itself in the overcommitment of women and the undercommitment of men to heterosexual relationships. These filmic undercurrents, like female culture and consciousness itself, were probably contradictory in effect, both encouraging women to express their anger while containing that rage (at least temporarily) within the confines of culture.

By no means do I assert that suspicion and distrust were the dominant emotions of women in this era. However, an analysis of noir women's films in the 1940s reveals a powerful undercurrent of distrust, hostility, and suspicion toward men. And, in the particular contradictions of women in this period, we can see an intensification of distrustful feelings, as well as the suppression of their more direct and potentially political articulation.

The "culture of pain" is not the creation of contemporary feminism. Historically it arose in response to a female oppression that may have imagined few alternatives, and expressed itself (in mediated form) through popular culture. The culture of pain is, often, a culture of defense and resignation. How, why, and under what social conditions the culture of pain gives birth to the "culture of transformation" is a key question for contemporary feminism.

NOTES

(1)   The preceding are quotes from undergraduate papers on "Sex Role Socialization," for Sex Roles in Modern Society, a sociology course I taught at SUNY-Binghamton, Spring 1977. All of the above quotes are either mother-daughter or grandmother-granddaughter confidences, and occurred in the period roughly 1950-1977.

(2)   See Karen Horney, Feminine Psychology, ed. and intro. by Harold Kelman (New York: Norton, 1967); Theodore Reik, Listening with the Third Ear (New York: Farrar, Straus, 1948); Phyllis Chesler, Women and Madness (New York: Avon, 1973); Mirra Komarovsky, Blue Collar Marriage (New York: Vintage, 1962); Joyce A. Ladner, Tomorrow's Tomorrow: The Black Woman (Garden City: Doubleday, 1971); Ntozake Shange, For Colored Girls Who Have Considered Suicide when the Rainbow is Enuf (New York: Macmillan, 1975); Barbara Gordon, I'm Dancing as Fast as I Can (New York: Bantam, 1979).

(3)   See E. Ann Kaplan (ed.), Women in Film Noir (London: British Film Institute, 1978), for a discussion of problems of classifying films noir. In her introduction, Kaplan discussed whether film noir constitutes a genre, generic development, subgenre or movement. As film noir embodies a variety of themes, I do not consider it a genre. However, it does employ a characteristic visual-narrative style. I feel the concepts of "generic development" or "movement" are more appropriate. Also see Alain Silver and Elizabeth Ward (ed.), Film Noir: An Encyclopedic Reference to the American Style (Woodstock, N.Y.: Overlook Press, 1979).

(4)   See Sylvia Harvey, "Woman's Place: The Absent Family of Film Noir," in Women in Film Noir, ed. E. Ann Kaplan (London: British Film Institute, 1978), p. 33; also see Stuart Kaminsky, American Film Genres (New York: Dell, 1974); Tom Flinn, "Three Faces of Film Noir: Stranger on the Third Floor, Phantom Lady and Criss Cross," in Kings of the Bs, ed. Todd McCarthy and Charles Flynn (New York: Dutton, 1975); Robert Sklar, Movie Made America (New York: Random House, 1975).

(5)   Janey Place, "Women in Film Noir," in Women in Film Noir, ed. E. Ann Kaplan (London: British Film Institute, 1978), p. 37.

(6)   Molly Haskell, From Reverence to Rape: The Treatment of Women in the Movies (New York: Holt, Rinehart, 1973), p. 179.

(7)   Michael Wood, America in the Movies (New York: Basic, 1975), p. 97.

(8)   Howard Barnes, quoted in Lawrence J. Quirk, The Films of Joan Crawford (New York: Citadel, 1971), p. 166.

(9)   Marjorie Rosen, Popcorn Venus (New York: Coward, McCann, Geoghegan, 1973), p. 240.

(10) Bergman won an Oscar for Best Actress in 1944; Huldschinsky, et al. received the award for Best Interior Decoration in Black & White; Gaslight was also nominated for Best Picture, Boyer for Best Actor, Lansbury for Best Supporting Actress, and Joseph Ruttenberg for Best Black and White Cinematography. Bergman also received a "Best Acting" award from the National Board of Review, and "Best Actress" from Golden Globe. Lansbury was named Best Supporting Actress and J. Carrol Naish Best Supporting Actor by the Golden Globe.

(11) In interviewing audience members (and from personal experience), I've found this term to be widely used and understood throughout the next 15-20 years after the film's release. This could be accounted for, in part, by its continued popularity on television and in revival houses.

(12) Gordon Gow, in Suspense and the Cinema (New York: Paperback Library, 1971) has analyzed the use of trains in suspense films. On the one hand, trains are escapist, spelling travel and wide open spaces. On the other hand, however, they are close and claustrophobic, providing a dual image of isolation/entrapment amidst freedom.

(13) Gavin Lambert, On Cukor (New York: G.P. Putnam, 1972), p. 183.

(14) Bosley Crowther, quoted in Tony Thomas, Films of the Forties (Secaucus, N.J.: Citadel, 1975), p. 48.

(15) Marjorie Rosen, Popcorn Venus, p. 236.

(16) When addressing audiences who have just seen one of these films (especially women), the "what if" structure continually reappears. Some audience members will yell to the too trusting young wife early in the film: e.g., "Don't do that, you jerk," "Don't open the closet," "Don't let him do that."

(17) For an earlier analysis of these and other related films see Andrea Walsh, "Films of Suspicion and Distrust: Undercurrents of Female Consciousness in the 1940s," Film and History, VIII, no. 1 (February 1978). See Diane Waldman, "Horror and Domesticity: The Modern Gothic Romance Film of the 1940s " (unpublished Ph.D. dissertation, University of Wisconsin-Madison, 1981) for a somewhat similar analysis.

(18) Mankiewicz called the ending a "boo-boo." Many viewers thought that Porter lied to save Deborah's face. Mankiewicz himself did not intend a "happy ending"; the next step for Porter and Lora Mae (in his fantasy) was to divorce. Other viewers, like General Douglas MacArthur (who wrote Mankiewicz asking who did run off with Addie), may have been totally confused. See Kenneth L. Geist, Pictures Will Talk: The Life and Films of Joseph L. Mankiewicz (New York: Scribner's, 1978), p. 145.

(19) Joseph C. Goulden, The Best Years, 1945-1950 (New York: Atheneum, 1976), p. 31.

(20) A Letter to Three Wives reveals stronger female influence in its production than the credits indicate. Vera Caspary (who is listed in the credits as "Screen Adaptation By") asked the Screen Writers Guild to decide that she should receive co-writing credit with Mankiewicz. The Guild ruled in Caspary's favor, but the egotistical Mankiewicz successfully contested the decision. Producer Sol Siegel, after Letter ... opened with great critical acclaim, declared "It's an outrage that all they can talk about is Mankiewicz on this picture. Mankiewicz had a crack at this material and couldn't lick it . . . . It wasn't till Siegel and Caspary came along that it came to life." See Kenneth L. Geist, Pictures Will Talk, p. 145.

(21) Simone de Beauvoir, The Second Sex (New York: Bantam, 1953), p. 237.

CONCLUSION

Traditional mothers and independent daughters, comically embattled career heroines and their lover-competitors, terrified wives and murderous husbands — what do these popular characters from 1940s women's films tell us about the American female experience in that era?

Taken separately and together, these classic characters and their narratives constitute the symbolic universe of a Hollywood "woman's narrative" reflecting, in its production and reception, the dynamics of a dominant culture challenged by residual and emergent social influences. Interpreted in the context of war-era social history, women's films provide a rich source for the analysis of undercurrents as well as maincurrents in female consciousness. A comic mood, a foreign or historical setting, a fantastic plot, a "happy ending" — can all "work" in films to allow for the expression of the unmentionable. In this light, popular culture can provide either or both an incubator and a safety valve for repressed and dissident sentiments.

The contrasting dynamic of dark and light, of despair and hope, of traditionalism and change, of suspicion and trust, colors the world of the women's film, a world in which the heroine must make difficult personal and moral choices or confront life crises. Within the maternal drama, female wisdom, nurturance, and resilience are celebrated within traditional feminine roles. In the traditional mother-independent daughter narratives, like I Remember Mama and Little Women, the hope and power of female bonding suggest an emergent feminism. Yet a darkness shadows the maternal theme: Mildred and Veda Pierce are the "dark mirror" to Marta and Katrin Hansen. In the career woman comedy, a similar contrast appears. Whereas films like His Girl Friday and Adam's Rib portray a more positive resolution of the tension between femininity and achievement, Lady in the Dark, the first Freudian musical (!), depicts the

195

conflict as irresolvable. Madness is the price Liza Elliott must pay for "flying in the face of nature." The films of suspicion and distrust, however, are colored by the darkness and paranoia of film noir. The myth of "love at first sight" and the romance of the feminine mystique are symbolically critiqued in these tales of domestic entrapment and female victimization.

What do these three complementary and contrasting types of women's film narratives suggest about audience consciousness? And how can one interpret the dynamic of light and dark, hope and despair? Taken together, these filmic fantasies suggest: that images of female power and bonding were most acceptable to women (and Hollywood) if coupled with domesticity; that the temporary matriarchy of many war families caused strain, exhaustion, and fear as well as pride; that women experienced an exhilarating sense of their own power at work, as well as strong conflict between femininity and achievement; that many women were attracted to heterosexual relationships marked by equality and a struggle for power; and that many women feared and distrusted men (individually and as a group) at the same time that they desired them. Clearly, all women were not represented equally in the "audience image" employed by the major studios. For lesbian, older, handicapped and minority women, their experience was much more likely to be ignored, stereotyped, or coded in concealing ways on screen. Despite this fact, however, one can trace significant currents of female consciousness within Hollywood's women's films.

If we situate the dominant themes of war-era women's films within the context of American society in the 1940s, we find that they do not stand alone. Poll data has revealed the persistence of traditional conceptions of masculinity and femininity, at the same time that it has documented the anger and injustice felt by women (25 percent of the women surveyed in a 1946 poll wished that they had been born male!). First person accounts, survey research, and histories of the period all have documented a sense of "rising expectations" and pride on the part of female war workers, as well as the multiple strains of the "double day." Social work literature has reflected a deep concern with the effects of wartime separation on men and women, husbands and wives, parents and children. Even the suspicion and distrust of wartime women toward men has revealed itself in newspaper advice columns and women's magazine articles. However, the dominant ideology of optimism and patriotism often downplayed its power and pervasiveness. Margaret Mead, often a national spokeswoman for the dominant culture, warned Americans against postwar hysteria:

Dramatic news, quintuplets and quads, double murders and triple suicides, bobby sox roundups and bluebeard lovers, all fall into place in peacetime, as events which spice the even round of life, life in which most babies are born one at a time, husbands and wives may sometimes feel like murdering each other but hardly ever do, most high school girls are studying their lessons, and most men find it quite enough to have married one woman, without looking for extra wives.(1)

The world of popular women's films sometimes challenges the dominant ideology, contrasting with the facilely reassuring message just mentioned by portraying domestic claustrophobia and female entrapment. It is in the exploration of the dark side, the under-currents of culture and consciousness explored in these films which are most revealing, opening up often unasked questions about female fear, anger, and confusion in this period.

The dominant themes of popular 1940s women's films can be seen as threads running through the lives of women in American culture. The common sense of American womanhood suggested by these filmic fantasies is complex, embodying dominant, residual, and emergent cultural currents. Although most of these films are not feminist by contemporary definition, they do depict powerful, competent, or intuitive heroines at the heart and center of cine-matic narrative. One might consider many of these films to embody a nascent or emergent feminism, expressing the positive aspects of female power, bonding, and autonomy without the coherence of a feminist ideology or the organizing power of a women's movement.

The interpretation of this study takes issue with those who view the 1940s as an era unmarked by significant changes in female consciousness. The absence of organized feminist protest on a mass scale and the persistence of traditional values and roles should not blind us to the manifestations of female anger and discontent and its potential for future articulation as a full-blown feminist ideology.

The nascent feminist consciousness of the 1940s, as revealed in the narratives of popular women's films, suggests a connection between Rosie the Riveter and her women's movement sisters of the 1960s. And the fact that many contemporary feminists testify to "loving 'women's films' " compels us to explore the reasons for the continuing power of these filmic texts in the lives of women. While we cannot immediately draw causal links between the 1940s and the 1960s, 1970s, and 1980s, these observations lead us to re-examine the culture and consciousness of American women in the war era.

A thorough examination of these issues would take one far beyond the bounds of this book — to a fuller examination of the 1940s and to an extensive analysis of the culture and society of America in the 1950s.(2) When and how dissident, repressed, and forbidden emotions cohere into a compelling counterideology is a pressing question. When does the "culture of pain," the "culture of fatalism" become the "culture of transformation"? When does an emergent culture threaten to become the dominant? But that is the subject of yet another study.

NOTES

(1)   Margaret Mead, "The Women and the War," in Jack Goodman, ed., While You Were Gone (New York: Simon and Schuster, 1946), p. 275.

(2)   Several cultural and social historians have suggested that feminist and other socially critical undercurrents "lurked" beneath the surface conformism of the 1950s. See Andrew Dowdy, The Films of the Fifties: The American State of Mind (New York: Morrow, 1973); Sara Evans, Personal Politics: The Roots of Women's Liberation in the Civil Rights Movement and the New Left (New York: Knopf, 1979); Brandon French, On the Verge of Revolt: Women in American Films of the '50s (New York: Ungar, 1978).

APPENDIXES

APPENDIX 1: COMPARISON CHARTS OF MARQUEE VALUES
OF WOMEN'S FILM STARS FOR AUDIENCES BY SEX,
AGE, AND SOCIOECONOMIC STATUS

The following charts are constructed from data collected by George Gallup and Associates in the 1940s. These charts describe "marquee value" (i.e., whether or not a specific star's name on a marquee alone would entice a person to see a film). See Gallup Looks at the Movies: Audience Research Reports, 1940-1950 (Wilmington, Delaware: Scholarly Resources, 1979). The following indicate for what percentage of audience these stars have "marquee value."

Ingrid Bergman

	1941-1942	1944	1946	1947	1949
Men	8	n.a.	37	48	49
Women	16		55	62	63
Women					
12-17	12		46	59	n.a.
18-30	18		59	63	65
31+	15		53	62	62
Upper-middle					
income	15		56	62	62
lower income	6		42	51	52
Cities of					
100,000+	15		50	57	55
10-10,000	10		43	54	53
Under 10,000	9		43	46	n.a.

Claudette Colbert

	1941-1942	1944	1946	1947	1949
Men	17	20.9	n.a.	25	29
Women	29	30.5		40	47
Women					
12-17	21	19.8		32	39
18-30	30	29.6		38	45
31+	34	41.9		47	55
Upper-middle					
income	28	31.1		35	41
lower income	22	23.2		31	36
Cities of					
100,000+	24	26.0		32.5	36
10-10,000	33	25.9		33	39
Under 10,000	23	29.2		35	n.a.

Joan Crawford

	1941-1942	1944	1946	1947	1949
Men	12	n.a.	15	28	21
Women	22		23	19	39
Women					
12-17	13		14	19	30
18-30	24		23	27	37
31+	24		29	35	49
Upper-middle					
income	17.5		22	25	32
lower income	20		18	23	28
Cities of					
100,000+	14		20	24	30.5
10-10,000	15		17	24	28
Under 10,000	17		20	22	n.a.

Bette Davis

	1941–1942	1944	1946	1947	1949
Men	35	30.3	30	26	25
Women	62	50.3	45	44	44
Women					
12–17	49	29.6	31	33	34
18–30	69	54.2	46	46	48
31+	57	58.5	52	50	49
Upper-middle					
income	50	47.4	45	42	37
lower income	42	38.5	35	32	32
Cities of					
100,000+	52	43	40	38.5	34.5
10–10,000	52	37.4	37	32	34
Under 10,000	52	39	36	30	n.a.

Joan Fontaine

	1941–1942	1944	1946	1947	1949
Men	5	16	12	17	22
Women	9	25	21	29	38
Women					
12–17	11	17	16	26	35
18–30	10	27	24	30	40
31+	6	27.9	20	30	38
Upper-middle					
income	8.3	24.9	21	28	32
lower income	5	15.7	15	20	39
Cities of		20	20	24	31
100,000+	12	15.5	14	24	26
10–10,000	9	13	14	17	n.a.
Under 10,000	7				

Greer Garson

	1941–1942	1944	1946	1947	1949
Men	9	37.3	38	32	26
Women	24	58	56	47	40
Women					
12–17	21	45.5	50	43	38
18–30	25	56.5	55	47	40
31+	26	71.8	61	50	41
Upper-middle					
income	20	58.6	55	44	35
lower income	12	43.4	44	37	31
Cities of					
100,000+	20	50	49	40	33
10–10,000	15	47	45	40	32
Under 10,000	20	40.7	52	38	n.a.

Katharine Hepburn

	1941–1942	1944	1946	1947	1949
Men	11	12.9	13	12	15
Women	26	21.9	22	25	29
Women					
12–17	17	10.5	16	14	21
18–30	28	23.9	23	28	33
31+	29	26.6	25	27	30
Upper-middle					
income	22	24.6	24	25	27
lower income	13	13.5	15	14	18
Cities of					
100,000+	22	19	19.5	20.5	22
10–10,000	21	15.6	17	18	21
Under 10,000	20	16.1	16	15	n.a.

Rosalind Russell

	1941-1942	1944	1946	1947	1949
Men	18	17.8	18	21	20
Women	29	34.4	27	33	32
Women					
12-17	24	22.8	19	25	25
18-30	31	36.2	28	32	31
31+	26	40.1	30	39	38
Upper-middle					
income	26	33.7	27	32	28
lower income	15	23.2	21	24	24
Cities of					
100,000+	29	31	25	28.5	26
10-10,000	27	23.3	20	24	26
Under 10,000	25	20.7	20	24	n.a.

APPENDIX 2:
THE 1930 PRODUCTION CODE

Preamble

Motion picture producers recognize the high trust and confidence which have been placed in them by the people of the world and which have made motion pictures a universal form of entertainment.

They recognize their responsibility to the public because of this trust and because entertainment and art are important influences in the life of a nation.

Hence, though regarding motion pictures primarily as entertainment without any explicit purpose of teaching or propaganda, they know that the motion picture within its own field of entertainment may be directly responsible for spiritual or moral progress, for higher types of social life, and for much correct thinking.

During the rapid transition from silent to talking pictures they realized the necessity and the opportunity of subscribing to a Code to govern the production of talking pictures and of acknowledging this responsibility.

On their part, they ask from the public and from public leaders a sympathetic understanding of their purposes and problems and a spirit of cooperation that will allow them the freedom and opportunity necessary to bring the motion picture to a still higher level of wholesome entertainment for all the people.

GENERAL PRINCIPLES

1. No picture shall be produced which will lower the moral standards of those who see it. Hence the sympathy of the audience shall never be thrown to the side of crime, wrong-doing, evil or sin.
2. Correct standards of life, subject only to the requirements of drama and entertainment, shall be presented.
3. Law, natural or human, shall not be ridiculed, nor shall sympathy be created for its violation.

I. Crimes Against the Law
These shall never be presented in such a way as to throw sympathy
with the crime as against law and justice or to inspire others with a
desire for imitation.

   1.   Murder
      (a)   The technique of murder must be presented in a way
            that will not inspire imitation.
      (b)   Brutal killings are not to be presented in detail.
      (c)   Revenge in modern times shall not be justified.
   2.   Methods of crime should not be explicitly presented.
      (a)   Theft, robbery, safe-cracking, and dynamiting of
            trains, mines, buildings, etc. should not be detailed in
            method.
      (b)   Arson must be subject to the same safeguards.
      (c)   The use of firearms should be restricted to essentials.
      (d)   Methods of smuggling should not be presented.
   3.   The illegal drug traffic must not be portrayed in such a
        way as to stimulate curiosity concerning the use of, or
        traffic in, such drugs; nor shall scenes be approved which
        show the use of illegal drugs, or their effects, in detail (as
        amended September 11, 1946).
   4.   The use of liquor in American life, when not required by
        the plot or for proper characterization, will not be shown.

II. Sex
The sanctity of the institution of marriage and the home shall be
upheld. Pictures shall not infer that low forms of sex relationship
are the accepted or common thing.

   1.   Adultery and illicit sex, sometimes necessary plot
        material, must not be explicitly treated or justified, or
        presented attractively.
   2.   Scenes of passion
      (a)   These should not be introduced except where they are
            definitively essential to the plot.
      (b)   Excessive and lustful kissing, lustful embraces,
            suggestive postures and gestures are not to be shown.
      (c)   In general, passion should be treated in such a manner
            as not to stimulate the lower and baser emotions.
   3.   Seduction or rape
      (a)   These should never be more than suggested, and then
            only when essential for the plot. They must never be
            shown by explicit method.
      (b)   They are never the proper subject for comedy.
   4.   Sex perversion or any inference to it is forbidden.
   5.   White slavery shall not be treated.
   6.   Miscegenation (sex relationship between black and white
        races) is forbidden.

7.   Sex hygiene and venereal diseases are not proper subjects for theatrical motion pictures.
8.   Scenes of actual childbirth, in fact or in silhouette, are never to be presented.
9.   Children's sex organs are never to be exposed.

III. Vulgarity
The treatment of low, disgusting, unpleasant, though not necessarily evil, subjects should be guided always by the dictates of good taste and a proper regard for the sensibilities of the audience.

IV. Obscenity
Obscenity in word, gesture, reference, song, joke or by suggestion (even when likely to be understood only by part of the audience) is forbidden.

V. Profanity
Pointed profanity and every other profane or vulgar expression, however used, is forbidden.

No approval by the Production Code Administration shall be given the use of words and phrases in motion pictures including, but not limited to, the following:

Alley cat (applied to a woman); bat (applied to a woman); broad (applied to a woman); Bronx cheer (the sound); chippie; cocotte; God, Lord, Jesus, Christ (unless used reverently); cripes; fanny; fairy (in a vulgar sense); finger (the); fire, cries of; Gawd; goose (in a vulgar sense); "hold your hat" or "hats"; hot (applied to a woman); "in your hat"; louse; lousy, Madam (relating to prostitution); nance, nerts; nuts (except when meaning crazy); pansy; razzberry (the sound); slut (applied to a woman); S.O.B.; son-of-a; tart; toilet gags; tom cat (applied to a man); traveling salesman and farmer's daughter jokes; whore; damn, hell (excepting when the use of said last two words shall be essential and required for portrayal, in proper historical context, of any scene or dialogue based upon historical fact or folklore, or for the presentation in proper literary context of a Biblical, or other religious quotation, or a quotation from a literary work provided that no such use shall be permitted which is intrinsically objectionable or offends good taste).

In the administration of Section V of the Production Code, the Production Code Administration may take cognizance of the fact that the following words and phrases are obviously offensive to the patrons of motion pictures in the United States and more particularly to the patrons of motion pictures in foreign countries:

Chink, Dago, Frog, Greaser, Hunkie, Kike, Nigger, Spic, Wop, Yid.

VI. Costume
1.   Complete nudity is never permitted. This includes nudity in fact or in silhouette, or any licentious notice thereof by other characters in the pictures.
2.   Undressing scenes should be avoided, and never used save where essential to the plot.
3.   Indecent or undue exposure is forbidden.
4.   Dancing costumes intended to permit undue exposure or indecent movements in the dance are forbidden.

VII. Dances
1.   Dances suggesting or representing sexual actions or indecent passion are forbidden.
2.   Dances which emphasize indecent movements are to be regarded as obscene.

VIII. Religion
1.   No film or episode may throw ridicule on any religious faith.
2.   Ministers of religion in their character as ministers of religion should not be used as comic characters or as villains.
3.   Ceremonies of any definite religion should be carefully and respectfully handled.

IX. Locations
The treatment of bedrooms must be governed by good taste and delicacy.

X. National Feelings
1.   The use of the flag shall be consistently respectful.
2.   The history, institutions, prominent people and citizenry of all nations shall be represented fairly.

XI. Titles
Salacious, indecent, or obscene titles shall not be used.

XII. Repellent Subjects
The following subjects must be treated within the careful limits of good taste.
1.   Actual hangings or electrocutions as legal punishments for crime.
2.   Third-degree methods.
3.   Brutality and possible gruesomeness.
4.   Branding of people or animals.

5. Apparent cruelty to children or animals.
6. The sale of women, or a woman selling her virtue.
7. Surgical operations.

REASONS SUPPORTING PREAMBLE OF CODE

1. Theatrical motion pictures, that is, pictures intended for the theatre as distinct from pictures intended for churches, schools, lecture halls, educational movements, social reform movements, etc., are primarily to be regarded as entertainment.

    Mankind has always recognized the importance of entertainment and its value in rebuilding the bodies and souls of human beings.

    But it has always recognized that entertainment can be of a character either HELPFUL or HARMFUL to the human race, and in consequence has clearly distinguished between:
    (a) Entertainment which tends to improve the race, or at least to re-create and rebuild human beings exhausted with the realities of life; and
    (b) Entertainment which tends to degrade human beings, or to lower their standards of life and living.
    Hence the moral importance of entertainment is something which has been universally recognized. It enters intimately into the lives of men and women and affects them closely; it occupies their minds and affections during leisure hours; and ultimately touches the whole of their lives. A man may be judged by his standard of entertainment as easily as by the standard of his work.

    So correct entertainment raises the whole standard of a nation.

    Wrong entertainment lowers the whole living conditions and moral ideals of a race.

    > Note, for example, the healthy reactions to healthful sports, like baseball, golf; the unhealthy reactions to sports like cockfighting, bullfighting, bear baiting, etc.

    > Note, too, the effect on ancient nations of gladiatorial combats, the obscene plays of Roman times, etc.

2. Motion pictures are very important as art.

    Though a new art, possibly a combination art, it has the same object as the other arts, the presentation of human thought, emotion and experience, in terms of an appeal to the soul through the senses.

    Here, as in entertainment,

    Art enters intimately into the lives of human beings.

Art can be morally good, lifting men to higher levels. This has been done through good music, great painting, authentic fiction, poetry, drama.

Art can be morally evil in its effects. This is the case clearly enough with unclean art, indecent books, suggestive drama. The effect on the lives of men and women is obvious.

Note: It has often been argued that art in itself is unmoral, neither good nor bad. This is perhaps true of the thing product of some person's mind, and the intention of that mind was either good or bad morally when it produced the thing. Besides, the thing has its effect upon those who come into contact with it. In both these ways, that is, as a product of a mind and as the cause of definite effects, it has a deep moral significance and an unmistakable moral quality.

Hence: The motion pictures, which are the most popular arts for the masses, have their moral quality from the intention of the minds which produce them and from their effects on the moral lives and reactions of their audiences. This gives them a most important moral quality.

1. They reproduce the morality of the men who use the pictures as a medium for the expression of their idea and ideals.
2. They affect the moral standards of those who, through the screen, take in these ideas and ideals.

In the case of the motion pictures, this effect may be particularly emphasized because no art has so quick and so widespread an appeal to the masses. It has become in an incredibly short period the art of the multitudes.

3. The motion picture, because of its importance as entertainment and because of the trust placed in it by the peoples of the world, has special moral obligations:
    A. Most arts appeal to the mature. This art appeals at once to every class, mature, immature, developed, underdeveloped, law abiding, criminal. Music has its grades for different classes; so has literature and drama. This art of the motion picture, combining as it does the two fundamental appeals of looking at a picture and listening to a story, at once reached every class of society.
    B. By reason of the mobility of a film and the ease of picture distribution, and because of the possibility of duplicating positives in large quantities, this art reaches places unpenetrated by other forms of art.
    C. Because of these two facts, it is dificult to produce films intended for only certain classes of people. The exhibitor's theatres are built for the masses, for the cultivated and the rude, the mature and the immature, the self-respecting and the criminal. Films, unlike books and music, can with difficulty be confined to certain selected groups.

D.   The latitude given to film material cannot, in consequence, be as wide as the latitude given to book material. In addition:

   (a)   A book describes; a film vividly presents. One presents on a cold page; the other by apparently living people.

   (b)   A book reaches the mind through words merely; a film reaches the eyes and ears through the reproduction of actual events.

   (c)   The reaction of a reader to a book depends largely on the keenness of the reader's imagination; the reaction to a film depends on the vividness of presentation.

E.   This is also true when comparing the film with the newspaper.

   (a)   Newspapers present by description, films by actual presentation.

   (b)   Newspapers are after the fact and present things as having taken place, the film gives the events in the process of enactment and with apparent reality of life.

F.   Everything possible in a play is not possible in a film:

   (a)   Because of the large audience of the film, and its consequential mixed character.
         Psychologically, the larger the audience, the lower the moral mass resistance to suggestion.

   (b)   Because through light, enlargement of character, presentation, scenic emphasis, etc., the screen story is brought closer to the audience than the play.

   (c)   The enthusiasm for and interest in the film actors and actresses, developed beyond anything of the sort in history, makes the audience largely sympathetic toward the characters they portray and the stories in which they figure. Hence the audience is more ready to confuse actor and actress and the characters they portray, and it is more receptive of the emotions and ideals presented by their favorite stars.

G.   Small communities, remote from sophistication and from the hardening process which often takes place in the ethical and moral standards of groups in large cities, are easily and readily reached by any sort of film.

H.   The grandeur of mass settings, large action, spectacular features, etc., affects and arouses more intensely the emotional side of the audience.

In general, the mobility, popularity, accessibility, emotional appeal, vividness, straightforward presentation of fact in the film make for more intimate contact with a larger audience and for greater emotional appeal.

Hence the larger moral responsibilities of the motion pictures.

REASONS UNDERLYING THE GENERAL PRINCIPLES

1. No picture shall be produced which will lower the moral standards of those who see it. Hence the sympathy of the audience should never be thrown to the side of crime, wrong-doing, evil or sin.
   This is done:
   (1) When evil is made to appear attractive or alluring, and good is made to appear unattractive.
   (2) When the sympathy of the audience is thrown on the side of crime, wrong-doing, evil, sin. The same thing is true of a film that would throw sympathy against goodness, honor, innocence, purity, or honesty.
   Note: Sympathy with a person who sins is not the same as sympathy with the sin or crime of which he is guilty.
   We may feel sorry for the plight of the murderer of even understand the circumstances which led him to his crime. We may not feel sympathy with the wrong which he has done.
   The presentation of evil is often essential for art or fiction or drama. This in itself is not wrong provided:
   a. That evil is not presented alluringly. Even if later in the film the evil is condemned or punished, it must not be allowed to appear so attractive that the audience's emotions are drawn to desire or approve so strongly that later the condemnation is forgotten and only the apparent joy of the sin remembered.
   b. That throughout, the audience feels sure that evil is wrong and good is right.
2. Correct standards of life shall, as far as possible, be presented.
   A wide knowledge of life and of living is made possible through the film. When right standards are consistently presented, the motion picture exercises the most powerful influences. It builds character, develops right ideals, inculcates correct principles, and all this in attractive story form.
   If motion pictures consistently hold up for admiration high types of characters and present stories that will affect lives for the better, they can become the most powerful natural force for the improvement of mankind.
3. Law, natural or human, shall not be ridiculed, nor shall sympathy be created for its violation.
   By natural law is understood the law which is written in the hearts of all mankind, the great underlying principles of right and justice dictated by conscience.
   1. The presentation of crimes against the law is often necessary for the carrying out of the plot. But the presentation must not throw sympathy with the crime as against the law nor with the criminal as against those who punish him.

2.   The courts of the land should not be presented as unjust. This does not mean that a single court may not be represented as unjust, much less that a single court official must not be presented this way. But the court system of the country must not suffer as a result of this presentation.

REASONS UNDERLYING PARTICULAR APPLICATIONS

1. Sin and evil enter into the story of human beings and hence in themselves are valid dramatic material.
2. In the use of this material, it must be distinguished between sin which repels by its very nature, and sins which often attract.
   a.   In the first class come murder, most theft, many legal crimes, lying, hypocrisy, cruelty, etc.
   b.   In the second class come sex sins, sins and crimes of apparent heroism, such as banditry, daring thefts, leadership in evil, organized crime, revenge, etc.

   The first class needs less care in treatment, as sins and crimes of this class are naturally unattractive. The audience instinctively condemns all such and is repelled.

   Hence the important objective must be to avoid the hardening of the audience, especially of those who are young and impressionable, to the thought and fact of crime. People can become accustomed even to murder, cruelty, brutality, and repellent crimes, if these are too frequently repeated.

   The second class needs great care in handling, as the response of human nature to their appeal is obvious. This is treated more fully below.
3. A careful distinction can be made between films intended for general distribution, and films intended for use in theatres restricted to a limited audience. Themes and plots quite appropriate for the latter would be altogether out of place and dangerous in the former.

   Note: The practice of using a general theatre and limiting its patronage during the showing of a certain film to "Adults Only" is not completely satisfactory and is only partially effective.

   However, maturer minds may easily understand and accept without harm subject matter in plots which do younger people positive harm.

   Hence: If there should be created a special type of theatre, catering exclusively to an adult audience, for plays of this character (plays with problem themes, difficult discussions and maturer treatment) it would seem to afford an outlet, which does not now exist, for pictures unsuitable for general distribution but permissible for exhibitions to a restricted audience.

I. Crimes Against the Law
The treatment of crimes against the law must not:
1. Teach methods of crime.
2. Inspire potential criminals with a desire for imitation.
3. Make criminals seem heroic and justified.

Revenge in modern times shall not be justified. In lands and ages of less developed civilization and moral principles, revenge may sometimes be presented. This would be the case especially in places where no law exists to cover the crime because of which revenge is committed.

Note: When Section I, 3 of The Production Code was amended by resolution of the Board of Directors (September 11, 1946), the following sentence became applicable:

Because of its evil consequences, the drug traffic should not be presented in any form. The existence of the trade should not be brought to the attention of audiences.

The use of liquor should never be excessively presented. In scenes from American life, the necessities of plot and proper characterization alone justify its use. And in this case, it should be shown with moderation.

II. Sex
Out of regard for the sanctity of marriage and the home, the triangle, that is, the love of a third party for one already married, needs careful handling. The treatment should not throw sympathy against marriage as an institution.

Scenes of passion must be treated with an honest acknowledgement of human nature and its normal reactions. Many scenes cannot be presented without arousing dangerous emotions on the part of the immature, the young, or the criminal classes.

Even within the limits of pure love, certain facts have been universally regarded by lawmakers as outside the limits of safe presentation. In the case of impure love, the love which society has always regarded as wrong and which has been banned by divine law, the following are important:
1. Impure love must not be presented as attractive and beautiful.
2. It must not be the subject of comedy or farce, or treated as material for laughter.
3. It must not be presented in such a way as to arouse passion or morbid curiosity on the part of the audience.
4. It must not be made to seem right and permissible.
5. In general, it must not be detailed in method and manner. III. Vulgarity; IV. Obscenity; V. Profanity; hardly need further explanation than is contained in the Code.

VI. Costume
General principles:
1. The effect of nudity or semi-nudity upon the normal man or woman, and much more upon the young and upon immature persons, has been honestly recognized by all lawmakers and moralists.
2. Hence the fact that the nude or semi-nude body may be beautiful does not make its use in the films moral. For, in addition to its beauty, the effect of the nude or semi-nude body on the normal individual must be taken into consideration.
3. Nudity or semi-nudity used simply to put a "punch" into a picture comes under the head of immoral actions. It is immoral in its effect on the average audience.
4. Nudity can never be permitted as being necessary for the plot. Semi-nudity must not result in undue or indecent exposures.
5. Transparent or translucent materials and silhouette are frequently more suggestive than actual exposure.

VII. Dances
Dancing in general is recognized as an art and as a beautiful form of expressing human emotions.

But dances which suggest or represent sexual actions, whether performed solo or with two or more; dances intended to excite the emotional reaction of an audience; dances with movement of the breasts, excessive body movements while the feet are stationary, violate decency and are wrong.

VIII. Religion
The reason why ministers of religion may not be comic characters or villains is simply because the attitude taken toward them may easily become the attitude taken toward religion in general. Religion is lowered in the minds of the audience because of the lowering of the audience's respect for a minister.

IX. Locations
Certain places are so closely and thoroughly associated with sexual life or with sexual sin that their use must be carefully limited.

X. National Feelings
The just rights, history, and feelings of any nation are entitled to more careful consideration and respectful treatment.

XI. Titles
As the title of a picture is the brand on that particular type of goods, it must conform to the ethical practices of all such honest business.

XII. Repellent Subjects
Such subjects are occasionally necessary for the plot. Their treatment must never offend good taste nor injure the sensibilities of an audience.

APPENDIX 3:
SELECTED POPULAR WOMEN'S FILMS OF THE 1940s

1940-41:
    The Grapes of Wrath (20th)+
    His Girl Friday (Columbia)
    Gone with the Wind (MGM)
    Rebecca (UA)
    All This and Heaven Too (WB)
    The Old Maid (WB)
    Philadelphia Story (MGM)
    Suspicion (RKO)
    Pride and Prejudice (RKO)
    Kitty Foyle (RKO)

1941-42:
    Mrs. Miniver (MGM)
    In This Our Life (WB)
    Somewhere I'll Find You (MGM)
    This Above All (20th)
    Woman of the Year (MGM)

1942-43:
    Claudia (20th)
    Now, Voyager (WB)
    So Proudly We Hail (Paramount)
    Watch on the Rhine (WB)

1943-44:
    Dragonseed (MGM)
    Gaslight (MGM)
    Letter from an Unknown Woman (Universal)

MGM – Metro Goldwyn Mayer; UA – United Artists; WB – Warner Brothers; 20th – Twentieth Century Fox

+The Grapes of Wrath is not a classic women's film; however, its major female character is the prototype for women's film heroines to follow.

Madame Curie (MGM)
Lady in the Dark (Paramount)
Mr. Skeffington (WB)
Since You Went Away (UA)
Song of Bernadette (20th)

1944-45:
    Meet Me in St. Louis (MGM)
    Mrs. Parkington (MGM)
    Affairs of Susan (Paramount)
    Tree Grows in Brooklyn, A (20th)
    Jane Eyre (20th)

1945-46:
    Dragonwyck (20th)
    Mildred Pierce (WB)
    My Reputation (WB)
    Tomorrow Is Forever (RKO)
    The Spiral Staircase (RKO)

1946-47:
    To Each His Own (Paramount)
    The Farmer's Daughter (RKO)
    Nora Prentiss (WB)
    Possessed (WB)

1947-49:
    I Remember Mama (RKO)
    Apartment for Peggy (20th)
    Johnny Belinda (WB)
    A Letter to Three Wives (20th)
    Little Women (MGM)
    Snake Pit (20th)

1949-50:
    Adam's Rib (MGM)
    Joan of Arc (RKO)
    Pinky (20th)
    The Heiress (Paramount)

FILMOGRAPHY

Adam's Rib (1949, MGM). Directed by George Cukor, written by Ruth Gordon and Garson Kanin, photographed by George Folsey, music by Miklos Rozsa, with Katharine Hepburn, Spencer Tracy, Judy Holliday, Tom Ewell, David Wayne.

Dragonwyck (1945, 20th Century Fox). Produced by Darryl F. Zanuck, directed and written by Joseph L. Mankiewicz, from a story by Anya Seton, photographed by Arthur Miller, edited by Dorothy Spencer, music by Alfred Newman, with Gene Tierney, Vincent Price, Spring Byington, Jessica Tandy.

Gaslight (1944, MGM). Directed by George Cukor, written by John van Druten, Walter Reisch, and John Balderston, from the play Angel Street by Patrick Hamilton, photographed by Joseph Ruttenberg, music by Bronislav Kaper, with Ingrid Bergman, Charles Boyer, Joseph Cotten, Angela Lansbury, Dame May Whitty.

Grapes of Wrath, The (1940, 20th Century Fox). Directed by John Ford, produced by Darryl F. Zanuck, written by Nunnally Johnson from the novel by John Steinbeck, photographed by Gregg Toland, edited by Robert Simpson, music by Alfred Newman, with Henry Fonda, Jane Darwell, John Carradine, Dorris Bowdon, Russell Simpson, Eddie Quillan, John Qualen, Grant Mitchell.

His Girl Friday (1940, Columbia). Directed by Howard Hawks, written by Charles Lederer and Ben Hecht (uncredited), from the play The Front Page (1928) by Ben Hecht and Charles Mac-Arthur, photographed by Joseph Walker, edited by Gene Havlick, with Cary Grant, Rosalind Russell, Ralph Bellamy, John Qualen, Helen Mock, Billy Gilbert, Alma Kruger, Abner Biberman.

I Remember Mama (1948, RKO). Directed by George Stevens, written by DeWitt Bodeen from the screenplay by John van Druten, adapted from the novel by Kathryn Forbes, photographed by Nicholas Musuraca, with Irene Dunne, Philip Dorn, Barbara Bel Geddes, Oscar Homolka, Ellen Corby.

Lady in the Dark (1944, Paramount). Directed by Mitchell Leisen, written by Frances Goodrich and Albert Hackett, from the play by Moss Hart, photographed by Raymond Rennahan, edited by Alma McCrorie, music by Kurt Weill, with Ginger Rogers, Ray Milland, Warner Baxter, Jon Hall, Mischa Auer, Barry Sullivan, Gail Russell.

Letter to Three Wives, A (1949, 20th Century Fox). Directed and written by Joseph Mankiewicz, adapted by Vera Caspary (from a story by John Klempner), produced by Sol Siegel, photographed by Arthur Miller, music by Alfred Newman, with Linda Darnell, Jeanne Crain, Ann Sothern, Jeffrey Lynn, Kirk Douglas, Hobart Cavanaugh, Florence Bates, Celeste Holm.

Little Women (1949, MGM). Directed and produced by Mervyn LeRoy, written by Andrew Solt, Sara Mason, and Victor Heerman from the novel by Louisa May Alcott, with Liz Taylor, June Allyson, Janet Leigh, Margaret O'Brien, Mary Astor, Peter Lawford.

Mildred Pierce (1945, Warners). Directed by Michael Curtiz, produced by Jerry Wald, written by Ranald MacDougall and Catherine Turney, photographed by Ernest Haller, edited by David Weisbart, music by Max Steiner, with Joan Crawford, Ann Blyth, Eve Arden, Jack Carson, Bruce Bennett, Lee Patrick, Butterfly McQueen, Moroni Olsen, Veda Ann Borg, JoAnn Marlowe.

Mrs. Miniver (1942, MGM). Directed by William Wyler, written by Arthur Wimperis, George Froeschel, James Hilton, and Claudine West, from the book by Jan Struther, photographed by Joseph Ruttenberg, music by Herbert Stothart, with Greer Garson, Walter Pidgeon, Teresa Wright, Helmut Dantine, Richard Ney, Dame May Whitty, Henry Travers, Reginald Owen.

Now, Voyager (1942, Warners). Directed by Irving Rapper, written by Casey Robinson, from the novel by Olive Higgins Prouty, photographed by Sol Polito, with Bette Davis, Claude Rains, Paul Henreid, Gladys Cooper, Ilka Chase, Bonita Granville, Lee Patrick.

Possessed (1947, Warners). Directed by Curtis Bernhardt, produced by Jerry Wald, from a story by Rita Weiman, written by Silvia Richards and Ranald MacDougall, photographed by Joseph Valentine, edited by Rudi Fehr, music by Franz Waxman, with Joan Crawford, Van Heflin, Raymond Massey.

Since You Went Away (1944, UA). Directed and written by John Cromwell, adapted from the book by Margaret Buell Wilder, photographed by Stanley Cortez and Lee Garmes, edited by Hal Kern, music by Max Steiner, with Claudette Colbert, Jennifer Jones, Joseph Cotten, Shirley Temple, Monty Wooley, Lionel Barrymore, Robert Walker, Hattie McDaniel, Nazimova, Agnes Moorehead, Keenan Wynn.

Sorry, Wrong Number (1948, Paramount). Directed by Anatole Litvak, written by Lucille Fletcher, from her radio play, photographed by Sol Polito, edited by Warren Low, music by Franz Waxman, with Barbara Stanwyck, Burt Lancaster, Wendell Corey, Ed Begley, Leif Erikson, Ann Richards, Harold Vermilyea.

Spiral Staircase, The (1946, RKO), Directed by Robert Siodmak, produced by Dore Schary, written by Mel Dinelli, from the novel by Ethel L. White, photographed by Nicholas Musuraca, edited by Harry Marker and Harry Gerstad, music by Roy Webb, with Dorothy McGuire, George Brent, Ethel Barrymore, Kent Smith.

Suspicion (1942, RKO). Directed by Alfred Hitchcock, written by Samson Raphaelson, Joan Harrison, and Alma Reville, from the novel by Francis Iles, edited by William Hamilton, music by Franz Waxman, with Joan Fontaine, Cary Grant, Dame May Whitty, Nigel Bruce.

To Each His Own (1946, Paramount). directed by Mitchell Leisen, written by Leisen and Charles Brackett, photographed by Daniel Fapp, edited by Alma Macrorie, music by Victor Young, with Olivia de Havilland, Roland Culver, Phillip Terry, Bill Goodwin, John Lund, Victoria Horne.

Tomorrow is Forever (1945, RKO). Directed by Irving Pichel, written by Lenore Coffee, music by Max Steiner, with Claudette Colbert, George Brent, Orson Welles, Natalie Wood.

Tree Grows in Brooklyn, A (1945, 20th Century Fox). Directed by Elia Kazan, written by Tess Slesinger and Frank Davis from the novel by Betty Smith, photographed by Leon Shamroy, edited by Dorothy Spencer, music by Alfred Newman, with Dorothy McGuire, Joan Blondell, Peggy Ann Garner, James Dunn, Lloyd Nolan, Ted Donaldson.

Watch on the Rhine (1943, Warners). Directed by Herman Shumlin, written by Dashiell Hammett, from the play by Lillian Hellman, photographed by Hal Mohr, music by Max Steiner, with Bette Davis, Paul Lukas, Lucile Watson, George Coulouris, Beulah Bondi, Geraldine Fitzgerald.

Woman of the Year (1942, MGM). Directed by George Stevens, produced by Joseph Mankiewicz, written by Ring Lardner, Jr. and Michael Kanin, photographed by Joseph Ruttenberg, music by Franz Waxman, with Katharine Hepburn, Spencer Tracy, Fay Bainter, Reginald Owen, Dan Tobin, William Bendix.

BIBLIOGRAPHY

Adorno, Theodor. Negative Dialectics. London: New Left Books, 1973.

_____. Prisms. (Trans. by Samuel and Shierry Weber.) London: New Left Books, 1973.

_____. "TV and the Patterns of Mass Culture." In Mass Culture. Eds. Bernard Rosenberg and David Manning White. New York: Free Press, 1957a, pp. 474-488.

_____. "A Social Critique of Radio Music." In Reader in Public Opinion and Communications. Eds. Bernard Berelson and Morris Janowitz. Glencoe, Ill.: Free Press, 1950, pp. 309-316.

_____. "On Popular Music." Studies in Philosophy and Social Science 9, 1 (1941): 17-48.

_____ and Max Horkheimer. Dialectic of Enlightenment. (Translated by John Cumming.) New York: Herder and Herder, 1972.

Althusser, Louis. For Marx. New York: Vintage, 1976.

_____. Essays in Self-Criticism. London: New Left Books, 1971.

_____ and Etienne Balibar. Reading Capital. London: New Left Books, 1970.

Amberg, George (ed.). The New York Times Film Reviews, 1913-70 (1 volume). New York: Quadrangle, 1971.

Anderegg, Michael. William Wyler. Boston: Twayne, 1979.

Anderson, Karen. Wartime Women: Sex Roles, Family Relations and the Status of Women During World War II. Westport, Conn.: Greenwood Press, 1981.

Anderson, Perry. "The Antinomies of Antonio Gramsci." New Left Review 100 (Nov. 1976-Jan. 1977): 5-78.

Andrew, J. Dudley. The Major Film Theories. New York: Oxford, 1976.

Anthony, Susan B. II. Out of the Kitchen - Into the War: Women's Winning Role in the Nation's Drama. New York: Stephen Daye, 1943.

Arnow, Harriette. The Dollmaker. New York: Avon, 1954.

Auerbach, Nina. Communities of Women. Cambridge: Harvard University Press, 1978.

Bahr, Stephen J. "Effects on Family Power and Division of Labor in the Family." In Working Mothers. Eds. Lois W. Hoffman and F. Ivan Nye. San Francisco: Jossey-Bass, 1974.

_____. "Comments on the Study of Family Power Structures: A Review, 1960-69." Journal of Marriage and the Family 34 (1972): 239-243.

Baker, M. Joyce. Images of Women in Film: The War Years: 1941-45, Ann Arbor: UMI Research Press, 1980.

Banner, Lois W. Women in Modern America. Englewood Cliffs, N.J.: Prentice-Hall, 1975.

Barthes, Roland. Image/Music/Text. New York: Hill and Wang, 1977.

_____. S/Z. New York: Hill and Wang, 1974.

_____. Mythologies. New York: Hill and Wang, 1972.

_____. Writing Degree Zero/Elements of Semiology. Boston: Beacon, 1970.

Basinger, Jeanine. "Ten That Got Away." In Women and the Cinema. Eds. Karyn Kay and Gerald Peary. New York: Dutton, 1977, pp. 61-72.

Bathrick, Serafina Kent. The True Woman and the Family-Film: The Industrial Production of Memory. Ph.D. dissertation, University of Wisconsin-Madison, 1981.

Baxandall, Rosalyn. "Who Shall Care for Our Children: The History and Development of Day Care in the United States." In Women: A Feminist Perspective. 2nd ed. Ed. Jo Freeman. Palo Alto: Mayfield, 1979, pp. 134-49.

_____, Linda Gordon, and Susan Reverby (eds.). America's Working Women: A Documentary History - 1600 to Present. New York: Random House, 1976.

Baxter, John. Sixty Years of Hollywood. New York: Barnes and Noble, 1973.

Benjamin, Walter. Illuminations. Ed. and Intro. by Hannah Arendt. New York: Schocken, 1968.

Bergman, Andrew. We're in the Money: Depression America and Its Films. New York: Harper & Row, 1971.

Berkin, Carol R. and Clara M. Lovett (eds.). Women, War and Revolution. New York: Holmes and Meier, 1980.

Bernard, Jessie. The Future of Motherhood. New York: Penguin, 1974.

_____. Academic Women. University Park: Penn State Press, 1964.

Bernikow, Louise (ed.). The World Split Open: Four Centuries of Women Poets in England and America, 1552-1950. New York: Random House, 1974.

Bogle, Donald. Toms, Coons, Mulattoes, Mammies and Bucks: An Interpretive History of Blacks in American Films. New York: Bantam, 1973.

Bradley, Verne. "Women at Work." National Geographic 86, 2 (1942): 103-220.

Braverman, Harry. Labor and Monopoly Capital. New York: Monthly Review, 1974.

Brownmiller, Susan. Against Our Will. New York: Simon and Schuster, 1975.

Campbell, D'Ann. "Was the West Different?" Pacific Historical Review (August 1978): 453-463.

_____. Wives, Workers and Womanhood: America During World War II. Ph.D. dissertation, University of North Carolina, 1979.

Campbell, Russell. "Trampling Out the Vintage: Sour Grapes." In The Modern American Novel and the Movies. Eds. Gerald Peary and Roger Shatzkin. New York: Frederick Ungar, 1978, pp. 107-118.

Canby, Vincent. "World War II Won't Fade Away – Not In the Movies, That Is." New York Times, July 3, 1977, p. 1.

Cantril, Hadley. Public Opinion: 1935-46. Princeton: Princeton University Press, 1951.

_____. Invasion from Mars: A Study in the Psychology of Panic. Princeton, N.J.: Princeton University Press, 1940.

Carroll, Berenice A., (ed.). Liberating Women's History: Theoretical and Critical Essays. Chicago: University of Illinois Press, 1976.

Carroll, Noel. "Address to the Heathen." October 23 (Winter 1982): 89-163.

Casty, Alan, ed. Mass Man. New York: Holt, Rinehart, Winston, 1968.

Cavell, Stanley. Pursuits of Happiness: The Hollywood Comedy of Remarriage. Cambridge, Ma: Harvard University Press, 1981.

Chafe, William. Women and Equality: Changing Patterns in American Culture. New York: Oxford, 1978.

_____. The American Woman: Her Changing Social, Economic and Political Roles, 1920-1970. New York: Oxford, 1972.

Chesler, Phyllis. Women and Madness. New York: Avon, 1973.

Chodorow, Nancy. The Reproduction of Mothering: Psychoanalysis and the Sociology of Gender. Berkeley: University of California Press, 1978.

Clarke, Simon, Terry Lovell, et al. One-Dimensional Marxism: Althusser and the Politics of Culture. New York: Allison and Busby, 1980.

Clawson, Augusta H. Shipyard Diary of a Woman Welder. New York: Penguin, 1944.

Clive, Alan. "Women Workers in World War II: Michigan as a Test Case," Labor History 20 (Winter 1979), 44-72.

Colton, Sara and Hawley Jones. "What's Right About the Movies," Harpers', 187, no. 1118 (July 1943): 146-151.

Corliss, Richard, ed. The Hollywood Screenwriters. New York: Avon, 1970.

Cowie, Elizabeth. "The Popular Film as a Progressive Text: A Discussion of Coma, Part I." M/F 1, no. 3 (1979): 59-82.

Cuber, John F. "The College Youth Goes to War." Marriage and Family Living 5 (Winter 1943): 5-8.

Custen, George. Film Talk: Viewer Responses to a Film as a Socially Situated Event. Ph.D. dissertation, University of Pennsylvania, 1980.

Czitrom, Daniel J. Media and the American Mind. Chapel Hill: University of North Carolina Press, 1982.

Dalton, (Susan) Elizabeth. "Women at Work: Warners in the 1930s." In Women and the Cinema, eds. Karyn Kay and Gerald Peary. New York: Dutton, 1977, pp. 267-282.

Damico, James. "Ingrid from Lorraine to Stromboli: Analyzing the Public's Perception of a Film Star," Journal of Popular Film, IV (1975): 3-20.

de Beauvoir, Simone. The Second Sex. New York: Bantam, 1953.

Deckard, Barbara. The Women's Movement: Political, Socio-economic and Psychological Issues. New York: Harper & Row, 1975.

Deming, Barbara. Running Away from Myself: A Dream Portrait of America Drawn from the Films of the '40s. New York: Grossman, 1969.

D'Emilio, John. Sexual Politics/Sexual Communities. Chicago: University of Chicago Press, 1983.

Dennis, Peggy. Autobiography of an American Communist. Westport, Conn.: Laurence Hill, 1977.

Deutsch, Felix. "Civilian War Neuroses and Their Treatment." Psychoanalytic Quarterly, XIII, no. 1 (1944): 300-312.

Dinnerstein, Dorothy. The Mermaid and the Minotaur: Sexual Arrangements and Human Malaise. New York: Harper & Row, 1977.

Douglas, Ann. The Feminization of American Culture. New York: Knopf, 1977.

Dowdy, Andrew. The Films of the Fifties: The American State of Mind. New York: Morrow, 1973.

Durbin, E.F.M. and John Bowlby. "Personal Aggressiveness and War." In War: Studies From Psychology, Sociology and Anthropology. New York: Basic, 1968, pp. 81-104.

Durgnat, Raymond. The Crazy Mirror: Hollywood Comedy and the American Image. New York: Dell, 1969.

_____. The Strange Case of Alfred Hitchcock. Cambridge: MIT Press, 1980.

Duvall, Evelyn Millis. "Loneliness and the Serviceman's Wife." Marriage and Family Living 7 (Autumn 1945): 77-81.

_____. "Marriage in War Time." Marriage and Family Living 4 (Autumn 1942): 73-76.

Elbert, Sarah. "The Persistence of Memory and the Education of Desire, The Women's Room and others," Working Papers, Fernand Braudel Center, Binghamton, New York, 1979.

_____. A Hunger for Home: Louisa May Alcott and Little Women. Philadelphia: Temple University Press, 1983.

Erens, Patricia (ed.). Sexual Stratagems: The World of Women in Film. New York: Horizon, 1979.

Evans, Sara. Personal Politics: The Roots of Women's Liberation in the Civil Rights Movement and the New Left. New York: Knopf, 1979.

Ewen, Elizabeth. "City Lights: Immigrant Women and the Rise of the Movies." Signs: A Journal of Women in Culture and Society 5, 3 (Spring 1980): 45-65.

Ewen, Stuart. Captains of Consciousness. New York: McGraw-Hill, 1976.

_____ and Elizabeth Ewen. Channels of Desire. New York: McGraw Hill, 1982.

Fekete, John. "McLuhanacy: Counterrevolution in Cultural Theory." Telos 15 (Spring, 1973): 75-123.

Filene, Peter G. Him/Her Self: Sex Roles in Modern America. New York: Harcourt, Brace, Jovanovich, 1974.

Fishel, Elizabeth. Sisters. New York: Bantam, 1979.

Flinn, Tom. "Three Faces of Film Noir." In Kings of the Bs, eds. Todd McCarthy and Charles Flynn. New York: Dutton, 1975, pp. 155-66.

Flitterman, Sandy. "That Once-Upon-A-Time . . . of Childish Dreams." Cine-Tracts, 4, no. 1 (Spring 1981): 14-26.

Fox, Frank. Advertising and the Second World War: A Study in Private Propaganda. Unpublished Ph.D. dissertation, Stanford University, May 1973.

Frank, Miriam, Marilyn Ziebarth, and Connie Field. The Life and Times of Rosie the Riveter. Emeryville, Ca.: Clarity Educational Productions, 1982.

Freeman, Jo (ed.). Women: A Feminist Perspective. 2nd ed. Palo Alto: Mayfield, 1979.

_____. The Politics of Women's Liberation. New York: McKay, 1975.

French, Brandon. On the Verge of Revolt: Women in American Films of the '50s. New York: Ungar, 1978.

French, Warren. Filmguide to the Grapes of Wrath. Bloomington: Indiana University Press, 1978.

Friedan, Betty. The Feminine Mystique. New York: Dell, 1963.

Friedman, Jean E. and William G. Shade, eds. Our American Sisters. Boston: Allyn and Bacon, 1973.

Gabin, Nancy. "They Have Placed a Penalty Upon Womanhood: The Protest Actions of Women Auto Workers in Detroit-area UAW Locals, 1945-1947." Feminist Studies 8, no. 2 (Summer 1982).

Gaines, Jane Marie and Charlotte C. Herzog. "Hildy Johnson and the 'Man-Tailored' Suit: The Comedy of Inequality, Film Reader: 232-246.

Gallagher, Dorothy. Hannah's Daughters. New York: Crowell, 1976.

Gallup, George, et al. Gallup Looks at the Movies: Audience Research Reports, 1940-1950. Wilmington, Delaware: Scholarly Resources, 1979.

Gans, Herbert. "The Creator-Audience Relationship in the Mass Media." In Mass Culture. Eds. Bernard Rosenberg and David M. White. New York: Free Press, 1957, pp. 315-24.

Gardner, Carl (ed.). Media, Politics and Culture: A Socialist View. London: Macmillan, 1979.

Genovese, Eugene. Roll, Jordan, Roll. New York: Random House, 1972.

Gerken, Mable. Ladies in Pants: A Homefront Diary. New York: Exposition Press, 1949.

Gilbert, Sandra M. and Susan Gubar. The Madwoman in the Attic: The Woman Writer and the Nineteenth Century Literary Imagination. New Haven: Yale University Press, 1979.

Giles, Nell. Punch In, Susie! A Woman's War Factory Diary. New York: Harper, 1943.

Gilligan, Carol. "In a Different Voice: Women's Conceptions of the Self and of Morality." Harvard Educational Review 47, 4 (1977): 481-517.

_____. In a Different Voice: Psychological Theory and Women's Development. Cambridge, Ma.: Harvard University Press, 1982.

Gledhill, Christine. "Recent Developments in Feminist Criticism." Quarterly Review of Film Studies (Fall, 1978): 457-93.

Gluck, Sherna. "Rosie the Riveter Revisited." Paper presented at the Fifth Berkshire Conference on the History of Women, June 1981.

Goffman, Erving. Gender Advertisements. New York: Harper, 1976.

Goldfarb, Lyn. Separated and Unequal: Discrimination Against Workers After World War II. Washington, D.C.: URPE, 1976.

Goodman, Jack (ed.). While You Were Gone: A Report on Wartime Life in the United States. New York: Simon and Schuster, 1946.

Gorbman, Claudia. "The Drama's Melos: Max Steiner and Mildred Pierce." Velvet Light Trap, no. 19: 35-39.

Gordon, Ann, Mary Jo Buhle, and Nancy Schrom Dye. Women in American Society: An Historical Contribution. Somerville, Mass.: New England Free Press, n.d.

Gordon, Barbara. I'm Dancing as Fast as I Can. New York: Bantam, 1979.

Gordon, Linda. Woman's Body, Woman's Right. New York: Grossman, 1976.

Gornick, Vivian. The Romance of American Communism. New York: Basic, 1977.

Goulden, Joseph C. The Best Years: 1945-1950. New York: Atheneum, 1976.

Gow, Gordon. Suspense in the Cinema. New York: Paperback Library, 1968.

Gramsci, Antonio. Letters from Prison. New York: Harper & Row, 1973.

_____. Modern Prince and Other Writings. New York: International, 1970a.

_____. Prison Notebooks. New York: International, 1970b.

Grant, Barry K. Film Genre: Theory and Criticism. Metuchen, N.J.: Scarecrow Press, 1977.

Griffith, Richard. "Cycles and Genres." In Movies and Methods. Ed. Bill Nichols. Berkeley: University of California Press, 1976, pp. 111-17.

_____ and Arthur Mayer. The Movies. New York: Simon and Schuster, 1970.

Griffiths, Coleman R. "The Psychological Adjustments of Returned Servicemen and Their Families." Marriage and Family Living 4 (Autumn 1944): 65-87.

Gussow, Mel. Don't Say Yes Until I Finish Talking: A Biography of Darryl F. Zanuck. Garden City: Doubleday, 1971.

Habermas, Jürgen. Theory and Practice (translated by John Viertel). Boston: Beacon Press, 1973.

Hagood, Margaret J. Mothers of the South: Portraiture of the White Tenant Farm Woman. New York: Norton, 1977.

Hall, Stuart, Bob Lumley, and Gregor McLennon. "Politics and Ideology: Gramsci." Working Papers in Cultural Studies 10 (1977): 45-76.

Hall, Stuart, Dorothy Hobson, Andrew Lowe, and Paul Willis (eds.). Culture, Media, Language. London: Hutchinson, 1980.

Hall, Stuart. "Encoding/Decoding" in Stuart Hall, et al. (eds.). Culture, Media, Language. London: Hutchinson, 1980, pp. 128-138.

Halliday, Jon. Sirk on Sirk. New York: Viking, 1972.

Handel, Leo. Hollywood Looks at Its Audience. Urbana: University of Illinois Press, 1950.

Handlin, Oscar. "Comments on Mass and Popular Culture." In Culture for the Millions? Mass Media in Modern Society. Ed. by Norman Jacobs. Boston: Beacon, 1959, pp. 63-70.

Harris, Barbara J. Beyond Her Sphere: Women and the Professions in American History. Westport, Conn.: Greenwood Press, 1978.

Hart, Hornell and Henrietta Bowne. "Marriage and the Family." Social Forces 22 (December 1943): 191-194.

Hartman, Mary and Lois W. Banner (eds.). Clio's Consciousness Raised: New Perspectives on the History of Women. New York: Harper & Row, 1974.

Hartmann, Susan M. "Prescriptions for Penelope." Women's Studies 6 (1978): 131-44.

_____. The Home Front and Beyond: American Women in the 1940s. Boston: G.K. Hall, 1982.

Haskell, Molly. From Reverence to Rape: The Treatment of Women in the Movies. New York: Holt, Rinehart, Winston, 1973.

_____. "Women in the Movies Grow Up," Psychology Today, 17, no. 1 (1983): 18-27.

Hattaway, Kymberly. "Did Rosie the Riveter Give Up Her Job?" Work, Family and Social Change: University of Michigan Papers in Women's Studies (1976).

Haygood, William Converse. "A G.I.'s Wartime Letters." Wisconsin Magazine of History 59 (1975-76): 101-34.

Hayner, Norman S. "Women in a Changing World." Marriage and Family Living (Summer 1943).

Hecht, Ben and Charles MacArthur. The Front Page. New York: Covici-Friede, 1928.

Hellman, Lillian. Pentimento. Boston: Little, Brown, 1973.

Higham, Charles and Joel Greenberg. Hollywood in the '40s. New York: Coronet, 1968.

Hill, Reuben. "The Returning Father and His Family." Marriage and Family Living 6 (Spring, 1944): 31-34.

Hinshaw, David. The Home Front. New York: Putnam, 1943.

Hochschild, Arlie Russell. "Making It: Marginality and Obstacles to Minority Consciousness." In Women and Success: The Anatomy of Achievement. Ed. Ruth B. Kundsin. New York: Morrow, 1974, pp. 194-99.

Hoffman, Lois W. and F. Ivan Nye (eds.). Working Mothers. San Francisco: Jossey-Bass, 1974.

Hofstadter, Beatrice. "Popular Culture and the Romantic Heroine." American Scholar 30 (1961): 98-116.

Honey, Maureen. "Temporary Equality: The Use of Magazine Fiction as Propaganda during World War II." Paper presented at the Fifth Berkshire Conference on the History of Women, June 1981.

Hoopes, Roy. Americans Remember: The Home Front. New York: Hawthorn, 1977.

Horner, Matina. "Toward an Understanding of Achievement-Related Conflicts in Women." Journal of Social Issues 28,2 (1972): 157-175.

Horney, Karen. Feminine Psychology. Ed. and intro. by Harold Kelman. New York: Norton, 1967.

Howe, Louise Kapp. Pink Collar Workers. New York: Avon, 1977.

Humphries, Jane. "Women: Scapegoats and Safety Valves in the Great Depression." Review of Radical Political Economics 8, 1 (Spring 1976).

Israel, Lee. "Women in Film: An Endangered Species." Ms. 5 (February 1975).

Jacobs, Norman, ed. Culture for the Millions? Mass Media in Modern Society. Boston: Beacon, 1959.

Jay, Martin. The Dialectical Imagination. Boston: Little, Brown, 1973.

Johnston, Claire. "Myths of Women in the Cinema." In Women and the Cinema. Eds. Karyn Kay and Gerald Peary. New York: Dutton, 1977, pp. 407-11.

_____. ed. Notes on Women's Cinema, Screen, Pamphlet Z.

_____. ed. The Work of Dorothy Arzner: Towards a Feminist Cinema. London: British Film Institute, 1975.

Jowett, Garth (for the American Film Institute). Film: The Democratic Art. Boston: Little, Brown, 1976.

Kael, Pauline. When the Lights Go Down. New York: Holt, Rinehart, Winston, 1975.

_____. Reeling. New York: Warner, 1972.

Kaminsky, Stuart. American Film Genres: Approaches to a Critical Theory of Popular Art. New York: Dell, 1974.

Kanter, Rosabeth Moss. Men and Women of the Corporation. New York: Harper & Row, 1977.

Kaplan, E. Ann. "Integrating Marxist and Psychoanalytical Approaches in Feminist Film Criticism." Milennium: Film Journal 6 (Spring 1980): 8-17.

_____. ed. Women in Film Noir. London: British Film Institute, 1978.

Kaufman, Debra and Barbara L. Richardson. Achievement and Women: Challenging the Assumptions. New York: Free Press, 1982.

Kavinocky, Nadina, M.D. "Medical Aspects of Wartime Marriages." Marriage and Family Living (Spring 1944).

Kay, Karyn. "Part Time Work of a Domestic Slave, or Putting the Screws to Screwball Comedy." In Women and the Cinema: A Critical Anthology. Eds. Karyn Kay and Gerald Peary. New York: Dutton, 1977, pp. 311-23.

_____ and Gerald Peary (eds.). Women and the Cinema: A Critical Anthology. New York: Dutton, 1977.

Kennedy, Susan Estabrook. If All We Did Was to Weep at Home: A History of White Working Class Women in America. Bloomington: Indiana University Press, 1979.

Komarovsky, Mirra. Women in the Modern World: Their Education and Their Dilemmas. Boston: Little, Brown, 1953.

_____. Blue Collar Marriage. New York: Vintage, 1962.

Lichtman, Sheila. "Experiences of Women's Wartime Employment." Paper presented at the Fifth Berkshire Conference on the History of Women, June 1981.

_____. Women at Work 1941-1945: Wartime Employment in the San Francisco Bay Area. Ph.D. dissertation, University of California-Davis, 1981.

Lowenthal, Leo. Literature and the Image of Man. Boston: Beacon, 1957.

_____. "Historical Perspectives of Popular Culture." In Mass Culture. Eds. Bernard Rosenberg and David M. White. New York: Free Press, 1957, pp. 46-58.

Lundberg, Ferdinand and Marynia Farnham. Modern Woman: The Lost Sex. New York: Harper, 1947.

Lutz, Alma (ed.). With Love, Jane: Letters from American Women on the War Fronts. New York: John Day, 1945.

Lynd, Helen Merrell and Robert S. Lynd. Middletown in Transition: A Study in Cultural Conflicts. New York: Harcourt, Brace, 1937.

MacDonald, J. Fred. Don't Touch that Dial! Radio Programming in American Life, 1920-1960. Chicago: Nelson-Hall, 1979.

Maccoby, Eleanor E., W.C. Wilson, and R.V. Burton. "Differential Movie-Viewing Behavior of Male and Female Viewers." Journal of Personality, 26 (1958): 259-267.

Marx, Karl. A Contribution to the Critique of Political Economy. New York: International, 1970.

Mazon, Mauricio. Social Upheaval in World War II: 'Zoot-Suiters' and Servicemen in Los Angeles, 1943. Ph.D. dissertation, UCLA, 1976.

McBride, Joseph (ed.). Focus on Howard Hawks. Englewood Cliffs: Prentice-Hall, 1972.

McLuhan, Marshall. Understanding Media. New York: McGraw-Hill, 1964.

McQuail, Denis (ed.). Sociology of Mass Communications. Baltimore: Penguin, 1972.

Mead, Margaret. "The Women and the War." In While You Were Gone. Ed. Jack Goodman. New York: Simon and Schuster, 1946, pp. 274-89.

Meisenhelder, Thomas. "The Social Meaning of 'Disaster' Films," paper presented at the American Sociological Association, August, 1979, Boston, Ma.

Mellen, Joan. Big Bad Wolves: Masculinity in the American Film. New York: Pantheon, 1977.

_____. Women and Their Sexuality in the New Film. New York: Horizon, 1973.

Meyer, Agnes. Journey Through Chaos: America's Homefront. New York: Harcourt, Brace, 1945.

Michel, Sonya. "The Reproduction of Privatization: Women, Families and Professionals during World War II." Paper presented at the Fifth Berkshire Conference on the History of Women, June 1981.

_____. "Contradictions of Privatization: American Families during World War II." Paper presented at the Society for the Study of Social Problems, August 1980.

Milkman, Ruth. "Women's Work and Economic Crisis: Some Lessons from the Great Depression," Review of Radical Political Economics 8,1 (Spring 1976): 73-97.

_____. "Organizing the Sexual Division of Labor: Historical Perspectives on 'Women's Work' and the American Labor Movement." Socialist Review 49, 10, 1 (January-February 1980): 95-150.

_____. "Redefining 'Women's Work': The Sexual Division of Labor in the Auto Industry during World War II," Feminist Studies 8, 2 (1982).

Mitford, Jessica. A Fine Old Conflict. New York: Random House, 1956.

Modleski, Tania. "The Search for Tomorrow in Today's Soap Operas: Notes on a Feminine Narrative Form." Film Quarterly 33, 1 (Fall 1979): 12-21.

_____. "The Disappearing Act: A Study of Harlequin Romances." Signs 5, 3 (1980): 435-48.

_____. "Never to be Thirty-Six Years Old: Rebecca as Female Oedipal Drama," Wide Angle (1982): 34-41.

Monaco, James. How to Read a Film. New York: Oxford, 1977.

Monroe, Day. "Using Family Resources Wisely in Wartime." Marriage and Family Living 5 (Summer 1943): 52-54.

Morella, Joe, Edward Z. Epstein, and John Griggs. The Films of World War II. Secaucus, N.J.: Citadel Press, 1973.

Moss, Myra. "The Use of Women as a Surplus Labor Force in World War II." Paper presented to the North Central Sociological Association, May 6, 1975.

Mouffe, Chantal (ed.). Gramsci and Marxist Theory. London: Routledge, 1979.

Mulvey, Laura. "Visual Pleasure and Narrative Cinema." In Women and the Cinema. Eds. Karyn Kay and Gerald Peary. New York: Dutton, 1977, pp. 412-28.

Nachbar, Jack, Deborah Weiser, and John L. Wright (eds.). The Popular Culture Reader. Bowling Green, Ohio: Bowling Green University Popular Press, 1978.

National Film Theatre of London. Women's Cinema. April-May, 1973.

Nichols, Bill (ed.). Movies and Methods. Berkeley: University of California Press, 1976.

O'Connor, John E. and Martin A. Jackson (eds.). American History/American Film: Interpreting the Hollywood Image. New York: Ungar, 1980.

Olsen, Keith W. "World War II Vets at the University of Wisconsin." Wisconsin Magazine of History 53 (1969-70): pp. 83-97.

Pauly, Thomas. "Gone With the Wind and Grapes of Wrath as Hollywood Histories of the Depression," Journal of Popular Film, III: 203-256.

Peary, Gerald and Roger Shatzkin (eds.). The Modern American Novel and the Movies. New York: Ungar, 1978.

Pendleton, Ann. Hit the Rivet, Sister. New York: Howell, Soskin, 1943.

Piers, Maria. "The Role of the Family in Preventing Delinquency." Marriage and Family Living (Spring 1942).

Pitcher, Evelyn Goodenough. "Male and Female." In And Jill Came Tumbling After: Sexism in American Education. Eds. Judith Stacey, Susan Bereaud, and Joan Daniels. New York: Dell, 1974, pp. 79-90.

Place, Janey. "Women in Film Noir." In Women in Film Noir, ed. E. Ann Kaplan. London: British Film Institute, 1978, pp. 35-66.

Polenberg, Richard. War and Society: The United States, 1941-45. New York: Lippincott, 1972.

Poster, Mark. Existential Marxism in Post-War France. Princeton, N.J.: Princeton University Press, 1975.

Powdermaker, Hortense. Hollywood: The Dream Factory. Boston: Little, Brown, 1950.

Powers, Tom. "His Girl Friday: Screwball Liberation." Jump Cut 17 (Spring 1978): 25-27.

Quick, Paddy. "Rosie the Riveter: Myths and Realities," Radical America 9 (July-Aug. 1975): 124-130.

Quirk, Lawrence J. The Films of Joan Crawford. New York: Citadel, 1971.

_____. The Great Romantic Films: From the Beginnings of the Sound Era to 1973. New York: Citadel, 1974.

Raushenbush, Winifred. How to Dress in Wartime. New York: Coward-McCann, 1942.

Reeves, Grace. "The New Family in the Postwar World." Marriage and Family Living 7 (Autumn 1945): 73-76.

Reik, Theodor. Listening with the Third Ear: The Inner Experience of a Psychoanalyst. New York: Farrar, Straus, 1948.

Reiter, Rayna (ed.). Toward an Anthropology of Women. New York: Monthly Review Press, 1975.

Renov, Michael. "From Fetish to Subject: The Containment of Sexual Difference in Hollywood's Wartime Cinema," Wide Angle 5, 1 (1982): 16-27.

Rhode, Eric. A History of the Cinema: From Its Origins to 1970. New York: Hill and Wang, 1976.

Rich, Adrienne. Of Woman Born: Motherhood as Experience and Institution. New York: Norton, 1976.

_____. Snapshots of a Daughter-in-Law. New York: Norton, 1960.

Riemer, Svend. "War Marriages Are Different." Marriage and Family Living (Fall 1944): 84-87.

Ringgold, Gene. The Films of Bette Davis. New York: Citadel, 1970.

Robertson, Patricia and Hawley Jones. "Housekeeping After the War." Harpers' 188 (1944): 430-37.

Roffman, Peter and Jim Purdy. The Hollywood Social Problem Film: Madness, Despair and Politics From the Depression to the Fifties. Bloomington: University of Indiana Press, 1981.

Rogers, Donald I. Since You Went Away. New Rochelle, N.Y.: Arlington House, 1973.

Rosaldo, Michelle Z. and Louise Lamphere (eds.). Woman, Culture and Society. Stanford: Stanford University Press, 1974.

Rosen, Marjorie. Popcorn Venus: Women, Movies and the American Dream. New York: Coward, McCann, Geoghegan, 1973.

Rosenberg, Bernard and David Manning White (eds.). Mass Culture: The Popular Arts in America. New York: Free Press, 1957.

Rosenberg, Marie Barovic and Len V. Bergstrom. Women and Society: A Critical Review of the Literature with a Selected Annotated Bibliography. Beverly Hills: Sage, 1975.

Rosenzweig, Sidney. Casablanca and Other Major Films of Michael Curtiz. Ann Arbor, Mich.: UMI Press, 1982.

Rosten, Leo. Hollywood: The Movie Colony, The Movie Makers. New York: Harcourt Brace, 1941.

Rothman, Sheila M. Woman's Proper Place: A History of Changing Ideals and Practices. New York: Basic, 1978.

Rubin, Lillian Breslow. Worlds of Pain: Life in the Working Class Family. New York: Basic, 1976.

Rupp, Leila J. Mobilizing Women for War: German and American Propaganda, 1939-45. Princeton, N.J.: Princeton University Press, 1978.

Russ, Joanna. "Someone's Trying to Kill Me and I Think It's My Husband." Journal of Popular Culture 6, 4 (Spring 1973): 666-91.

Russo, Vito. The Celluloid Closet: Homosexuality in the Movies. New York: Harper & Row, 1981.

Ryan, Mary P. Womanhood in America: From Colonial Times to the Present. (2nd ed.). New York: New Viewpoints, 1979.

_____. "The Projection of a New Womanhood: The Movie Moderns in the 1920s." In Our American Sisters. (2nd ed.). Eds. Jean E. Friedman and William G. Shade. Boston: Allyn and Bacon, 1976, pp. 366-84.

Sarris, Andrew. The John Ford Movie Mystery. Bloomington: Indiana University Press, 1976.

Satterwhite, Joseph N. "The Tremulous Formula: Form and Technique in Godey's Fiction." American Quarterly 8 (1956): 99-113.

Scheuer, Steven H. The Movie Book. London: Ridge Press, 1974.

Scott-Smith, Daniel. "Family Limitation, Sexual Control and Domestic Feminism in Victorian America." In Clio's Consciousness Raised. Eds. Mary Hartman and Lois W. Banner. New York: Harper & Row, 1974, pp. 119-36.

Seiter, Ellen Elizabeth. The Promise of Melodrama: Recent Women's Films and Soap Operas. Ph.D. dissertation, Northwestern University, 1981.

Shaffer, Robert. "Women and the CP-USA, 1930-40." Socialist Review 45, 9, 3 (May-June 1979): 73-118.

Shange, Ntozake. For Colored Girls Who Have Considered Suicide When the Rainbow Is Enuf. New York: Macmillan, 1975.

Silver, Alain and Elizabeth Ward (eds.). Film Noir: An Encyclopedic Reference to the American Style. Woodstock, N.Y.: Overlook Press, 1979.

Sinclair, Jo. "I Was on Relief," Harpers,' 184 (January 1942): 161-163.

Sklar, Robert. Movie Made America. New York: Random House, 1975.

Skold, Karen Beck. "The Job He Left Behind: American Women in the Shipyards During World War II," in Women, War and Revolution, eds. Carol R. Berkin and Clara M. Lovett. New York: Holmes and Meier, 1980: 55-75.

Smith, Joan. "Preparing for Armageddon: Labor is Mobilized for War," unpublished paper, 1976.

Sochen, June. Herstory: A Woman's View of American History. New York: Alfred, 1974.

Steinbeck, John. The Grapes of Wrath. New York: Viking, 1964.

Steinfels, Margaret O'Brien. Who's Minding the Children: The History and Politics of Day Care in America. New York: Touchstone, 1973.

Stine, Whitney (with Bette Davis), Mother Goddam. New York: Hawthorn, 1974.

Straub, Eleanor. "United States Government Policy Toward Civilian Women During World War II." Prologue 5 (Winter 1973): 240-254.

_____. Government Policy Toward Civilian Women During World War II. Ph.D. dissertation, Emory University, 1973.

_____. "The Impact of World War II on Sex Roles: Women in the Civilian Labor Force." National Archives Women's History Conference (1976).

Susman, Warren (ed.). Culture and Commitment, 1929-1945. New York: George Braziller, 1973.

Talbot, David and Barbara Zheutlin. Creative Differences: Profiles of Hollywood Dissidents. Boston: South End Press, 1978.

Taylor, John Russell. Hitch. New York: Pantheon, 1978.

Thomas, Tony. The Films of the Forties. Secaucus, N.J.: Citadel, 1973.

Thompson, Edward P. The Poverty of Theory and Other Essays. New York: Monthly Review, 1978.

Thomson, David. America in the Dark: The Impact of Hollywood Films on American Culture. New York: Morrow, 1977.

Tobias, Sheila and Lisa Anderson. "New Views of Rosie the Riveter." Unpublished paper, 1975.

_____. "What Really Happened to Rosie the Riveter: Demobilization and the Female Labor Force, 1944-47." New York: MSS Modular Publications, 1974. Module 9.

Trey, Joan Ellen. "Women in the War Economy: World War II." Review of Radical Political Economics 4, 3 (July 1972): 40-57.

Trilling, Diana. Reviewing the Forties (introd. by Paul Fussell). New York: Harcourt, Brace, Jovanovich, 1978.

Tuchman, Gaye, Arlene Kaplan Daniels, and James Benet. Hearth and Home: Images of Women in the Mass Media. New York: Oxford, 1978.

Tudor, Andrew. "Genre and Critical Methodology." In Movies and Methods. Ed. Bill Nichols. Berkeley: University of California Press, 1976, pp. 118-25.

Turim, Maureen. "Gentlemen Consume Blondes," Wide Angle, 1, no. 1 (1979): 52-59.

Viviani, Christiane. "Who Is Without Sin? The Maternal Melodrama in American Film, 1930-39," Wide Angle, 4, no. 2 (1981).

von Miklos, Josephine. I Took A War Job. New York: Simon and Schuster, 1943.

Vorse, Mary Heaton. "The Girls of Elkton, Maryland," Harpers', 186, no. 1113 (February 1943): 347-354.

Waldman, Diane. "Critical Theory and Film." New German Critique 12 (Fall 1977): 39-60.

_____. Horror and Domesticity: The Modern Gothic Romance Film of the 1940s. Ph.D. dissertation, University of Wisconsin-Madison, 1981.

Walsh, Mary Roth. "Doctors Wanted: No Women Need Apply:" Sexual Barriers in the Medical Profession, 1835-1975. New Haven: Yale Press, 1977.

Ward, Clyde H., M.D. "Kilroy Was Here: A Reflection of History in Some Language Fads," Psychoanalytic Quarterly XXXI (1962): 80-88.

Weibel, Kathryn. Mirror, Mirror: Images of Women Reflected in Popular Culture. Garden City: Doubleday, 1977.

Weisbord, Vera Buch. A Radical Life. Bloomington: Indiana University Press, 1977.

Weitzman, Lenore. "Sex Role Socialization." In Women: A Feminist Perspective. 2nd ed. Ed. Jo Freeman. Palo Alto: Mayfield, 1979, pp. 153-217.

Welsch, Janice R. An Analysis of the Film Images of Hollywood's Most Popular Post World War II Stars. Ph.D. dissertation, Northwestern, 1975.

Welter, Barbara. "The Cult of True Womanhood." American Quarterly 18 (1966): 151-74.

Westin, Jeane. Making Do: How Women Survived the Thirties. Chicago: Follett, 1976.

Wilkinson, Virginia Snow. "From Housewife to Shipfitter." Harpers' 187 (Fall 1943): 325-37.

Williams, Raymond. Marxism and Literature. London: Oxford University Press, 1977.

_____. Culture and Society. London: Chatto and Windus, 1958.

Wolfenstein, Martha and Nathan Leites. Movies: A Psychological Study. Glencoe, Ill.: Free Press. 1950.

Wollen, Peter. Signs and Meaning in the Cinema. Bloomington: Indiana University Press, 1967.

Women's Studies Group. "Relations of Production: Relations of Reproduction." Working Papers in Cultural Studies 9 (Spring 1976): 95-118.

Wood, Michael. America in the Movies. New York: Basic, 1975.

Wood, Robin. Howard Hawks. New York: Doubleday, 1968.

"Working Women and the War: Four Narratives," Radical America, 9, 4/5 (1975), pp. 133-161.

Wright, Will. Sixguns and Society: A Structural Study of the Western. Berkeley: University of California Press, 1975.

Wylie, Max. "Washboard Weepies," Harpers' 185, no. 1110 (Nov. 1942): 633-638.

Yates, Gayle Graham. What Women Want: The Ideas of the Movement. Cambridge: Harvard University Press, 1975.

INDEX

abortion, 65, 68, 120
achievement, female, 156, 159-60; see also femininity-achievement conflict
achievement, maternalized, 139
Adam's Rib, 24, 25, 28, 30, 139, 147-52, 158, 159-60, 161
adolescence and adolescents, 100-101, 106ff, 111
Adorno, Theodor, 19
adultery, 170; see also infidelity
agriculture, 54-55, 58
Alcott, Louisa May, 30
All This and Heaven, Too, 25
Althusser, Louis, 11, 19, 21
Anderson, Karen, 3, 15, 67, 86
Anderson, Lisa, 83
anger, female, 4, 184, 190; see also suspicion and distrust, films of
antifeminism, 76, 77, 78, 139, 160, 161
Arden, Eve, 124, 130
armed forces, women in, 51, 66
Arthur, Jean, 33
Arzner, Dorothy, 31, 33
aspirations, female, 75
assertiveness, female, 139
Astor, Mary, 90
attendance, film, 37; see also audience research statistics
audience, film, 4, 13-14, 15, 31, 35, 36-43, 90, 131, 159, 160; male, 24, 35
audience research statistics, 201-5
autonomy, female, 56, 67-68, 72, 103, 109-10, 117, 128, 129, 131, 132, 157, 159, 169, 170

baby boom, 68

Back Street, 25, 30
backlash, conservative, 133
backlash, male, 60, 61, 66, 150; and management, 60-61
Backstage Wife, 30
Baker, M. Joyce, 17
Barthes, Roland, 21
Bathrick, Serafina, 45, 133, 135
"battle of the sexes," see conflict, male/female
Beavers, Louise, 28
Benjamin, Walter, 19
Bergman, Ingrid, 29, 38-39, 176-82; popularity statistics, 201; scandal of, 38
Bertolucci, Bernardo, 8, 12
birth control, see contraception
birth rate, 68
black actresses, 28
black women, 56, 58
The Blue Dahlia, 169
Bloch, Ernst, 9
Blyth, Ann, 124, 129
Bogle, Donald, 28
bonding, female, 1, 4, 24, 27, 72, 106, 109, 110, 111, 119-20, 126, 130, 131, 133, 143, 183, 186, 189
bonding, male, 24
boomtowns, 58
"box office draw," 12, 31, 95, 111-12
Bradley, Verne, 54
Bringing Up Baby, 34
Browne, Ray, 18
business, women in, 127
business hours, 64

Cain, James, 128, 169

ABOUT THE AUTHOR

ANDREA WALSH lives in the Boston area and teaches sociology at Clark University. Her research and teaching interests are focused on the areas of women's studies, gerontology, and mass communications. She received her M.A. from the New School for Social Research and her Ph.D. from State University of New York at Binghamton. Previously she taught at City University of New York, Cornell University, and SUNY-Binghamton, and has been active in the women's movement over the last decade.